UNDERSTANDING
CHILD
MOLESTERS

UNDERSTANDING
CHILD
MOLESTERS

Taking Charge

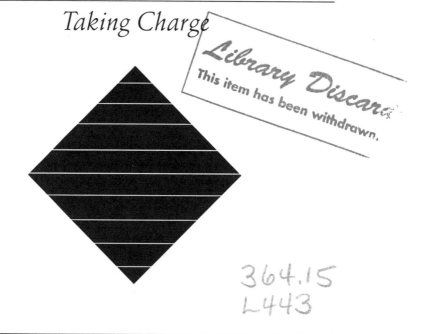

Eric Leberg

Foreword by
Lucy Berliner

SAGE Publications
International Educational and Professional Publisher
Thousand Oaks   London   New Delhi

For information address:

SAGE Publications, Inc.
2455 Teller Road
Thousand Oaks, California 91320
E-mail: order@sagepub.com

SAGE Publications Ltd.
6 Bonhill Street
London EC2A 4PU
United Kingdom

SAGE Publications India Pvt. Ltd.
M-32 Market
Greater Kailash I
New Delhi 110 048 India

Printed in the United States of America

Library of Congress Cataloging-in-Publication Data

Leberg, Eric.
    Understanding child molesters: Taking charge/Eric Leberg.
        p.   cm.
    Includes bibliographical references (p.   ) and index.
    ISBN 0-7619-0186-8 (cloth: acid-free paper).—
    ISBN 0-7619-0187-6 (pbk.: acid-free paper)
    1. Child molesters—United States—Psychology.   2. Child
molesters—Legal status, laws, etc.—United States.   3. Child
molesters—Rehabilitation—United States.   4. Child sexual
abuse—United States—Prevention.   I. Title.
    HV6570.2.L42   1997
    364.15′554′019—dc21   97-4754

97 98 99 00 01 02 03 10 9 8 7 6 5 4 3 2 1

Acquiring Editor:	C. Terry Hendrix
Editorial Assistant:	Dale Mary Grenfell
Production Editor:	Astrid Virding
Production Assistant:	Karen Wiley
Typesetter/Designer:	Marion Warren
Cover Designer:	Candice Harman
Print Buyer:	Anna Chin

Contents

Foreword

It is a fact of life that individuals who commit sex offenses against children live among us. They are co-workers, neighbors, parishioners, and respected members of the community. And they all have families. They are our parents, our brothers and sisters, our children. What this means is that we all have an opportunity to protect children from sex offenders.

Yet the greatest difficulty we face as a society that is trying to deal with the problem of sexual offending is that we have trouble reconciling our views about sex offenders in the abstract with our attitudes toward sex offenders whom we know. Virtually all citizens believe that sexual abuse of children is a heinous crime that should be punished severely. Legislatures pass increasingly harsh laws and the community demands that child molesters receive long sentences. Ex-offenders are widely believed to represent a continuing danger to children. When it comes to someone we know being convicted, or even being accused, of a sex offense, all of a sudden it becomes less clear how he or she should be treated.

Sex offenders are often able to garner the support of the community or family members. Sometimes, even when there is no doubt about guilt or in cases where the offender has confessed, supporters will assert that the accused could not possibly have committed the crimes or does not fit the profile. Family and friends will "go to bat" on behalf of certain offenders. It will be claimed that this offender is not like other sex offenders and is not a danger to the community, that the crimes were not so serious or were a case of bad judgment, that he or she does not deserve the punishment the law dictates. The fact that children have been sexually assaulted and potentially harmed is disregarded, overlooked, or minimized.

The reason that people react this way is because sex offenders are more like us than they are not like us in many cases. The majority of child molesters are not antisocial and deviant in all aspects of their lives. They may be quite ordinary in most ways. They may even have positive attributes and qualities. It is very hard to integrate the public persona of sex offenders with the image or idea of them being sexual with children. This dissonance is often resolved in favor of the less disturbing interpretation that people are more or less what they seem, not that they have sordid, secret lives.

The other big problem that we have in protecting children from sex offenders is that we expect the government to do it for us. When there is a reoffense, the police, the prosecutors, the judges, the community corrections officers, and the law are blamed. It is clear that these authorities do have responsibility and that they sometimes fail in carrying out their obligations. But when it comes right down to it, it is those who know and interact with sex offenders who can do the most to prevent sex offenders from reoffending.

That is what this book is all about. Eric Leberg, an experienced community corrections officer, offers the knowledge and resources not only to protect children from known sex offenders but also to identify signs of potential relapse or increased risk in these offenders and to help them refrain from the behaviors that can lead to sex offending. When those who come in contact with known sex offenders understand the psychology and behavioral patterns of sex offenders, they are in a position to make a constructive difference.

The basic message is that knowledge is power. Not only is it important to know how sex offenders operate in general, but it is also important to know that there are other potential sources of information on individual offenders. Convicted sex offenders often have official reports and evaluations completed about them that may be available. If they are in treatment, it may be possible to obtain a waiver of confidentiality. The probation, parole, or community corrections officer may be able to provide information about the legal conditions imposed on the offender or other key insights into the warning signs of relapse.

Access to some or all of this information may be restricted, but those who are involved in relationships with sex offenders are perfectly within their rights to insist that the offender permit free exchange of information among the professionals involved. Most offender treatment specialists welcome the involvement of family members. Family participation in creating a protective environment around an offender that inhibits reoffending and that reinforces treatment lessons increases the likelihood of a successful outcome.

Protecting children from known sex offenders is a shared responsibility. After all, the best protection would be ensuring that a sex offender is never alone with a child, and only friends and family can make sure this never happens. Community corrections officers, treatment providers, and community members who are informed about sex offenders and who are alert to manipulations and deceit can together make the world much, much safer for children.

Lucy Berliner
Harborview Center for Sexual
Assault and Traumatic Stress
University of Washington

Preface

The Purpose of This Book

The purpose of this book is to explain how manipulative child molesters are and to provide some guidelines as to what those who know a convicted child molester can do to reduce the odds that he will victimize anyone again. This is important because child molesters often continue to interact with their families and acquaintances long after they have been convicted. If readers who know a convicted child molester do not become informed of how devious the typical offender is, they and their children are susceptible to further victimization.

This purpose is accomplished in two ways: (a) revealing child molesters' deceptiveness, and (b) informing readers of strategies for short-circuiting their methods of deception. Chapters 1 through 6 describe in detail how child molesters use denial, secrecy, blaming, and manipulation to set up not only their victim but everyone around them as well. By the end of Chapter 6, the reader will come to understand that these offenders have developed their skills of deception to a very advanced degree. Recognizing this is the first, yet crucial, step in taking charge of the child molester's life to prevent reoffending.

Chapters 7 through 10 deal specifically with what is needed to reduce the chances for reoffending. These chapters provide an in-depth look at the criminal justice system and explain how the reader can benefit from investigations and supervision of convicted child molesters by the corrections agency. The chapters detail what documents exists in the offender's official file and how the reader can obtain those documents. Chapters 7 through 10 also deal with the mental health treatment programs for sex offenders by describing the sex offender evaluation report, what elements a treatment program includes, and how the reader can benefit from this information.

Knowing what information exists and how to obtain it is vital for understanding the offender and for establishing controls to prevent reoffense. This information is particularly important for those families making efforts to reunite with an offender involved in a sex offender treatment program. Failing to get this information can result in disastrous consequences.

Who Should Read This Book

This book is primarily written for nonprofessionals and as a primer for professionals who are new to the field. It is written for wives of child molesters and their relatives, friends, neighbors, and acquaintances and for all those persons who want to know more to protect themselves and their children. Many other groups of people will find this work valuable reading as well. These groups include employers, ministers, educators, and medical personnel. As this book demonstrates, all persons who have even brief but regular contact with the offender can play a significant role in protecting children and discouraging reoffense by the molester.

Interested professionals will find this book useful as an introduction to the major issues applicable to working with these offenders. Invariably, professionals who are new to the field are astonished by the never-ending variety of child molesters' deceptions, contrivances, and manipulations. Chapters 7 through 10 will be especially valuable to them because they explain national trends and changes in the criminal justice system that are taking place at an increasing pace. These chapters also discuss specific documents that professionals should know about and explain the powers and limitations of the courts over child molesters.

This book will not replace good therapy. If your husband, boyfriend, or relative has been convicted of a sexual offense, your experience has, without doubt, been traumatic. For you, this book can be an important beginning in your effort to understand what happened to you. However, you should make every effort to get a therapist of your own who can help you understand your specific situation and who can help you deal with the unique problems that you will be facing. If you have not been able to get your own therapist, this book can still be useful, but do not assume that it will be a substitute in any way for an experienced professional counselor. Becoming involved in a counseling program is important because it helps reduce your isolation and, as you will discover, isolating family members is a primary tool of the sex offender.

This book is based on the author's 25 years of experience working with every type of child molester. In addition, it is based on the most current and widely accepted views about child molesters. References throughout the work demonstrate that these ideas are accredited by professionals working in this field. The references are also included for those who wish to pursue further reading.

Acknowledgments

There are many, many persons without whom this work could never have been completed. While I cannot name everyone who has helped on a project that took over 5 years to complete, I do wish to name some of you who have been so important to me. First, I wish to thank Chase Riveland, Secretary of the Washington State Department of Corrections. It was Chase who encouraged me and all of us in the field of corrections to expand our view of what corrections is and what we can do, not only for offenders but for victims and for the community as a whole. Similarly, I wish to thank his staff, in particular supervisor Chuck Wright, for technical assistance and review of the manuscript. Michael O'Connell, A.C.S.W., a noted sex offender therapist, also provided important feedback to improve the manuscript. My colleagues, Jack Johnsen and Joel Eskes, have provided continued support and encouragement in the long process of writing this book. All of the members of the informal professional group we call the Community Team on Child Sexual Abuse also provided inspiration over the years, particularly adding to my determination to persevere and to my belief that something can be done to combat child sexual abuse. Thanks also to Walter Leberg, K. C. Canfield, Donna Parker, John Nolte, Craig Donaldson, Barbara Huffman, Bill France, and to my basketball buddy at the Everett Y.M.C.A., Ray Carson. I wish to express my deepest appreciation to the members of the Washington State chapter of the American Professional Society on the Abuse of Children (APSAC) and to Lucy Berliner, in particular, with whose support and encouragement I knew that this book would become a reality. Finally, I wish to thank my family and wife, Carolyn, for her constant encouragement and all others who have expressed interest and support in ways large and small along the way. Thank you.

Introduction

◆ ◆ ◆

BURT

Usually, I drive our car home from work myself, but on this occasion I had asked my wife, Carolyn, to drive. I hadn't broken the news to her yet that a colleague of mine had been brutally murdered. It would be months, in fact, before I gave her the full details. She wasn't always happy about my job as a probation and parole officer, and she worried at times about the seriousness of criminals on my caseload. I knew, though, that I'd have trouble concentrating on traffic, so I told her that I just had too much on my mind and was tired after a long day at work.

Six blocks from the office, I noticed a convicted child molester, whom I'll call Burt, walking toward us. I was Burt's parole officer. (The names used in this book are fictitious, and the identities of all persons have been altered to protect the privacy of the offenders and their victims.) That Burt was walking on a public street was ordinarily of little concern. However, Burt was talking to a young newspaper boy, about 10 years old, I judged. That was alarming. Burt had molested 10-year-old boys before. The rules of his parole prohibited him from any kind of contact with minor children. For Burt, simply stopping on the street to talk to a child was a parole violation.

Burt was a predatory child molester. Most sex offenders molest their own children, their neighbors' children, or kids they know. Burt, on the other hand, would seek out children he had never known, near schools, parks, and on the streets. Sometimes runaways, sometimes not. Sometimes normal, well-adjusted children who, for one reason or another, happened to be defenseless.

Twenty years as a probation officer had taught me to avoid heroics. I always tried to keep my work as low key as possible. In this business, enough problems develop in spite of our best efforts. The last thing I wished for was inadvertently to provoke some unstable offender such as Burt to do something impulsive that everybody later regrets. Now, however, there was no time to plan: Some kind of action was absolutely necessary.

"Stop the car! There! Now! Park it there!" I said as I pointed to an empty space in a no-parking zone. Opening the passenger's door before the car was completely stopped (a foolish act in retrospect, though my mind and blood were already racing), I waited for a car to pass and then hopscotched my way through rush hour traffic.

Burt didn't see me, but the paperboy's eyes met my own. Burt's gaze was glued to the paperboy. The parolee seemed like a spider caught in his own psychological web, oblivious to everything around him. "Burt . . . You, Burt!" I said in a loud but controlled voice, just as there was a break in traffic and the clamor of automobiles subsided momentarily. His attention, obviously, would not be easily drawn from the boy. My sharp speech, however, finally caught Burt's attention and I could see in his demeanor the immediate shift to his con-artist, manipulative personality the instant he recognized me. He quickly began to calculate what he needed to say to try to appease and control me. He tried to conceal his utter surprise and stammered, "I'm learning this paper route . . . You know I, . . . I'm taking a second job. I have to earn more money."

Then Burt glanced nervously at the paperboy and back at me. He began to weigh what kind of trouble he was facing. Would I arrest him? Would I revoke his parole and send him back to prison to face abuse by other prisoners? Sex offenders rehearse how to manipulate their victims and also how to control everybody else, including adults, who might attempt to foil their plans. They constantly consider and plan what to do if anyone gets suspicious. Burt suddenly became aggressive, and he began a verbal attack aimed at hooking me into an argument right there on the street as traffic sped by.

The paperboy was watching everything. Everything he saw, I knew, would be extremely important later. He didn't know it yet, but he would be my primary witness at Burt's parole hearing. His testimony, regardless of how young he might be, was vital to convicting Burt of a parole violation. I could not assume, though, that the paperboy would be a willing and capable witness. In the criminal justice field you can never assume a witness can or will testify for you. You have to nurture your witness from the start. You have to guard their testimony and sometimes even their personal safety. Whatever I did, I could not traumatize the boy. At this point I had no idea whether he had met Burt just this afternoon or whether Burt had already begun sexually molesting him.

Burt's voice was rising. He was becoming increasingly argumentative and officious. He glanced sideways to see what impression he was making on the paperboy. He began to smile coyly, thinking he was making headway in his courtroom there on the sidewalk. I interrupted Burt with a cool voice, "Be quiet Burt. You can't do this. You have to leave this area now."

Burt was tall, obese, had his shirt unbuttoned to his navel, wore a yellow gingham bandanna around his throat, and had crooked front teeth. He had three tiny sapphire stones in one ear lobe, and a gold ring hanging from the other. His eyes protruded, bright blue, staring out from a mane of flaming red hair.

Burt refused to quit talking and to leave the area, claiming "a perfect right to freedom of movement in a free country."

I looked at the paperboy. He began to look frightened. "I'm losing him," I thought and was forced to shift my focus from Burt to the paperboy. "I'm . . . I'm Burt's parole officer." As I spoke, I drew my identification from inside my coat pocket showing him my badge. I asked, "What's your name?" "Jimmy," he said in a clear voice, his face reflecting an alertness that suggested he knew who I was, which puzzled me. "I'm quitting my route and Burt's taking it over."

Convicted felons who have been to court and who have sat through many trials, men who have spent years in prison with others of a similar fate, learn quite a bit about the law, but they usually think they know a great deal more than they do and press for every advantage they can muster when sparring verbally with legal authorities of any variety, whether police, probation officers, lawyers, or judges. Burt was no exception: the consummate jailhouse lawyer. He interrupted Jimmy with a hint of anger in his voice: "You can't stop me. After all, you're the one who's making me get into that phony counseling program, and I don't need counseling anyway. You're probably just getting a kickback from the counselor. It's a setup. You're just another corrupt public official. This whole thing is your fault! I'd be fine if you'd just back off, chill out, and let me take care of my own rehabilitation! But you've gotta interfere! It's all because of you that I need to take a second job to pay for some chickenshit therapy. So, you *can't stop me.* That would be unlawful deprivation of livelihood. And besides, you can't violate me for not being in therapy if you keep me from working." Burt's last retort was intended to manipulate the conversation by switching the subject from my demand that he leave the area to the volatile issue about being in sex offender counseling.

There are two preeminent goals that convicted child molesters harbor above all others. First, more than anything else, sex offenders try to get permission to be with children, especially their victims. "Don't you trust me?" they plead. "All I'm asking for is a second chance. Be reasonable!" In truth, their "second chance" is more likely their fifth, tenth, or hundredth chance. As they have learned, it is an effective ploy, especially against anyone who has not yet learned how to deal effectively with sex offenders.

The child molester's second goal is to avoid counseling. Burt was no exception. By now I had heard enough from Burt. He was hitting full stride as jail house lawyer, but I had lost patience and now I needed to act decisively. I needed to determine whether Jimmy had already been molested by Burt, and I needed to decide whether or not to arrest Burt right there on the street. I also needed to find out who Jimmy was, who his parents were, and what had happened between him and Burt. I had to communicate something to my wife, still waiting across the street in the car, watching, wondering. Most of all, I needed to be sure that Jimmy would be safe.

I had no handcuffs, no cellular phone, and no weapons. Probation and parole officers in my agency are prohibited from carrying firearms. Words truly are our best, and usually our only, weapon. Because I had no way to call police for immediate assistance, I decided to make sure that Jimmy was safe. This meant letting Burt go for the time being.

"Just a minute, Jimmy," I said and turned to Burt, stepping into his space deliberately to make him feel uncomfortable. "You do not have my permission to be here. Whatever you say will change nothing. You cannot learn this paper route. You must leave this area immediately or face the consequences." I was deliberately ambiguous when I said, "face the consequences."

Burt didn't know what I meant, but my tone of voice now suggested it wouldn't be pretty.

Burt hesitated. He didn't believe my first warning. Burt wanted to argue more, insisting that he needed more money than he earned from his job as a lot boy at a car dealership to pay for sex offender counseling. "If you don't leave right now, Burt, I'll arrest you right here on the spot. Understand?" No ambiguity. Truthfully, I wasn't sure quite how I would have managed it. A lot of probation work is done by the seat of your pants. In most tough situations, you learn to improvise. You learn to think, talk, and plan your strategy all in the same breath. And then you cross your fingers and hope whatever you've cooked up works. This time it worked. Burt got the message and left, heading up the street and around the corner, fussing and fuming about violations of his civil rights, filing a grievance against me with the Department of Corrections, and writing to the governor, all the while glancing back at Jimmy.

When I turned to Jimmy, he was beginning to cry. Fortunately, I had worked with a lot of children as a social worker before coming to corrections. This work included spending a great deal of time with a lot of kids who needed to cry. I reassured Jimmy that things were safe now, we were going to find his parents, and everything was going to work out okay. He began to wipe away his tears, but his breathing was still strong and he bit his lower lip. I asked whether Burt had done anything to hurt him. "No," Jimmy said, "but he was talking about sex and real bad things. I don't want to see him again, ever. And he wanted to come with me Saturday morning. I didn't know what to do." On Saturdays, I remembered, the paper was delivered in the mornings. "He won't bother you again, Jimmy, I'll see to that. But I don't think it's a good idea for you to continue delivering the papers today, do you?"

Though Burt was by now out of view, I was concerned that he might still linger in the area, and I was not about to let Jimmy continue on the paper route alone. I remembered when I was Jimmy's age how responsible I felt about my own paper route and what might happen if the papers didn't get delivered. Jimmy seemed to have that same sense of responsibility. As it turned out, he said he was also afraid that Burt might still be in the area somewhere. Not finishing the paper route gave him an obvious sense of relief.

"But I don't know about the papers," Jimmy said, motioning to his paper bag strapped over his shoulders. I offered to call the newspaper for him and let them know that he couldn't finish the route. Jimmy immediately said that he knew a lady customer who lived nearby whose phone we could borrow. He said again that he was afraid that Burt might still be around, somewhere. By now, daylight was fading, the gray sky threw a gloom over the street, and even a visual check for Burt would be inadequate for Jimmy's safety.

Moments later on the phone I spoke to the delivery supervisor at the newspaper and briefly explained who I was and what had happened. I was grateful the delivery supervisor cooperated. Maybe he was concerned because he hadn't checked out Burt's background before setting Burt and Jimmy up. Ironically, a simple phone call to the local Department of Corrections would have alerted them to Burt's history as a predatory child molester. But the newspaper, like most of the general public, doesn't know where to begin to protect itself from convicted sex offenders.

Jimmy and I left the remaining papers at the lady's house, though I don't think she fully understood what was going on. She probably wondered if I were really a child molester. Jimmy lived quite a distance away, but his mother worked in a drug store just down the street and around the corner. To everyone's good fortune, she had not left work yet. But when I offered to drive him down to talk to his mother, pointing to my wife waiting across the street in our car, Jimmy gave me a rather nervous look. He told me that he would rather walk, since it wasn't that far. It struck me only later that he was not about to get into cars with a stranger, even one with a badge and a wife. We walked down to the drug store. Jimmy's mother was there and I explained the circumstances to her. We made an appointment to talk more the next day at their home. I especially wanted Jimmy's father to be involved because I needed Jimmy's testimony at Burt's parole hearing and I knew that I couldn't get it if everyone didn't agree.

I met with Jimmy and his parents the next afternoon. "Jimmy," I began, "do you know what a parolee is?" I expected him to say no and then I would explain in basic terms what a parolee was, what the Parole Board was, and what a parole hearing was all about. "Sure, I know what a parolee is," he said. "It's a man who's been in prison, but has to follow rules when he gets out." I was speechless, but Jimmy put me at ease this time. While his parents sat watching comfortably, Jimmy described how he had actually been inside the state penitentiary many times. His aunt was a nurse in a prison across the state. Because Jimmy spent summers at the aunt and uncle's ranch, he had gone inside "the walls" often to meet his aunt at quitting time. As we sat in the family living room, Jimmy related his experiences. "They used to throw things out the bars and yell awful things. It was really bad. Sure, I know what parolees are."

I explained who Burt was and we talked about Burt's parole hearing. The Parole Board would decide whether to send Burt back to prison. Jimmy was, in fact, by now anxious to testify. He seemed to glow with pride at being a citizen, someone who could contribute to society in an important way.

Earlier that morning, before meeting with Jimmy and his parents, I had arrested Burt at the car dealership. A few weeks later, Jimmy confidently testified at the parole hearing about what Burt had said and done for several days while "learning the paper route." Fortunately, Burt had not molested Jimmy. Burt's parole was revoked. He was returned to prison.

❖   ❖   ❖

Each year, hundreds of thousands of children are sexually molested. Thousands of child molesters are also apprehended and convicted every year. For example, 100,100 persons were arrested for sexual offenses in 1988. Between 1978 and 1988 the number of arrests for those crimes had increased by 45% (Jamieson & Flanagan, 1989, pp. 481-489). Of those offenders who are sentenced to prison, the majority serve less than half of their full sentence before they are released to the community under some sort of supervision such as parole (Jamieson & Flanagan, 1989, p. 640). Although prisons are burgeoning with convicted sex offenders, an even greater number are either released on parole or are never sent to prison. Instead, they are sentenced to "probation" after a brief jail sentence and are allowed to return to the community (Brecher, 1978). Surprisingly, those offenders who rape children typically serve even less time than those who rape adult women.

The most common child molester sexually assaults his own children or those of someone he knows. The assaults take place within a social network of well-meaning and well-intentioned adults, who, because of the molester's manipulations, never suspect a thing. When released from jail or prison, the molester usually returns to that same place he left and continues to interact with that same group of people.

What this means is not only that millions of people are acquainted with the victims of child sexual abuse but also that they know and continue to interact with the men convicted of molesting these children. These people include the wives, parents, relatives, friends, neighbors, employers, and clergy for the offenders, to mention only a few groups. Despite this fact, the public fails to understand the child molester and what can be done to protect children from him, or to prevent him from reoffending when he returns to the community. Prison is certainly an appropriate way to control many convicted sex offenders, such as those like Burt. But as the figures indicate, prison is only a temporary option, and releasing the offender to an unsuspecting group of friends, family, and acquaintances who have little knowledge about sex offenders is a poor choice.

There is a better way, which is to build a knowledgeable network of people around the offender who know his past, his patterns of offense, and what can be done to protect children from him. This is especially important when considering the growing belief among professionals that many sex offenders can be helped through carefully conducted counseling programs (Marshall & Barbaree, 1990). This belief means that the number of child molesters released will continue to increase. A crucial part of successful treatment dictates that those who know the child molester are aware of his background and prepared to do what is necessary to increase the safety of all involved.

Until now, no comprehensive work has been written for the general public about who the child molester is, how he can be helped, and how he can be controlled. A considerable body of research and many fine textbooks about sex offenders have been published for professionals who work with sex offenders. For example, Marshall, Laws, and Barbaree's (1990) *Handbook of Sexual Assault* is an excellent overview of state-of-the-art thinking about sexual assault. But their book is highly technical and is addressed to professionals in the field. Literature and training programs are proliferating for law enforcement officials to understand typical profiles of sexual offenders and, for example, how offenders use computers and the Internet as a means of enticing victims. Also, many books and articles have been written to assist victims during their recovery. Legislatures across the nation are drafting new laws in an attempt to gain control over sex offenders. However, no one has yet tackled the knotty problem of spelling out in simple language who the convicted child molester is, how he can be helped, how he can be controlled, and how the legal maze called the criminal justice system works.

The purpose of this book is to fill this void. It is written for all of those persons who may not be professionals in the field but who still want to know more about the convicted sex offender so that they can make safer decisions for themselves, for children, and for offenders with whom they have contact. What can be done to help make the community safe from the convicted child molester? How should people talk to the offender to be sure that they are not overlooking clues that he is about to reoffend? What should they do to maximize his benefits from counseling? The purpose of this book is to answer these and many related questions.

Stated briefly, most child molesters are men and those men usually molest a child they know. The victim could be their own child or children, or a stepchild, or a relative's child, or a child of their neighbor. Fortunately, men such as Burt, the truly predatory offenders, are actually the exception rather than the rule. But nearly all sex offenders, including those such as Burt, maintain regular contact with their family and friends even after conviction and release from jail or prison.

The sex offender's wife is the adult who most often carries the heaviest burden of facing and dealing with the offender himself. In today's society, even for families without sexual abuse, it can be financially and socially devastating for a mother to be suddenly abandoned by her husband and left alone to support her children, facing the odds alone in a world that often turns a cold shoulder to single-parent families, especially the single mother. It is no surprise, then, that the mother will often wonder whether counseling can cure her husband, so that her family can be restored to wholeness, despite the anguish of sexual abuse (Herman, 1981). But what should she do, especially to ensure her own children's safety?

The child molester's other acquaintances also face the dilemma of what they should do. Although the offender fears that once caught and convicted he will be ostracized by everyone he knows, experience shows that this does not happen often. Relatives, friends, employers, neighbors, ministers, and a host of other acquaintances will continue to interact regularly with the offender after he is released from jail or prison. At present, these acquaintances most often do so without talking openly with the offender about his sexual offense and without communicating with each other. But should they remain silent on these matters?

What the convicted child molester wants most is that everyone accepts him back into society with no awareness, knowledge, or discussion of his crime or crimes. When a person does have some idea of his history, he hopes that person will accept on blind faith his denial or distorted admission of guilt. For a variety of reasons, he hopes he will never be questioned about his crime again. He hopes that everyone will be too afraid, or embarrassed, to talk openly to him or about him. He hopes that no one will bother to call his

probation officer or his therapist to find out what the rules are that
he must follow. Ironically, maintaining secrecy works not only
against the interests of children and society as a whole but also against
the welfare of the sex offender himself.

The chances are good that the child molester will get his wish
and that he will remain a mystery to others, because as a society we
seldom talk openly about child sexual abuse. "How could anyone be
sexually stimulated by a child?" people frequently ask in total
disbelief. But answers are seldom forthcoming. The question itself
seems so shocking that no real discussion occurs. Some demand
simplistically that child molesters be castrated and locked up forever.
For some, "three strikes" or even "two strikes" and life without
parole are too many. Some localities are proposing laws that would
make one offense of child molestation punishable by life without
parole. Although such strong reactions are understandable, extreme
pronouncements such as "castration" and "life without parole" stifle
informed, intelligent discussion, and ignore the unfortunate realities
of child sexual abuse. In fact, extreme statements may even promote
the child molester's goal, because they inhibit informed, intelligent
discussion. Consequently, the child molester too often gets his way:
People do not talk.

Reading this book should help uncover some of the mystery that
surrounds the child molester. This book will both identify the
common characteristics and kinds of child molesters and suggest how
to talk with the child molester in ways that can reduce his chances
to reoffend. Also, the book will show how the reader can positively
contribute to the therapist's efforts to help when the offender is in
therapy. The book will discuss ways to improve communication
among those who know the child molester, and will describe how
controls are used to take charge of the offender to reduce his chances
to reoffend. The book will explain the role that the probation officer
plays in the offender's life, what role the therapist plays, how the
court system works, and what you, the reader, can do to get the full
story about any convicted child molester who you may have an
ongoing acquaintance with.

The ideas in the book are based on current research and thinking by the top experts who study and treat sex offenders. It also

draws on the practical experiences of the author after 20 years of day-to-day investigation and supervision of literally hundreds of sex offenders.

The book will include a variety of stories that are typical of sex offenders that have occurred repeatedly. There is virtually no unique sex offender story. The examples described in this book have occurred scores of time, however unique and incredible they may seem at times. The identities of offenders and victims have been disguised to protect their right to privacy. The case examples are designed to make the reader fully aware of how the sex offender might be attempting to deceive and manipulate those around him in any one of a wide variety of circumstances.

It must be stressed that this book focuses on *convicted* child molesters. It would be a serious mistake to try to apply these ideas to someone you simply suspect of being a child molester (but who has not been charged or convicted) because many of the characteristics of child molesters, such as living a life of secrecy, are common to many law-abiding, well-adjusted individuals. When you know a child molester who has been convicted, this book should point the way to dealing more effectively with that person. If you suspect that someone may be a child molester, you should make your suspicion known to the police.

The basic assumption of this book is that knowing the truth about the offender will make you, your children, and everyone else's children safer. Finding out the truth about a child molester may prove somewhat awkward, and at times even embarrassing and emotionally painful, because you will invariably discover that the child molester's criminal behavior is more extensive than you ever suspected. You will also likely discover that the offender has been lying about himself to try to cover up secrets of which he was ashamed. However, by uncovering his falsehoods, you will be able to make far better and safer decisions for the welfare of everyone.

This book is written for the nonprofessional reader. No academic or professional training is needed to understand the ideas presented. The author has included references that support the ideas and concepts presented for several reasons. First, much is written that either sensationalizes or perpetuates myths about child molesters.

The references allow you, the reader, to check for yourself whether the ideas in this book are supported by experts in the field. Just as you should verify information about sex offenders (which is a major theme of this book), you should also consider double-checking what authors write about sex offenders. Your local public library can help you locate the books and articles cited here. Most are currently and widely available. If you are involved in mental health counseling yourself, or if you know such a counselor, the counselor may also be able to suggest additional reading. Such trained counselors are also able to answer questions you may have about the literature you read, to help keep ideas in proper perspective.

Because many trained mental health counselors will suggest that their clients read this book, they too need to be sure that the ideas are sound. They themselves may also want further access to the professional literature this book is based on. References allow those professional readers who wish to know more the opportunity to expand their knowledge. The more that we all know and learn about the convicted child molester, the greater our chance as a society to significantly impact child sexual abuse.

The Setup

The setup is the pattern of all behaviors that the child molester uses to create opportunities to molest children. He carefully lays the groundwork to avoid detection and disclosure in advance, before he begins molesting. He continues to strengthen his elaborate plans after molestation has begun by manipulating others, usually without their awareness, to make molesting easier. In his mind, everyone, adults and children alike, are the enemy with the power to send him to prison if they catch him and reveal his sexual abuse of innocent children. He sets up the victim, the victim's mother, neighbors, relatives, professional colleagues, fellow church members, and others, each in a deliberate manner, because every one of them has the potential to catch him and turn him in. The setup consumes nearly all of his waking hours and is the motivation behind nearly everything he does. With practice, often years of practice, he becomes quite skillful. Thus, those around him usually fail to notice and understand his motive: child molestation. Dan's story illustrates how one child molester set up virtually an entire community.

❖   ❖   ❖

DAN

Dan was a middle school teacher and counselor who was widely respected for his abilities and dedication to his students. He received numerous awards and had developed a reputation as the man to go to when a difficult job needed to get done. He developed close relationships with the parents of his pupils and became involved in the personal lives of his students and their families. Because he was divorced, he had plenty of spare time to dedicate himself to serving his students and his profession.

Fellow teachers appreciated Dan because if there was an especially time-consuming or demanding job to be done, for example, evening work to plan special student programs such as dances, assemblies, or seasonal festivities, Dan was willing to give up his personal time to help out. He always had a positive attitude and never complained. Counselors from other schools would call on him for advice because he knew so much about the home life of his students and their siblings in other nearby schools. In a crunch, Dan was even willing to baby-sit for a family in crisis when the family was being counseled by one of his colleagues.

It was not remarkable, then, that Dan offered to take several pupils camping, some of them troubled girls living in single-parent homes. He developed a close relationship with several of the girls. Sometimes when one of the girls could not go along, Dan would still take the others camping. Sometimes only one girl could go, but even so he would try not to disappoint her. He felt he had to show dependability to teach it.

When it was finally discovered that Dan had been sexually molesting one of his students, the community was shocked. Parents refused to believe it was true. Students told everyone that the girl had a reputation for lying, truancy, and using alcohol and drugs. But then another girl revealed that she too had been molested by Dan. She came forward on her own because she still liked Dan and wanted to see him get some help. She too was accused of being a liar and troublemaker. Students told their parents that she wasn't to be believed either.

When Dan was placed on administrative leave pending the outcome of the investigation, the other teachers were suddenly faced with taking over all of the special activities that he had been responsible for, including grounds patrol during recess and lunch, after school sports, field trips, and the year-end school picnic. It was difficult for them to believe that anyone who had dedicated his life to students could really be a child molester. They, as the parents and students, hoped that the allegations would prove to be untrue and that he would quickly be returned to full-time duties. They and school officials soon realized the tremendous amount of work that he had carried on his shoulders alone: It now fell onto theirs.

Months later, Dan admitted to his attorney that he had, in fact, molested the girls. Unknown to teachers, parents, and students at the time of the first accusations, he admitted to a long history of sexually molesting students, some who were too embarrassed to come forward at that time and others at previous schools who knew nothing about the current charges. Dan told his attorney that he felt ashamed. He knew he needed help. He had tried to control the problem by changing school districts, but he kept getting into the same situations as before. He tried to make up for what he had done by dedicating himself more and more to helping students, especially students from broken homes, disadvantaged students, students really in need of help. He thought working harder for them would "repay" them in some way for how he had abused others. He had never forced any of the children to have sex with him, he said, and never pressured them in any way. He said that he did not think any of the students had suffered severely and that most of the students had shown considerable improvement from his involvement with them. Many of the students knew about what had been going on, he said, and many of his victims, mostly early adolescent girls, had initiated sexual activities with him.

In his defense, he asked that his fellow teachers and supportive parents send letters on his behalf to the probation officer writing the presentence investigation report that the judge would use to decide his sentence. Over 75 letters were received from students, parents, teachers, counselors, and administrators. The majority of the letters expressed the belief that "Dan could not have done this," despite the fact that Dan had confessed. (Dan failed to inform the students, parents, and teachers that he had already pleaded guilty to the two current charges, as well as admitting many other incidents of molestation.) Other letters made no reference to Dan's crimes at all, but simply talked about what an extraordinary teacher he had been for the school, the students, and their families. Many letters included statements criticizing the victims, stating, for example, "If Dan in fact did anything wrong at all, I'm sure that the girls are to blame too. Everyone knows that they are liars, and that they use drugs and are a bad influence on the other students at school." One of the letters said, "If Dan had not been available to baby-sit my two younger ones, I could never have made it to counseling with my oldest daughter. How can anyone question this man's integrity and dedication to others?" Only two letters (both from female students) showed any awareness that Dan was, in fact, guilty.

❖   ❖   ❖

Dan's story illustrates how skillfully child molesters can set up victims and everyone that they know to reduce their chances of getting caught. Dan chose victims who were especially vulnerable and needy, victims the community was already predisposed to disbelieve, so-called troublemakers. He also reinforced the perception that he was a caring and helpful person by performing services valuable to his community. The damage to the community, no doubt, exceeded his positive works because of the expense and moral disillusionment he caused. It was all possible because of how effective Dan was.

Setting up those around him is a "way of life" for the child molester. A hobby in itself may be an outlet for recreation, but it can also be a way to attract children. Volunteering for a charity may earn money for a worthwhile cause, but it can also bring the offender into closer contact with children. Because of his fear of punishment, the child molester becomes an expert at creating smoke screens that blind everyone to his true motivation. His fear of prison motivates him to manipulate those around him and permeates virtually everything that he does with other people.

The child molester does not quit setting people up, even after he is caught, tried, and convicted. He knows too well how many times he tried to quit molesting before, making promise after promise to his victim that this was the "last time," only to strike again. Therefore, he knows he might fail again and at some future date he may really need some allies on his side: a child who won't tell, a mother who will need his income and won't disclose to authorities, a probation officer or judge who will go easy on him. The child molester continues to set others up long after he has been convicted. It is simply not a habit that is easy to give up once he has dedicated so many years to refining this skill.

To make it easier to recognize when the offender may be setting up people in his life, the present chapter will discuss three aspects of this kind of behavior, including isolating the victim, grooming behaviors, and new relationships. A theme that runs throughout any discussion of these topics is secrecy. Secrecy is so fundamental to child sexual abuse that a later chapter will deal with it exclusively. Secrecy is, in fact, so important that a Harvard University professor, Dr. Judith Herman, includes it as an integral part of her definition of incest itself. Dr. Herman (1981) says that incest is "any sexual relationship between a child and an adult in a position of paternal authority . . . that had to be kept a secret" (p. 70). Isolating his victim, grooming those around him, and developing new relationships all contain direct and indirect elements of secrecy. The direct secrecy is, of course, the mere fact that sexual molestation itself takes place in secret. The indirect element is more pernicious: Everything the offender does has its own secret purpose, its special manipulative value that others are usually completely unaware of. As author and educator Anna Salter (1988) writes, "The one denominator this author has seen is that the offenders often choose the one child in the family who is unlikely to tell" (p. 61).

Isolating the Victim

Mother-Child Barriers

Often the molester creates barriers between the victim and the victim's mother. Testimonies of scores of child molesters attest to the fact that they will deliberately damage the mother-child relationship to make molestation easier. These barriers may be physical, such as moving the victim to a room far from where the mother sleeps or encouraging the mother to take a trip to a distant city, leaving the offender alone with the victim. Other barriers are psychological, such as threatening the victim if she discloses the sexual abuse to her mother.

The significance of these barriers can be seen from many standpoints. From one perspective, victims often carry as much anger and hostility toward their mothers as they do toward the fathers who abused them (Herman, 1981, pp. 80-83). This fact illustrates how devastating and unjust child sexual abuse can be on family members other than the victim. It is clear that barriers between family members created by the molester must be eradicated to restore a healthy, nurturing family life. Breaking down these barriers through open, supportive communication reduces the possibility of further sexual abuse. Professionals who work with incestuous families agree on the need to restore the relationship between the mother and the daughter/victim in order for the healing process to occur.

Isolating the child from the mother can cause severe psychological trauma to the child. The degree of trauma varies depending upon a variety of factors, including the response of the mother and others once the abuse is disclosed, the nature and extent of the molestation, how long it lasts over time (weeks, months, years), the unique emotional development of the child, and a host of other circumstances. The degree to which he is willing to erect walls of isolation around family members illustrates how little regard the child molester has for the welfare of others.

The ways to isolate are seemingly endless. Offenders will offer to baby-sit, for example, both in their own and in others' homes, providing convenient moments when the children and mother are physically separated. They will design floor plans and assign children's rooms so that the targeted child's bedroom (the child he wants to molest) is the farthest from the parents' bedroom. He will encourage campouts in the backyard, knowing that the mother dreads sleeping outdoors, so that he can molest in private, without being interrupted. He will offer to take his victim places that he knows the mother does not want to go or cannot go because of other commitments.

Whenever possible, the offender will choose a victim who is already socially isolated to some degree. These children may seldom talk privately with their mothers. They may perform poorly in school and will try to limit or avoid direct communication with teachers whenever possible. They may resist talking to counselors. Also, they often have few close relationships with other adults. Finally, researchers have found that victims of child sexual abuse consistently have fewer friends than nonabused children (Finkelhor, 1979).

Whether or not the child is isolated, the child molester can still create barriers. Judith Herman (1981) agrees, "As the daughters reached adolescence, they often became more assertive and rebellious. The fathers responded with intense jealousy, bordering on paranoia. They did whatever they could to seclude and isolate their daughters and to prevent them from developing normal relationships with peers" (p. 91). For example, the child molester will create tension between the mother and daughter, by pointing out, or even fabricating, information about the daughter to provoke criticism from the mother. Or he may tell the mother that she is not strict enough and should be more demanding of the daughter, even though the mother may already be demanding enough. After creating arguments between the mother and daughter, the offender can confide secretly in the daughter, telling her to ignore her mother, that she's only going "through a phase," and he will offer to "make Mom back off." He then advises the mother to soften her stance. When Mom does back off, the daughter feels indebted to her father, but the chasm grows wider between the mother and the daughter. He will cause more strife between them later, insisting privately to the mother that she not allow her daughter to stay overnight at her best girlfriend's house, thus incurring the daughter's anger. Then, he will encourage the mother to spend the evening away from home, "to help reduce the tensions around the house." Once alone with the daughter, he comforts her by figuratively stabbing the mother in the back, undermining what little authority she might still have retained after the series of feuds between the mother and the daughter.

In a parallel fashion, the offender may create barriers between the victim and her peers. For example, the offender will refuse to let the child's friends visit the home, especially after sexual abuse has begun. He will forbid the victim to visit her friends as well. The offender may make unreasonable demands regarding clothing (wearing old or unfashionable styles) and makeup (prohibiting its use when it is generally accepted by other parents and children for her age), causing the victim to appear "different" to school mates and causing her to be avoided or shunned. To make matters worse, because the initial trauma of being sexually abused is great, the victim may then withdraw from her friends while she sorts out her predicament. (For in-depth discussions of the effects of child sexual abuse see Finkelhor, 1979; Herman, 1981; Meiselman, 1979.)

Ironically, the victim is often willing to comply with demands that friends not visit because the trauma of being molested is not something that she is anxious to tell others about. She is afraid, ashamed, embarrassed, confused. She may feel profoundly guilty for the molestation itself, and she may feel worthless, a person of no value to anyone, as if she were "spoiled goods." Victims of sexual abuse find themselves in a whirlwind of negative, confusing, and often contradictory emotions, all of which occur simultaneously. Quite understandably, being around friends raises the victim's anxiety even further. Noting the change in her behavior, her friends may suspect something. She may fear that they will press her into telling them her troubles. She may perform poorly in school, quit talking to classmates, and become even more isolated than she was at first. Even in those cases where a child can maintain some degree of social contact with others until the fact of her abuse is disclosed, she finds herself profoundly isolated, especially from the person who should be most able to help her, her mother. Her mother, however, not knowing about the abuse, is essentially helpless to take preventive action at this point.

Sibling Barriers

Unfortunately, the child molester's devious work usually does not stop with isolating the victim from her mother and her friends. He begins to construct barriers between the victim and her sisters and brothers. For example, the offender may blame the victim for causing problems in the family but withdraw privileges from all the children in the family. This action causes the siblings to resent the victim. At the same time, he then secretly coerces the victim to engage in further sexual acts with him. The victim's sense of helplessness is increased. She cannot control her relationship with the person who is assaulting her, and furthermore, she cannot control her relationships with her brothers and sisters. She is assaulted from all sides now.

The wall of misunderstanding created between the victim and her siblings often takes years to unravel, if, indeed, it is ever unraveled at all. The secrecy of being molested often persists for years after the children are grown and have left the home. Sometimes several children are molested in a single family without ever knowing that their siblings are also being molested.

Barriers between siblings are sometimes so effective that an offender can molest one daughter after another in the following way: The father will molest the eldest girl until she becomes old and savvy enough to call a halt to the abuse by simply warning him that if he doesn't stop, she will inform the authorities and he can "rot in prison for the rest of his life!" She also warns him that if she ever learns of him laying a hand on any of her younger sisters, she will make things worse for him than the police ever could. What she does not realize is that her younger sisters are just as subject to the power of isolation as she was. Knowing this, the father begins molesting the second daughter, isolating her through a variety of threats, bribes, and coercion. The second daughter, not realizing this happened to her older sister, similarly matures and calls a halt to the abuse, giving the father the same warning, but just like her older sister, she does not realize that the father can successfully isolate the youngest sister as he did the older ones. Thus, the sexual assaults are transferred again to the third daughter in a family of victims. Regrettably, such experiences are not unique, and they illustrate the tremendous power that child molesters can have through isolating the victims and siblings from one another.

Isolating can occur in many ways. Besides punishment, bribery and special favors are commonly used to isolate a victim. For example, after punishing everyone for something the current victim did, the offender may later give privileges to the other siblings and tell them he favors them because of their good behavior. This creates a sense of superiority in the siblings' minds. They are more likely to isolate and shun the victim, as children will do, not because it is reasonable and just, but merely because they have been successfully manipulated. Then the offender may create secret rewards for the victim to enlist her cooperation with the sexual abuse. He will buy her presents, take her to special places, and give her special privileges without letting the others know.

Creating barriers between the victim and sibling or friends is crucial to setting up the family, because victims often disclose sexual abuse not to their mothers but to someone else, frequently their sisters, brothers, or close friends (Herman, 1981). But the distorted patterns of reward and punishment so disrupt the children's relationships that even if the victim discloses the abuse to her brothers or sisters, her siblings do not have the knowledge, skills, or perhaps even the desire to respond appropriately. Nonabused children are often concerned about what they will lose if the molester "gets in trouble." When they are recipients of special favors, treatment, or rewards from him, they are not anxious to see him get in any kind of legal trouble or leave the home. Thus, the child molester's efforts to isolate the victim from others not only has a profound impact on the victim's well-being but also affects how everyone in the family gets along.

Grooming Behaviors

Grooming is the offender's plan to make the victim less likely to resist, to make others unaware of what he is doing, or even to make them likely to help him, without their knowledge, to molest a child. Grooming behaviors in combination with isolating the victim form a powerful weapon that enables child molesters to assault victims sexually. Grooming often (though not always) involves pleasure for the victim. The trauma of sexual assault combined with this pleasure is powerful because it confuses the victim's senses about what is actually happening. As the case of Dan the school teacher illustrated, child molesters groom not only the victim but also the mother and siblings, and other people outside the victim's home, including relatives, neighbors, professional acquaintances, ministers, counselors, and probation officers. In fact, an entire community can be groomed. The child molester is able to concentrate his energies so effectively that, without their knowing it, everyone in a community or town can be set up in advance to believe the offender is innocent, no matter what the evidence suggests.

On its surface, grooming often is pleasurable and it reduces anxiety, concern, or fear. For that reason, people sometimes enjoy being groomed without knowing its sinister purpose. Dan groomed his professional colleagues by doing all of the additional work involved in extracurricular activities. This brought them considerable relief. He took children camping who otherwise would perhaps have never slept in a sleeping bag and tent. This brought pleasure to those parents unequipped to provide such experiences for their children. Furthermore, Dan made school programs function smoothly, bringing professional satisfaction to school administrators. Because grooming is so useful and effective, child molesters will take extreme measures to groom effectively. Three kinds of grooming will be discussed here:

1. Physically grooming the victim
2. Psychologically grooming the victim and her family
3. Grooming of the social environment or the community

The following examples may surprise some readers but they are in fact typical of what hundreds of child molesters do every day.

Physical Grooming

Physically grooming the victim usually begins with behaviors that children and adults would usually consider "normal" and appropriate. The child molester will wrestle, tickle, cuddle, hug, or play touching games with the victim, often in the presence of the mother or other adults and children. Thus, he not only secures the approval of the adults but lends an air of legitimacy to the activity. The victim can be convinced later that because she and the offender played this way in front of adults, there can be nothing wrong with playing this way when they are alone.

Later, usually when alone but sometimes even discreetly in the presence of other adults, the child molester begins to touch the private areas of the victim's body, her buttocks, between her legs, her vagina, and her breasts or the thighs, penis, and testicles if the victim is a boy. At first, he may touch the child over her clothing, and then later, under her clothing. With a younger child, the offender may set the victim on his lap. At first, the offender may have no erection discernible to the child and the physical contact seems normal. Later, because he is sexually aroused by children, he may develop an erection. The younger child usually does not understand what is occurring, and will have virtually no idea that the offender is becoming sexually aroused by the contact. Depending upon the age of the child, the offender's erection may have no particular significance or may even be an object of curiosity, and the child molester can be counted on to exploit this curiosity. He can engage in small talk, tell jokes, and engage in positive emotional interaction with the child. The child often derives pleasure from such activities.

Thus far, if the victim shows no discomfort, embarrassment, or resistance, and they are alone, the offender may start talking about his erection in a manner intended to confuse the child without causing any alarm. He will adopt a tone of voice and manner of speech that conveys the idea that it is entirely normal for adults and children to talk about penises, erections, and sexuality together. He will always be gauging the child's reaction and reassuring the child that their activity is acceptable. He will even try to make the conversation fun and will deliberately set out to put the child at ease. This approach brings the discussion of sex out in the open to whatever degree the child is comfortable with.

Because sexuality is not a topic that is usually discussed openly in our society, it is not difficult for the offender to control any conversation regarding sex with a child. Through this particular grooming process, the child is led to believe that everything is perfectly normal and acceptable. If no resistance is shown, and especially if he can manipulate the child into expressing curiosity about his erection, the offender proceeds further, suggesting that the child "check it out" (i.e., touch his erect penis) by touching his erection over his clothing or by reaching in his pockets or inside his trousers. He makes the child feel safe by making her think that she is in charge of initiating the activity. He takes deliberate steps to make sure she is not frightened in any way, and he does his best to see that she derives some pleasure, often simply by satisfying a curiosity in her that he has set out to create.

If the victim appears uncomfortable or resists in any way, the offender can retreat, going back to whatever activity the child was last comfortable with, where the child showed no resistance. This reduces the anxiety and resistance of the child, and the child is subtly led to believe that everything is "safe." Then the offender applies the pleasurable reward, for example, a hug, some candy, a toy, or a promise for allowing the sexual behavior to have gone on that long, that far.

In this pattern of "reach and retreat," the offender proceeds to a point where the child feels uncomfortable or resists, and he then retreats or backs off from the approach that he was using to an activity that is not threatening to the child. In this way, the offender has given some degree of pleasure to the potential victim and has also found out how far he can go, what border he can cross, the next time he approaches the child. During subsequent efforts, the child will be less uncomfortable and he can apply rewards more effectively, reminding the child, if necessary, that nothing bad happened last time and a reward awaits the child for just "a little more cooperation."

More than one therapist has reported that a typical ploy by the offender is to train children to reach inside his pockets to get candy, and later the offender will cut the pockets out of his pants and urge the children to reach farther until they touch his genitals, thereby giving him sexual pleasure. This shows the extreme and deliberate step-by-step grooming process some offenders use to involve children in sexual abuse. *One should never underestimate the degree of sophistication that child molesters will use to entice children, and when the reach-and-retreat approach is rewarded, the effect is very powerful.*

Psychological Grooming

Physical grooming is often accompanied by psychological grooming. Psychological grooming refers to all of the verbal statements (or other communication) that the offender uses to reduce the child's resistance and lessen the likelihood that she will disclose the molestation. The offender uses his verbal advantage and life experiences to manipulate the child in whatever way he chooses. For example, the offender may carry on playful chatter, distracting the child from inappropriate behavior such as touching her breasts or genital areas. Even though a child may show some discomfort when her grandfather strokes her vagina through her clothing, she may nevertheless ignore her discomfort and be quite interested when he tells her that her birthday is coming soon and he has a special surprise planned for her. In this way, the offender mixes physical with psychological grooming, using a steady stream of verbal chatter. This strategy proves to be a very effective combination with many children and explains why some children, especially those who are isolated, lonely, or withdrawn, are such easy prey for the child molester.

Psychological grooming is effective because the victim is usually not inclined to bring up embarrassing or dangerous topics. Although victims of sexual abuse usually want to bring the abuse out in the open to make the offender stop, they also fear revealing the abuse because of the potential criticism, blame, and risk it may bring to themselves (Herman, 1981). By using psychological grooming, the offender invades the victim's personal space, her body, confuses her psychologically about what is happening through his distracting verbal chatter, and protects himself from all suspicion. Even if the child does find the strength to object to the abuse, the offender can simply say she is mistaken. "We're simply wrestling like we've always done," he will claim defensively, implying that the victim is guilty somehow for accusing him of misbehavior, which is another form of psychological grooming. If the victim accepts this response ("It's what we've always done"), or is momentarily confused and does not immediately act to prevent the sexual touching, the offender can touch her inappropriately again and again. And by now, he has gathered all the information he needs about how far he can carry the abuse without the child calling a halt to it or breaking the secrecy.

During these moments of confusion, however, the offender is not relaxing. He is, in fact, plotting his next steps to progress further with the abuse. He is also preparing a new litany of explanations for his molestation. His responses all play upon the psychological vulnerability of his victim. He may claim, for example, "It is fun." "It doesn't hurt." "This is just to teach you what dirty little boys might do to you." "It's for your own good." "I wouldn't harm you." "This is our own special secret." "You tell me when to stop, but not just yet." "It's too late now, it's already happened, but I'll stop now if you want me to because I love you and care about you so much."

Psychological grooming with older children occurs as well, although the dynamics may be different because of the older children's reasoning abilities and because the older children can more quickly recognize the inappropriateness of the abuse. With older children, emotional appeals, arguments, threats, and blaming the victim are more common. Inducing guilt paves the way for cooperation. To feel good about herself, an older daughter may feel that the best thing to do is to comply. But it is a double bind. Coerced by intimidation, she feels guilty about rejecting her father's wishes but she also feels horrible if she is molested. The father's persistence will often win out in this psychological dilemma as he applies more and more pressure. And she cannot comment on her dilemma.

Depending upon the circumstances, the incestuous father will often claim it is his right to have some sexual activity with his daughter because he works so hard to pay the bills and "to keep the family together." This latter subtle threat implies that if the daughter does not comply with his sexual demands, the father may leave the family. An older child often clearly understands what financial hardship might result from the breadwinner leaving the family. This is a common and powerful psychological ploy. Victims of father-daughter incest frequently say they believed it was their responsibility to hold the family together by tolerating the sexual abuse (Herman, 1981).

An important aspect of psychological grooming is the offender blaming the victim. Typical examples are, "You know it was wrong to do this." "You're to blame, you should have stopped us." "You were old enough to know better." "You know how powerful a man's sex drive is." "It was your responsibility to stop it before it went so far." "You'll be in bigger trouble than me if you tell." "I'll go to prison for 20 years if you tell! Do you want that on your conscience?" "I'll tell your mother that you seduced me, and you know she'll take my word over yours." "You've read the newspapers! You know what'll happen to me if you tell. Castration and life with no parole! Do I deserve that?"

Such claims are simply intended to make the child feel guilty. They capitalize on the child's immaturity. What child could understand and argue about such issues on an adult's level? The mention of such volatile issues here, as in other places, is another ploy the offender uses to silence his victims and others whom he may be grooming.

The child molester's claim that the victim was responsible for the molestation identifies a crucial fact of child sexual abuse: Children are not able, either legally or psychologically, to give consent in a sexually abusive relationship. The offender's claim that the victim "allowed it to happen" completely distorts the nature of the adult-child relationship. From a legal standpoint, child sexual abuse laws make it clear that consent is not an issue. Even if the child agrees to sex with an adult, the act would still be against the law in every state. The laws make this distinction abundantly clear (Finkelhor, 1979).

Sometimes an offender turns the tables and threatens to tell the victim's mother about the abuse, blaming the victim for everything. This is a painful and ironic paradox because children do not understand that telling the mother might be the best thing that could happen for them. Children lack the maturity to understand this. The child is thus effectively isolated from the person she most needs to protect her, her own mother.

Rewards, bribes, and granting wishes are also important aspects of psychological grooming. Thus, touching something hard (an erect penis) in the child molester's pants is a small price to pay for a 4- or 6-year-old victim who has been promised a special reward such as the doll she has been hoping for all year. Gradually, however, touching "something hard" in the offender's pants may progress to more advanced forms of sexual abuse, from fondling genitals beneath clothing, to fondling during complete nudity, to actual intercourse. The reach-and-retreat pattern occurs in the psychological as well as the physical arena. The offender may bring up sexual matters in groups where adults and children (including the victim) are present, but later be far more graphic about sex when talking alone with the victim to see how much she will tolerate before she shows she is uncomfortable. He learns how far he can go by laying the groundwork for how he discusses sexual issues beforehand, in a larger group with other adults present.

The process of psychological grooming, like physical grooming, is often subtle and gradual. Each time the child molester initiates an inappropriate behavior with the victim, he tests whether he can encroach a little farther and watches to see whether the victim resists more strongly. If he has successfully chosen a victim who will not resist very much, he can encroach farther. The fact that he gradually encroaches on the victim works to his advantage because he is able to lodge powerful arguments against the child if she does begin to object. For example, "We did this yesterday, and it didn't hurt you." "It's okay, everyone knows you sit on my lap." "Everyone saw us, there's nothing wrong." "Don't you love me? This is okay between people who love each other they way we do." "I love you, and this is how we show our love for each other." This grooming takes place at a pace determined by how cautious a person the offender is and how much resistance the victim is able to generate.

The following are other commonly heard grooming tactics: "This is our special secret. You must keep our secret. No one must ever know about this, that way we can do many fun things together." "Don't tell anybody or then I won't be able to buy you any more dollies [clothes, beer, etc.]." "Mom will be angry." "Mommy will make me stop buying you presents." " The police will make me leave home, so don't let her or anybody else know." Also, he may promise to stop the abuse: "I promise that this is the last time that I will ever do this to you. I will never do it again!" The promise to stop frequently reassures the victim, although in reality, the promise is seldom kept. There may be a brief lull in the abuse, but the abuse inevitably resumes, usually until the child is old enough to make good on her promise to tell or runs away.

The effectiveness of psychological grooming explains in part why it is possible for the child molester to abuse children sexually for so long without being discovered. When the offender seeks no further gratification than fondling the victim without causing her severe discomfort and the rewards (or severe threats) are sufficient, the offender may be able to continue molesting for months and even years (Herman, 1981).

Intimidation may also be a conscious part of psychological grooming. Although he often appears to those outside the family to be generous, cooperative, and loving, within his home he is frequently the tyrant, using whatever traditional male power roles are necessary to intimidate family members (Herman, 1981). He may at times coerce his victim by physically assaulting her, assaulting other family members, or simply by threatening violence against others. For example he might say, "Something could happen to your kitten, Fluffy." "You wouldn't want me to lose your dolly, Tinkerbell, would you?" "Your friend Ginny couldn't visit you any more. You know, Ginny could even somehow disappear forever. They might not be able to find her at all if you don't do what I tell you." "I know how much you love Mommy. You wouldn't want to be responsible for getting her hurt, would you?" "I'll kill your mother if you don't let me do what I want, and you better not tell. It's your duty."

How frequently the offender threatens to assault, and even to kill, is surprising only until one recalls his social situation. He lives a dual life. He has convinced the world that he is a caring, reasonable, sympathetic, even timid, but productive citizen because he keeps his job and pays his bills. Inside the home he is quite the opposite. He frequently threatens family members because he deeply fears getting caught. If caught, he believes that he faces society's worst punishment: becoming a child molester sentenced to prison to face the scorn and abuse by society's most frightening and violent criminals, drug dealers, robbers, and murderers. In the offender's mind, a small lie such as threatening to kill someone is justified because it spares him the harshest punishment that he knows, being raped in prison. The child molester's mental life is filled with such distortions and twisted logic.

It is frightening for a child to think that her own mother might be harmed if her mother finds out about the sexual abuse. To compound this fear, *the offender makes it the victim's own responsibility to make sure her mother never finds out about the abuse.* If the victim fails in her inflicted "responsibility" to keep the mother from knowing, in her own mind she would be responsible for any harm that befell her mother. The psychological harm can be severe—a child living in constant fear that she would be responsible for injury to her mother. It is no wonder that the long-term harm to some victims of sexual abuse has been so well documented (Browne &

Finkelhor, 1986). The severe trauma of such threats also explains the error of suggesting that the victim is partially to blame "for letting it go on so long." The victim should never be blamed. The offender is fully and solely responsible for his actions of child sexual abuse.

Many victims are sexually abused by more than one child molester. Stepfathers, boyfriends of the victim's mother, and other men are quickly able to identify a child who has been sexually abused before. Previous victimization makes those children especially vulnerable. Often the previous abuse was never disclosed to the child's mother. If it was disclosed, the new offender can easily assess his own risk by determining what happened. Was the previous offender prosecuted or was he allowed to continue the abuse until the mother found some reason to simply force him to leave? Noted sociologist David Finkelhor (1979) writes that there is great reluctance of families to report reoffenses, even by formerly convicted relatives. Child molesters do not hesitate to capitalize on circumstances when children were previously abused and when their mothers were reluctant to help prosecute the offender. In such cases, the new offender can plan his own strategies to be less harsh than the previous offender. By his using bribes and rewards rather than physical force and intimidation, the victim may feel relieved simply from knowing that she is not going to reexperience the pain and serious injury that she previously had to endure. If her previous complaints failed to stop the past abuse, she may resign herself to the new abusive situation because, on the surface, it seems at least better than what she had to go through before. The new offender recognizes that she has learned to be helpless and takes every advantage of it.

Often, psychological grooming takes an outwardly positive appearance, although its purpose is still to abuse the victim. For example, the child molester may arrange to spend "special" time playing, traveling with, entertaining, or just listening to and talking with a child who already feels lonely, isolated, and neglected. He may introduce his own problems, giving the child a sense of importance by asking for her advice. Gradually, he will build an emotional rapport with the child until she feels a need to be with him for her own emotional comfort. The offender may talk about problems between himself and the victim's mother. He will subtly introduce the idea that the victim can comfort him, a "grown-up," and give emotional support and love to him, love that the mother should give but cannot or will not because she has problems of her own. Subtle suggestions that the victim is mature for her age stimulates her to begin thinking that she is able to act sexually in a mature manner with the offender.

Often children want to feel they are unlike the children around them and to believe that they are mature beyond their years. They especially want to be treated as if they were already adults. The offender's approach takes advantage of this desire. It leads to physical grooming, hugging and kissing, and then to whatever activity the victim will allow, through persuasion or by force. A child can even be convinced that being forced into a sexual relationship is an acceptable part of any adult sexual relationship. "This is how adults do it," he may tell her. By so doing, the child molester casts the coercion and force in a completely different light, suggesting to the child that the force itself is proof that she is truly an adult now. A liaison is created between the offender and the child based on the child's isolation, vulnerability, and her premature sexualization that the offender deliberately created and exploited. Even though such grooming appears positive, it is nothing more than another strategy designed to molest the child.

While grooming the victim, the offender also grooms the victim's mother. It appears that, more often than not, grooming the mother may be accomplished through threats and coercion, against all family members, rather than through bribes and rewards as has already been discussed. In families studied by Dr. Judith Herman, grown victims of father-daughter incest reported a high incidence of fathers who intimidated family members, especially the mothers. Just as the victims themselves tend to be isolated, the wives of child molesters are often found to be isolated from friends and family and lack strong connections to the community outside their homes. Such women are especially vulnerable to threats and force. The child molester has a very important reason to control the victim's mother: He must be able to get rid of her whenever he wants to molest the daughter undisturbed. It is no wonder, then, that many offenders frequently choose as wives women who have been raised in abusive families— they are more likely to submit fully to his coercion. Just as the molester will select an already vulnerable child to victimize, he will also seek out a vulnerable woman.

Once this is done, the offender can then choose from a wide arsenal of tactics to groom in the most negative ways. Anger, intimidation, and violence have been discussed. Another way is by encouraging the mother to drink alcohol. This serves two purposes. First, it "gets rid of" the mother during times that he wants to molest the child, for example, when she is passed out or falls asleep from the effects of alcohol. He will be certain that alcohol is available to the wife when he wants it to be there. He will encourage her alcoholism by reassuring her that she is not an alcoholic if others suggest that she should take a second look at her drinking pattern. He wants her to continue to drink and become incapacitated. He will reassure her that he is able to take care of the kids when she becomes drowsy from alcohol and wants to go to bed early. He may encourage her by reassuring her that she is able to return to moderate drinking if she has quit drinking. He does whatever it takes to cripple a woman with alcohol who may be especially susceptible to alcoholism.

The second purpose is to create an alibi in alcohol. In the offender's mind, those who know the family are not as likely to believe the mother if she ever accuses him of sexually abusing her daughter if they think she is an alcoholic. While he secretly encourages her to continue drinking, to others he confides his concern: "I just can't get her to quit. I've talked about getting treatment and going into a hospital, but my words fall on deaf ears." He may tell stories to friends about finding alcohol hidden in the home and he himself may become abstinent, or at least publicly so, to further persuade acquaintances that he is doing everything possible for the family's welfare. Underneath the outward appearance, however, may lurk a concerted effort to disable the wife and persuade the circle of friends that the mother is the family's "problem." If she ever accuses him of abuse, or supports her daughter's disclosure of abuse, he has a ready-made alibi: His accuser is an alcoholic.

The child molester can isolate the wife as effectively as he can isolate his victims. He undermines her self-confidence by criticizing her appearance, intelligence, social grace, or her personality. He may set her up to fail in social situations and then reassure her that it's okay that she doesn't feel comfortable going out or having guests in. While he reminds her that they can find ways to entertain each other alone, he also subtly reminds her about her social failures. At other times, isolating her can also take a negative tone. He may discourage his wife from developing close relationships outside the home altogether and especially discourage her from developing friends who might drop by the home unannounced. Unexpected guests are a particular inconvenience and even a threat to the offender, who may be molesting his child at home alone. Friends also provide the opportunity for the wife to talk to others about her family and how it functions. She can ask more objective persons whether they have noticed anything wrong or unusual about her family situation. Is it common for their husbands to threaten them or the children, or frequently to spend time with one of the children alone, or to develop long-term disinterest in sexual activity? Such conversations make grooming more difficult because they provide a basis for the spouse to evaluate her situation and possibly become more suspicious about the family itself.

However, there are clearly times when the husband wants his wife to be gone from the home, so that he can molest his daughter in privacy. Therefore, at these times he pushes his wife into activities outside the home where there is little chance that the wife will discuss child sexual abuse or family matters with anyone. Child molesters are particularly threatened by churches that often adopt proactive programs for prevention of child sexual abuse. Instead, they choose churches that teach blind obedience to the father's authority and when they are active members themselves, they may discourage thoughtful discussion about abuse, either by extreme statements about castrating all child abusers, or by claiming that members of "this faith" simply don't do such things (i.e., commit child sexual abuse), despite the known fact that child sexual abuse is found in all social groups, including all religious affiliations.

The husband may also groom the wife in positive ways by encouraging her to participate in activities outside the home. School activities, Parent-Teacher-Student Associations, college programs, hobby clubs, and other social outlets that take the mother away from the house provide an effective barrier, that of distance, between the unsuspecting but protective mother and her children. The more time-consuming and highly structured the activity, the better for him because it leaves him alone with his victim for specified periods of time.

Grooming the Social Environment

We have looked at how the offender physically grooms the victim and how he psychologically grooms both the victim and her mother. Most offenders, however, take grooming one step farther and groom persons outside the home. As with the school teacher, Dan, some offenders spend considerable energy grooming their friends, relatives, acquaintances, and professional associates, either to foster situations in which they can molest or to create allies who will aide them in their defense if allegations are made against them.

Dan's case illustrates a primary offender strategy of making others so dependent that they will resist any suggestion of child sexual abuse. The same strategies that Dan employed are used in a variety of organizations, particularly those that involve children. Involvement in churches provides abundant opportunities for environmental grooming, because children's religious education and recreational activities are such an important part of church life and churches rely on the voluntary help of their members. The offender will offer to do the "dirty work," supervising children during chores at family retreats or during times that other adults participate in special activities, "sacrificing" his own plans for the weekend. He will quietly volunteer when no other adult seems willing or able to assist. To avoid suspicion, he will also involve himself in adult activities when children are conspicuously absent.

Furthermore, the offender will strive diligently to make his efforts a true success and significant contribution to the organization.

Everyone knows he really works! Mere effort is appreciated, but real success fosters dependency between the organization and the child molester. Those organizations often reward the child molester with public recognition for his service, not suspecting the hidden purpose behind his work. As a result, it is very difficult for those who know an offender to believe that he could be guilty of child molestation; his guilt means extra work for them. It is a kind of social double jeopardy. They discover that they have been betrayed by a friend, and they have to take over the work that he managed so well. It is no wonder that they want to believe he is innocent.

The power of grooming the community is widely recognized by experts in the criminal justice system. Kenneth Lanning of the FBI training academy in Quantico, Virginia, writes in a manual for law enforcement officers that

> prosecution of many child molesters may not be welcomed by their communities, especially if the molester is a prominent citizen. Citizens may protest, and community organizations may rally to the support of the offender and even attack the victims. City officials may apply pressure to halt or cover up the investigation. (Lanning, 1986, p. 31)

Grooming the social environment continues even after an offender confesses or is convicted. Typically, the child molester will conceal significant parts of his sexual offense history. He will minimize or lie about the seriousness of his crimes. He will distort what he actually did. He will bury any admission he makes under scores of rationalizations and excuses. A common grooming tactic is to tell others that he was convicted of assaulting someone who attacked him in a tavern, but he injured the other man so badly, nobody would believe it was self-defense. Then, if acquaintances do talk about him, they spread his lies among themselves, enhancing his prestige and lowering their suspicion about what his true crime was. When asked directly, he will indicate it was unpleasant and he doesn't want to talk about it anymore, saying, for example, that "it's in the past." If anyone knows his offense was child molestation, he will claim that he was coerced into a confession or that he wanted to spare the family of the humiliation of a public trial and he thought it was better to "take a fall, even though innocent; do some jail time, and get it all behind me instead of airing the family's dirty laundry in public." He can put a real damper on any further discussion through some shocking story about how he saw some "real" sex offender raped in jail by a gang of hoodlums. The result is usually that his acquaintances do not talk about him much and when they do, they are spreading misinformation. Thus, an entire network of friends, family, and acquaintances can be groomed by the child molester even when he intimates his conviction was for child sexual assault. Ironically, he can paint a picture of himself as the victim who is willing to suffer to spare his family any grief. He may even believe, in his own distorted way, that he actually is the victim and that others should feel sorry for him for suffering on behalf of his family. This attitude will not change until he has entered an effective program that addresses his distorted beliefs about himself and others.

A common approach to grooming groups of people is to play into their prejudices and misconceptions. Because news media stories about injustices in the criminal justice system are commonplace, the child molester will claim that he was just such a victim, treated unfairly by "the system." He will give details that sound significant but were essentially irrelevant at trial, effectively distorting the listener's perception of the court system. By maintaining his pleasant, meek appearance while making himself out as the victim, he can usually be persuasive. He will be courteous, helpful, agreeable to most requests or concerns, and will generally project an air of confidence mixed with personal indignation that he is being treated unfairly, claiming that his constitutional rights were denied to him. Listeners understandably believe the litany of distorted facts and explanations because he has pointed out stories that they themselves have heard or seen in the media, and they are only amazed that he is not more indignant and angry than he appears.

He, however, knows that he is walking a tightrope. If he invokes too much sympathy among his audience, they may band together to act in his defense by calling the prosecuting attorney to protest. Such an action could result in these persons learning the true nature of his crimes. Thus, the child molester provides enough information to nurture their sympathy without sparking them to take any true action.

New Relationships

After being convicted, the offender continues his efforts to groom mothers with children, his new potential victims. Up to the point of apprehension, grooming served him well, often helping him escape detection for literally years while his molestation took place. More grooming is especially likely when the offender begins a new romantic relationship. Such relationships typically occur when the offender's wife divorces him and refuses to allow him any contact with the children or his victim(s). At that point, after being released from jail or prison, the offender's approach is first to nurture an emotional and/or sexual relationship with a woman who is to some degree dependent on others for many of her needs. She may be unable to maintain her home and personal needs, or she have a multitude of other family responsibilities, including those essential to her children's welfare. The offender begins to help her out, typically by performing routine maintenance chores such as repairing her car or washing machine, or by fixing the plumbing. He will often support her financially as well as emotionally, recognizing that survival in itself is a lonely journey for any single parent. It is no difficulty for the child molester to listen to and sympathize with a mother facing hardship and poverty and to provide timely advice, not to mention intimate, sexual comfort. Sometimes the single mother may have problems with an emotionally disturbed child and she thinks or even says aloud that her child "needs a father figure." The stage may now be set for a new grooming process leading to new victims.

Once the offender has begun meeting the mother's emotional and physical needs he may disclose his criminal conviction, but usually in the most minimal and calculated way. For example, after a long day of backbreaking work for her, when she is especially

grateful for his help, he may mention that he is currently on probation and he is terribly ashamed of his past. He may stop here for now.
She will not pursue the matter lest she show ingratitude for his
generosity. Later, without sharing the details, he may let her know
that he "abused" children, in some vague way, but that he has
"learned his lesson," a very common expression among child molesters who want others to believe they were "cured" by a jail
experience. Or, he may say that he "assaulted" someone, not mentioning at this time that the assault was sexual in nature and against
a child. He may later describe himself as an "ex-offender," a term
that conveys the sense of something that happened many years ago
and implies that his past behavior no longer matters, that it is of no
consequence.

If he should disclose his history of sexual abuse, he will usually
indicate that he is no longer a threat to children. To her, he may claim
that the offense was alcohol related and because he no longer drinks
alcohol, he can now control his alcohol, or he has been saved in a
religious sense, he has therefore solved any problem he may have
had with children in the past. Or he may state that because he has
completed an alcohol treatment program he has been "rehabilitated." He can then provide a number of diversionary details about
his time in jail or prison that are so shocking the listener quickly
changes the subject away from the fact of his criminal history to "the
system" and how unfairly it treats people.

If he does tell her that he sexually molested a child, he will
emphasize his sincerity to make amends for his crime, claiming, for
example, that "I will never repeat my mistake, so help me God! It
was a one-time thing, a mistake, I really don't know how it happened
but I want to just put it all behind me." "I've done my time and I've
learned my lesson! Talking about it can't change what happened. I
can't change the past. Nobody can. So it won't do any good talking
about it." "Just give me a chance to prove myself by what I do now,
not by my past." Along with these declarations, the offender will say
that he does not want to discuss it further. Particularly, he does not
want to discuss in detail the grizzly facts or pattern of his sexual
assaults. His intent is to control all conversation completely. He

wants to control how much is said whenever and if ever the subject is discussed. He wants to determine who will be included in the conversation and who will know what details afterwards.

More important, he will manipulate any listener away from getting corroboration about what he says because it will invariably reveal his lies and distortions. He will reveal certain details but ask that the listener promise not to discuss the matter with anyone else. If pressed to reveal too much, he may threaten to terminate the relationship or become emotional and take a victim stance in a subtle effort to persuade the listener to back off. The intent is to reduce the flow of information and eliminate communication among those persons who know him.

Control of the discussion is easily accomplished. In reality, few people wish to pry into the details of an offender's sex life. Most people are uncomfortable discussing sexual issues openly, and the child molester capitalizes on this fact as he does on so many other opportunities. A simple admission, such as "Yes, I molested my daughter," is usually so shocking that the listener is relieved if the offender does not want to discuss it further. Unless a person has learned some of the defenses and manipulations of the child molester (e.g., by reading this and other books, or consulting with a therapist or professional), it is difficult to maintain any control of the conversation with the offender. The child molester generally remains in control through "shocking" disclosures and other manipulations. He may disclose to a new girlfriend that he molested his daughter and gain her confidence in his "honesty," without revealing the fact that he also molested his son, their three cousins, and 10 of their friends.

Although not all child molesters deliberately attempt to shock or intimidate others, the power of shocking others is not lost on child molesters. They know that aggressive disclosures can frighten people and squelch discussion. For this reason, as well as the fact that child molesters are notoriously dishonest, one should not rely on the facts that a child molester voluntarily presents. It is certainly important to let the offender talk about himself to whatever extent he chooses and to pay attention and remember what he is saying. However, one should never conclude that he has given the full truth. It is absolutely

necessary to get the facts from another party, such as the sex
offender's probation officer or counselor. How to do so will be
discussed in depth in Chapters 7 through 10 of this book.

Grooming a new girlfriend occurs not just verbally. The offender
will be careful to maintain his best behavior around her children so
that he will appear to be an even better father figure than the
mother's past husband or boyfriend. Due to his helpful acts and good
deeds, the mother gradually becomes convinced that he could never
be a threat to her own children. To her, he seems so much more open
and sincere than any man she has known before. (Contrary to
popular belief, child molesters often have good empathy for others;
they simply fail to use what empathy they have to stop themselves
from assaulting children.) With relative ease, the child molester can
turn a potential adversary (a mother with children) into his advocate,
an ally whose very children he may one day molest.

Sometimes the offender may emphatically repeat the concern
that he must never offend against any children or even be alone with
children ever, ever again. This is actually cunning use of reverse
psychology. The more he insists that he is concerned about the
welfare of her children, the more the mother can believe in his
sincerity and, more important, the more she will come to believe that
he poses no risk at all to her children. She begins to tell him directly
and to tell any others who may now know about him, that she simply
cannot believe he would ever repeat his mistake. She points to all
the evidence she has accumulated. Without knowing it, she has
cleverly been groomed by the child molester.

"He hasn't tried to hide a thing from me. He has been completely
open and honest from the beginning. Don't you believe that a person
can change?" she asks anyone who questions why she, a mother with
children, would associate with a convicted child molester. These,
however, are the exact lines that the child molester has been cleverly
feeding her. Then, she begins persuading herself more strongly than
ever, sometimes even over the offender's very own objections, that
he is no risk to her children. All along, this is exactly what he
intended to do. He continues to build this relationship by being "the
man in her life," and he gradually becomes the man in the children's

lives as well. He continues to help her in whatever ways he can and makes every effort, outwardly, to build strong relations with her children. Then, he agrees—reluctantly, on the surface—to spend more time with her children. At first, he agrees to baby-sit the children when she needs to go shopping. Later when other child care plans fall through, he agrees to baby-sit over the weekend while she visits a sick relative in another city. Almost without effort, he has become a primary caretaker for her children. He has successfully and totally groomed her. Thereafter, he keeps a lookout for opportunities to exploit the family, to be alone with the children, to groom the children, and then to molest them.

What the child molester fears is complete, open, and honest communication among those who deal with him such as his wife, his parents, the probation officer and his counselor, his employers, his neighbors, his friends, and his new girlfriend. He fears that the facts about him will be shared openly. Sharing complete and accurate information means the end of his secrecy. Ironically, ending secrecy is exactly what is needed both to protect children from further abuse and to see that the offender gets the help he truly needs. Later in this book the reader will find out how to obtain such information. Armed with the facts, those who know, work with, and live with convicted child molesters will be able to make more informed, better decisions. These decisions will help make the lives of children and families safer and will increase the odds that those who know the offender can really and effectively help him to keep from repeating his crimes of sexual molestation.

Denial

Denial is a characteristic of virtually all convicted sex offenders. For our discussion here, denial is meant to include all communication by the offender in which he insists that he did not commit the crime, gives reasons or "proofs" intended to persuade others of his innocence, or attempts to minimize or distort the extent of his sexual deviance. The polygraph examination (commonly known as a lie detector test) is of growing interest to therapists who treat convicted child molesters for several reasons. The most important is that polygraph examinations encourage the offender to admit more and more important information about himself. The more accurate the information about the offender, the more appropriate the treatment can be. However, denial by the offender often does not cease even years after conviction. Those who know the offender and who are aware of his use of denial can be more helpful in assuring the safety of children and the success of the offender in treatment and in avoiding reoffense.

❖ ❖ ❖

GEORGE

George was a meat cutter. He had molested his two daughters, ages 7 and 9, until one of them told a school counselor. George moved out of his home and his wife divorced him. At his attorney's encouragement, George contacted a counselor in town, explained what had happened, and asked about arranging a counseling program. The counselor was experienced in many other fields but had only treated a few sex offenders. He interviewed George regarding his background, read the police reports and statements by his daughters, and decided that he could treat George safely in the community. George pleaded guilty to the charges and was put on probation after serving 90 days in work release so that he could keep his job. Afterwards, he was released on probation with the requirement that he complete counseling, obey the law, and follow the directions of his therapist and probation officer.

The probation officer had an uneasy feeling about George. Her intuition told her that there was more to George's story than George had so far disclosed to anyone. She asked the counselor to have George take a polygraph examination to see whether George had been completely truthful about his sexual history.

The counselor objected. He felt insulted that a probation officer would suggest how he, a licensed counselor, should proceed with psychological treatment. Furthermore, he felt that he had the skills and experience to understand and treat George appropriately. He believed that he had the skills to make George admit the truth, however slow and painful it might be for him. The counselor had good credentials and was respected by other professionals in the community, and he was dedicated to treating George successfully.

In this case, the probation officer was not questioning the authority of the counselor. Her concern was not so much for

George's successful treatment (although that certainly was important to her, too), but rather for the safety of children. She
felt that if George had hidden any important secrets from his
past, those problems might remain untreated. She did not know
whether George had lied. Perhaps he had been entirely truthful,
but she had learned that on matters of personal safety, she
should not ignore her intuition. And in George's case, she felt
uneasy following each interview with him. Perhaps it was the
way he seemed to avoid eye contact with her. Maybe it was the
way he said treatment was "going fantastic!" She knew that, at
best, sex offender treatment was a personally painful experience for child molesters, because they had to deal openly with
the destruction they had caused their children while admitting
shameful and embarrassing acts they had committed against
helpless children with total disregard for their welfare. When
treatment is going well for child molesters in the truest sense,
they seldom, if ever, describe it as "fantastic." They are more
likely to say something along the lines of, "I'm learning some
things I didn't think enough about before."

The probation officer also knew that some counselors
(although certainly not all of them) used polygraph examinations with good results, and she felt that a polygraph examination was a good idea in George's case. After a long series of
unsuccessful telephone calls and letters to try to persuade the
counselor to change his mind, the probation officer decided
that she would ask for a court hearing to consider making a
polygraph examination a requirement of probation. This would
also allow the counselor the opportunity to argue in court
against the polygraph examination and the matter would not
become an ongoing power struggle between the two professionals. The date for a court hearing was set.

Once the hearing was set, the counselor changed his mind.
Knowing that other therapists sometimes used polygraph examinations, he felt uncomfortable claiming in court that one
was completely unnecessary in George's case. After consulting
with some of his professional colleagues who treated greater

numbers of sex offenders than he did, he reversed his decision, as was his prerogative. He advised George that after consulting with his professional colleagues, he felt a polygraph examination was really a beneficial idea. It would resolve any question the judge might have regarding George's truthfulness and would give George an opportunity to demonstrate to everyone his commitment to change. The examination would also improve George's relationship with his probation officer because suspicion would no longer characterize the basic tone of their interviews. The polygraph examination was scheduled for just a few days later.

The morning before the examination, George requested an emergency session with the therapist. George reassured the therapist that he had been completely truthful about molesting his daughters but that there were a few other aspects of his sexual history that he had lied about. He said that he was sexually aroused by animals. Ever since he was a young boy living on a farm, he had been having sex with farm animals. Further, when he went hunting, he found that he was also sexually aroused by game that he had shot. George told the counselor that his sexual appetite for animals was so consuming that he had mentally catalogued every farm animal he could see from the highway while driving home from work. George had always thought that this made him so extremely abnormal that no therapist would ever accept him in to a treatment program, so he lied about it during his evaluation with the therapist because he was afraid of being sent to prison.

Polygraph examinations of sex offenders usually consist of two parts: the preexamination interview and the polygraph test itself. During the preexamination interview, the examiner will sometimes ask the offender to specify the frequency and nature of sexual crimes and then to list the frequency and nature of all other forms of sexual activities he has experienced in his life. The examiner may even read from a standard, lengthy list, asking whether the offender has participated in any of a wide variety of sexual activities. Upon learning from George that he had a wide variety of unusual sexual experiences, George's counselor took a new sexual history from George. He asked questions and wrote down all that George disclosed. Then, the counselor sent this information to the polygrapher and consulted with the examiner to be sure that the right material was covered in the examination.

Although George had disclosed a long history of bestiality (sex with farm animals and wild game that he had hunted), the test results indicated that George was attempting to deceive the polygrapher. After showing him the results, George begrudgingly admitted that he had molested not only his daughters but his young nephew as well. Because it had happened over 10 years ago, George had hoped his polygraph examination would not show any deception when he was tested. He was afraid, he said, that he would be prosecuted for molesting the nephew, though the nephew had never disclosed the abuse to his parents and the family moved to another state shortly after it happened. The polygrapher consulted with the therapist about the results and what George had to say, and they agreed to give another polygraph examination at a later date.

When it was verified during the second polygraph examination that George no longer appeared to be attempting to deceive anyone about his sexual history, the counselor decided to refer George to another counselor who was more experienced in dealing with problems that were so far outside the realm of his professional expertise.

After the results of the interviews and polygraph examinations, the enormous complexities of George's case became clear to everyone involved. All of the professionals involved in George's case now had many significant decisions to consider; for example, whether it was appropriate for George to continue in his profession as a meat cutter, whether he should be prosecuted for the years-old abuse of his nephew, and whether he should lose the privilege of probation and be sent to prison. The court decided to allow George to continue on probation, leaving the choice of occupation to the therapist. The prosecutor decided not to prosecute the case involving George's nephew. The goals of treatment were radically changed, now taking into consideration that George had a history of attraction to young boys as well as sexual arousal to animals. These aspects of his past would probably never have become known without the polygraph examination.

❖   ❖   ❖

We have now looked at how the offender sets up others so that he can molest his chosen victim(s). The next few chapters will describe characteristics common to nearly all sex offenders. The first of these, as shown in George's case, is denial. Subsequent chapters will deal with the use of secrecy, blaming, and manipulation. Numerous experts have described the characteristic of denial that is common to virtually every convicted child molester (Schwartz, 1988b). There is nearly unanimous agreement among specialists who treat them that child molesters deny committing offenses when they are first caught and sometimes for a long time afterwards as well. Some persist in their denial even though there is overwhelming evidence against them.

One offender, Jim, had served many years in prison. The entire time, he denied that he had ever had sex with his niece. Although his wife left him, his mother stood by him insisting on his innocence. Each time that Jim became eligible for parole, his plans were turned down by the parole board. Then he was interviewed carefully by a parole officer who took the time to visit him in prison and talk to him at length about his case. After a three-hour interview of quiet but persistent and thoughtful questions by the parole officer, Jim admitted that he had in fact committed the offense. Jim told the parole officer that no one else had ever taken so much time to probe his story, to scrutinize his denials, and to cross-examine his alibi. Jim knew that admitting his crime might in fact reduce his chances for parole, but parole had been denied so many times before that he had grown weary of trying to "live a lie" after 7 years, even if it meant confessing to his mother and letting other relatives know that he was indeed guilty after all.

When first accused, the sex offender usually denies his offense adamantly. As Michael J. Dougher, Ph.D., writes,

> Decisions [about sex offenders] require an adequate information base which can only be acquired through thorough assessment procedures. Moreover given the fact many, if not most sex offenders tend to lie about their offenses and are unreliable and deceptive in their verbal reports, the importance of a thorough assessment cannot be overemphasized. (1988, p. 77)

Michael Dougher is writing about the decisions regarding how to treat sex offenders in prison. However, his remarks are equally applicable to those dealing with a convicted child molester who is free in the community. It is not difficult to understand why denial would characterize the child molester's thought patterns and communication with others. The social stigma against them is one of the strongest known in our society. It is so strong, in fact, that they are stigmatized in jails and prisons by other offenders. Just as many law abiding citizens do, other criminals see sex offenders as a particularly despicable group of criminals. With the increased public awareness of the problem of sexual deviance, child molesters are confronted daily with widespread disapproval in newspaper stories, magazine articles, and television and radio programs. Headlines cry out for harsher punishment of child molesters. As a result, the offenders are confronted everywhere with harsh attitudes. Along with everyone else, they hear their own friends and relatives condemn child molesters. Many of these people say that they believe society should "Lock them up forever, castrate them, and throw away the key!" Such disapproval contributes to their tremendous fear of being caught, convicted, and incarcerated. It strengthens their resolve to deny any involvement in sexual abuse, whatever the evidence against them suggests.

What most people fail to understand is how often people unwittingly encourage the child molester's denial even after he has actually been convicted in court and despite sometimes overwhelming, incontrovertible evidence against him. These individuals, however, normally do not realize that they are being manipulated by the offender in ways described in the preceding chapter. Nor are they aware that they are encouraging the child molester's denial to the detriment of everyone, including the offender himself.

One way that this can happen, for example, is when the child molester tells a friend that his wife has pulled the "final trick" in their divorce by claiming that he sexually abused their daughter. "This way," he claims, "she can lay stake to the home, the cars, and get high alimony from me for years to come." As discussed in the preceding chapter, the friend is unlikely to ask what, exactly, it is that he has been accused of doing. After all, few people want to ask for the graphic details about anyone's sexual activities, let alone the details about an actual case of child molestation by someone they know. The friend virtually never asks, "Joe, what's the evidence against you?" Instead, the friend innocently responds, "I'm sorry, I hope things work out okay. That's really too bad."

But child molesters often distort what they hear others say. As a result, to the sex offender, this friend's simple offer of sympathy means he has fooled the friend and persuaded him of his innocence. In reality, the friend may have come to no conclusion about the allegations at all. Or if the offender believes in his own innocence (e.g., that molesting his daughter was really only sex education), he may leap to the conclusion that the friend has carefully weighed all the evidence and has also come to the belief that he is totally innocent.

Furthermore, because it was so easy to persuade his friend of his innocence, the offender begins to believe that he can convince many others of his innocence as well. And if he can convince his wife of his innocence, she might even be willing to take him back, stop the divorce action, and let him move back into the home. If he can convince his wife, she might be able to pressure the child into saying it was all "a mistake."

The acquaintance has innocently encouraged the offender to believe that there is hope in denial. The pattern of denial will continue long after it has begun, even after conviction, and sometimes throughout an offender's counseling program, unless the counselor insists that he must quit denying, or he will be kicked out of treatment and returned to court where he could conceivably be given more jail time, or worse, be sent to prison. As the prison inmate, Jim, illustrated, denial may not cease for 5 or 10 years, and sometimes offenders never cease denying their offense. (Denial is, of course, a valid, legal defense. For our purpose, however, we are discussing convicted child molesters who ultimately resist all other methods of determining the truth of their cases, such as an open examination of all of the evidence or polygraph examination.)

The importance of requiring the offender to admit to his sexual assaults is well known to therapists who specialize in the treatment of sex offenders. As long as he denies his offense, no meaningful sex offender therapy can occur. A recent survey of therapists in four states demonstrated that therapists universally require the child molester's candid acknowledgment of sexual assaults before they permit him to enter their programs for treatment (Green, 1988).

Although it may be extremely difficult, wives, friends, and other acquaintances should not discuss his denials, alibis, and whitewashed explanations of sexual assault with the convicted child molester. Instead they should encourage him to talk with his therapist about these matters or speak with his attorney. This approach can help promote involvement in an effective therapy program. Prior to conviction, there are in fact other avenues the wife can take that will not feed into the offender's pattern of denial. This involves letting others evaluate and decide the matter as objectively as possible. In many communities the sex offender can participate in an evaluation for sexual deviance that is verified by a polygraph examination. The wife can insist that the husband participate in such an evaluation. This takes the issue and any arguments out of the realm of interpersonal persuasion and personal conflict ("If you really loved me, you, of all people, would believe me!") and places matters in the far more objective arena of trained professionals.

The matter of polygraph examination, it must be stated, is not without some controversy and will be discussed in depth in Chapter 10. Prior to taking a polygraph examination, child molesters often object on the basis that these examinations send innocent men to prison. However, the results of polygraph examinations are used in court only extremely rarely and then only with the child molester's permission. More often, the concern is that guilty men can sometimes beat the polygraph examination and appear innocent of crimes they actually did commit. Experience with hundreds of polygraph examinations shows repeatedly that men who fail the polygraph at one point in time nearly always admit later that they were lying.

A comprehensive review of the scientific evidence regarding polygraph examinations by the U.S. Congress's Office of Technology Assessment concludes that although the scientific research does not support polygraphs in employment screening, their use in criminal investigations cannot be so easily ruled out (Office of Technology Assessment, 1983). The American Medical Association's Council on Scientific Affairs (*Journal of the American Medical Association,* 1986) goes a step further:

> It is established that classification of guilty can be made with 75%-97% accuracy, but the rate of false-positives [finding someone guilty when they really are innocent] is often sufficiently high to preclude use of this test as the sole arbiter of guilt or innocence. This does not preclude using the polygraph test in criminal investigations as evidence or as another source of information to guide the investigation with full appreciation of the limitations in its use. (p. 1172)

In certain specialized treatment programs that require polygraph examinations, breaking the offender's denial pattern often happens more quickly. Ironically, once the offender admits his offense, he finds to his surprise that his world does not fall apart. Rather, he receives support for his willingness to begin looking at himself honestly, especially when he is in group therapy, with beneficial results for himself, his family, his wife, his victim, and for other children as well. Once the offender stops denying his sexual crimes, he can begin to look at other issues in his life. Until then, he remains absorbed in his effort to convince others of his innocence. Once he openly acknowledges his guilt, he can begin to look at his own unacceptable personal and sexual life, his abuse of his wife and children, his habit of keeping secrets from others, and his history of manipulating others for his own selfish ends. Only then can truly effective treatment begin.

Secrecy

In its most basic sense, secrecy means simply not telling others what is happening or what has happened. For child molesters, secrecy is much more sophisticated. For them secrecy refers also to how child molesters recover once the truth has been revealed. It includes how they perpetually attempt to cover up the truth in their communication. From this perspective, five stages of secrecy can be observed:

1. *Total denial*
2. *Misunderstood intentions*
3. *Minimal admission with an explanation*
4. *Partial disclosure*
5. *Full disclosure*

Secrecy does not end automatically, even under the best of circumstances, with the most motivated offender, because secrecy has become ingrained in the child molester's personality. Nevertheless, the slow process of dismantling secrecy is essential both for the safety of the children and for the community at large, as well as for therapy for the offender to be effective.

❖   ❖   ❖

BEN

Ben was the assistant pastor at a large urban church. His job was to direct the young teens' recreation and religious education program. He had worked with an assistant to help him for a while, until the church budget forced a staff cutback. The assistant was eliminated and Ben was alone in his responsibilities with the youth of the church. Ben took over the entire job on his own, without complaint. Often he drove children several miles to and from a variety of church programs and activities. Ben found many opportunities to talk with some of the teens alone. Although he had never talked about sexual abuse during any of the group activities (at this time, personal safety programs regarding sexual abuse for students were rare), he began asking some of the teens about "sexual responsibility." As he drove them around, it was easy for him to expand such discussions to include his own sexual experiences. Before long, it was common for Ben to talk explicitly about sex with teenage girls alone in his car or the church van while driving them home.

Ben was young, in his twenties, a little overweight but still handsome, and had grown close to many of the teens. He had no problems and there were no complaints about how he managed the programs. He began to talk with Sally, a 12-year-old girl who lived with her mother, about his own "lack of sexual experience." He asked her if she thought there were something wrong with him that he had never been married. He wondered aloud whether he were attractive to women. He showed more and more emotion as he talked with Sally while shuttling her between church and home. Her mother worked Sunday evenings, which provided a convenient excuse for him to drive Sally home. Often he would take a group home and Sally would be the last he would drop off. Other times, Sally was the only one who needed a ride.

Slowly but surely, Ben made Sally feel that she had a unique ability to bolster his ego. It was not long before they were kissing and petting heavily in the car before they got home. Sally was anxious to relate to a father figure, and her crush on Ben grew. She kept their relationship a secret from her mother and others in the church. Sometimes Ben would drop Sally off before others on the way home, just for appearances' sake. He explained to her that sometimes he felt what they did was wrong, and at other times, that he wanted to be alone with her, but he didn't want people to get suspicious. Sally understood.

So did Jean, Mary, and Bertha. So did plenty of other young teenage girls at the previous church where Ben had worked. Ben had so successfully created a web of secrecy that he had been able to molest scores of young teenagers sexually, using basically the same approach ("Prove to me that there is nothing wrong with me sexually") for over 4 years before being caught. It was later discovered that Ben had also become sexually involved with some of the girls' mothers as well. Ben had refined his skill at keeping his life secret to a fine art.

❖ ❖ ❖

Chapter 1 dealt with how the sex offender uses the setup to molest victims while deceiving their families and entire communities. This chapter will explore how he continues to use secrecy when the first allegations of child sexual abuse against him are made, and how he continues to use secrecy during the period of prosecution and even after conviction. As listed above, five stages of secrecy in this special sense can be identified with child molesters; each will be explored in this chapter. At times, these five stages can occur in a regular progression from one to the next, as if they were a predictable pattern. At other times, some offenders move quickly to the fifth stage of full disclosure, yet others maintain their dependence on secrecy throughout their lives and remain in total denial despite often overwhelming evidence and a criminal conviction against them. (For an extensive discussion of patterns of disclosure by sex offenders, see Salter, 1988, chap. 8.)

Total Denial

A common and not surprising reaction by the child molester to the initial allegations of sexual abuse is total denial of any sexual misconduct of any sort. While doing this, the offender also assesses who will believe his denials and whether his plans to set up and groom everyone will pay off. He begins to implement the manipulative strategy he has been planning for so long. For example, the offender may remind his wife of the tremendous financial losses they face if "she allows" the allegations to proceed, because he will, naturally, have to hire an expensive lawyer. He might tell her that they may have to separate, and that she and the daughter will be responsible for the suffering the family will face if she "doesn't stop the prosecution from going forward."

Offenders who remain in the state of "total denial" frequently are sentenced to prison because those who do deny all culpability in their crimes are generally viewed by courts and therapists as virtually untreatable and, therefore, unsafe in the community. After all, counseling is generally used to help people solve problems. Sex offender therapy is to help child molesters solve sexual problems, among other problems. If an offender denies the sexual offense, how can sex offender therapy be of any help? A child molester may have financial problems, employment problems, problems with self-esteem, or other problems in getting along successfully in life. But these problems do not lead a man to molest a child. Although it is not believed by every person who treats sex offenders, there is broad consensus among those who work with convicted child molesters that therapy must address sexual issues. If a child molester remains in total denial even after conviction, there is little or no basis for any meaningful sex offender counseling to take place.

Occasionally, a judge does try to arrange for a community-based treatment program rather than prison for a molester who remains in total denial. When this happens, a variety of results can follow. The judge may require mental health counseling in hopes that a therapist can "work the magic cure" or somehow persuade the offender to eventually admit to sexual problems and deal with them honestly. Unfortunately, therapists have little success when they try to work with offenders who remain in total denial. What is a therapist to counsel a child molester for when he has "no sexual problem"? There is no scientific evidence that shows offenders who deny their sexual assault can benefit in any way from a counseling program for sexual deviance.

When therapists do attempt treatment of deniers, the result is often a meandering discussion between the therapist and the offender about past problems, current unhappiness, problems with low self-esteem, and difficulties adjusting to being "labeled" a child molester. Therapists recognize that denial remains a problem, but they hope that they can "break through" the denial by establishing a supportive relationship with the offender. In more than 20 years of experience, I have never seen such efforts meet with any success.

Furthermore, convicted child molesters who maintain total innocence generally cause ongoing grief to their families. In one case, an offender was convicted by a jury of molesting his daughters' girlfriends. Because there had been a history of discord between the families, the wife believed the offender's story that the children were "coached" to make up lies about being molested by him. Within 6 months, however, the wife discovered him touching his own son's penis and when she talked to her other children, they said he had been having sex with them. Before he was arrested the second time, he committed suicide.

The grief and hardship brought upon families by offenders who remain in total denial is usually less tragic than this example, but is often full of turmoil and sometimes just as devastating. The offenders often remain bitter toward their wives, their children, toward non-supportive friends and relatives, and toward society in general and if allowed to be with their children, their presence can become an ongoing psychological victimization of the children, especially to any child who was sexually assaulted. In addition, their presence creates an ongoing sense of anxiety to extended family members who are uncertain what or whom to believe.

A wife who chooses to remain with the child molester who is in denial risks suffering such unpleasant experiences. She may feel unresolved anger that her child was molested or self-doubts about whether she failed to protect her children. She may even wonder if she herself is "crazy" for not being able to figure out whom to believe. Sometimes wives and relatives simply choose to refuse to look at the evidence and instead accept the offender's total denial. This may contribute to their own distorted view of themselves and their family and the repression of their true feelings. Dealing with a convicted child molester who remains in total denial can tear apart the fabric that holds the family together.

Misunderstood Intentions

After totally denying the molestation, an offender may see that denial will not work—when, for example, the evidence is too strong against him, or the victim is believed despite his efforts to undermine her or his credibility, or the mother stands by the child and does not waver in her defense of the victim. The offender's next step is often to explain that "something" may have happened, but it was not his intention to molest the child sexually. This is the period of misunderstood intentions.

A variety of explanations emerge. The offender has been preparing his defense for months, if not years, and he has sorted through the most plausible "explanations." For example, he may claim that he did touch his daughter, but that it was "accidental." He may have stumbled into her bedroom, but he was drunk and disoriented. Or he was only trying to teach her about "sexual abuse" so that he could be sure it wouldn't happen to her. Or he was only "rough-housing" with her, and she thought more really happened than actually did.

If the victim was a boy, he may claim that he had had men try to molest him when he was a child and he wanted to make sure the young boy could defend himself, but that the boy needed to understand clearly what it was he was defending himself against.

Here, the offender may admit a small part of the allegation and offer a plausible explanation. He will try to appear supportive of the child but insist that he was just misunderstood by her. Then, he will promise never to do anything similar, appearing very sincere and apologetic, placing the victim in a particularly difficult bind. When the mother accepts the offender at his word, she (the victim) may be stranded, alone, needing to repeat the graphic details of the sexual abuse to authorities and others that the offender is refusing to discuss. Perhaps she didn't tell the worst of the abuse in the first place. It was, without doubt, extremely difficult for her to disclose the subject of sexual abuse to begin with. To then find herself accused of misunderstanding her father's "good" intentions places her in an extremely vulnerable position, because she is now arguing from a defensive position herself.

A powerful aspect of misunderstood intentions is the offender's apology and promise that it will not happen again. He will sound absolutely sincere because he is so frightened. His cover of secrecy has nearly been destroyed by the disclosure. He is on the verge of having his worst nightmares come true: going to prison forever as a convicted child molester. By now, he may even begin to believe the excuse that he was misunderstood. In his twisted logic, he may tell himself that the sexual abuse was instructive to her; she will be able to protect herself better in the future. Child molesters, it must be understood, actually believe such faulty logic. Above all, he will sound completely sincere to everyone in his promise to avoid any and all situations in the future that are even remotely suggestive of child sexual abuse. For the moment, at least, he is sincere and absolutely believes he will never touch a child sexually again. Seeing his fear and a sincerity that she has never seen before may persuade the victim to take back her story. She may come to believe his promises to avoid any questionable situations with her. Unfortunately, experience shows that he will break this promise if he is not controlled by others.

During the stage of misunderstood intentions, the power and control is almost exclusively in the hands of the child molester. He has been preparing himself for years to counterattack any allegations of child sexual abuse. He has excuses prepared in advance. He is ready for combat with nearly any foe. He has intellectual superiority over his victim and he will usually have little difficulty outwitting any response she is likely to give. She, on the other hand, is poorly equipped to argue with an adult about sexual issues and is probably severely embarrassed to have brought up the subject to begin with. If she does not have total support from her mother, she is in one of the most difficult positions in her life: battling a well-prepared and intellectually superior abuser to try to persuade her mother she is telling the truth when the mother is already frightened that her daughter's accusations may be true.

The number of "misunderstood intentions" is vast, almost as vast as the ways that offenders can bribe or intimidate their victims. Some typical examples are, "I was only trying to educate her about sexual abuse." "I was drunk and may have touched her but not intentionally." "I was only playing." "I was trying to protect her. I thought it would teach her to resist." "I wanted to know if anyone had done that before." "I thought a back rub would comfort her." "I was going to take her into another room." "I thought she was having a bad dream so I was going to wake her." "I was concerned that her boyfriend was too sexually aggressive." "She seemed too uncomfortable about sex, and I was only trying to . . ." "She seemed too permissive about sex, and I was warning her . . ."

Obviously, there are similarities between misunderstood intentions and total denial. In both instances, the offender denies any sexual problem. The impact of the offender's claim of misunderstood intentions on the family members can be as disruptive as total denial and sometimes even more so. Claiming misunderstood intentions can contribute significantly to the family's confusion and reinterpretation of events. As a result, everyone may begin to question and doubt themselves.

Minimal Admission With an Explanation

At times, the evidence against the child molester is overwhelming. No rational person could deny that some form of sexual abuse must have occurred. The offender sees that denials will be flatly rejected by the adults who know him, particularly the victim's mother. This occurs most often when there is more than one victim or if there have been similar allegations in the past and the offender sees that the excuses he tried before will not hold up this time. Under such circumstances the offender may admit a small part of the allegations, usually the least offensive part, and deny the rest. He then will offer a variety of explanations to try to shift the attention and blame to someone else. He may, for example, explain that he was helpless in the act of committing the sexual molestation because his own sexual needs were not being met by his wife and he was, in essence, forced into an act of desperation by his wife. He may say, "Okay, I did go to bed with her one night and yes I did fondle her breasts, but I swear I did not touch her vagina and I didn't have intercourse with her, for crying out loud. She is my daughter, after all. And she's only 10 years old. What kind of man do you think I am, anyway? And besides, you've refused to have sex with me for over a year! What am I supposed to do? I am a man, after all!"

As the above example illustrates, minimal admissions are often coupled with attempts to blame someone else. Blaming others is a hostile and aggressive act that is deliberately intended to confuse others. It can be used by the offender to shift attention away from himself and the sexual assault. Offenders who minimize prefer to focus on others' problems rather than their own. Also, they try to generalize the problem, pulling others into the turmoil of responsibility to make their own sexual impulses and behavior seem to be a small part of a larger problem.

Because the offender is still minimizing his guilt, he will desperately try to maintain secrecy through aggressive verbal taunts and accusations that sidetrack all meaningful discussion. The offender is often extremely well prepared to taunt aggressively and accuse others for the simple reason that during the time that he has been grooming and molesting, he has been justifying his own behavior by watching for every misdeed in those around him. Thus, he will remember the number of times that the wife refused his demands for sex, the times she got intoxicated, or the times she didn't clean the house to his satisfaction or forgot his birthday wishes or left her dirty socks on the floor. He'll remember the times the children fought, disturbed his sleep, came home late, did poorly in school, wasted their allowance, spilled milk during dinner, or failed to take his advice "when they knew they should have." To each of these events he will attach some value judgment that, although it may be absurd, again deflects the discussion away from his sexual abuse of his child or children.

The verbal manipulations are intended to provoke an emotional response in the listener, making it difficult to stick to the subject at hand, his sexual abuse of a child. He tries to avoid talking about what really happened and especially avoids the frightening admission that he is sexually aroused by children. He avoids admitting that his own sexual impulses are out of his control. He avoids facing the truth that he jeopardized the health and well-being of a child so that he could satisfy his own selfish, sexual desires.

An important aspect of the minimal admissions during this stage is that they energize the offender. Not only is he frightened, but he may become combative. He will discover an energy that prepares him for the fight of his life. In a very realistic sense, he has been "in training" similar to an athlete, rehearsing for the time he would be confronted by accusers. He has both prepared the excuses and has built up his psychic energy to defend himself tenaciously. In his own mind, no matter what he says or does, whether he lies, bribes, threatens, or even physically assaults his family members, he believes profoundly that his actions are justified to avoid going to prison. He is ready to fight. For these reasons, other family members, but especially the victim and her mother, should not stand alone against the offender's counterattack. Family members need professional support from the beginning, even though their husband, father, and loved one may now appear to be "cooperating" by admitting bits and pieces of the picture that he previously had denied.

Again, when the offender admits something happened but says that he was misunderstood, he is not truly progressing toward solving the problem. The minimal admission stage is only further manipulation to get the victim and supportive persons to back off, lower their guard, and retreat from responsible action. Professional support is necessary before the offender will give up his ongoing efforts to conceal what he really did.

Partial Disclosure

Misunderstood intentions are characterized by the fact that the child molester denies that there was any sexual intention on his part. Essentially, he is claiming that he is completely innocent of any wrongdoing. Such disclosures that there was contact of some kind with the victim, even if misunderstood, however, may lead to further disclosures by the offender. If at this point the offender progresses to admitting some sexual motivation, a "partial disclosure" where he acknowledges in a small way that he did something wrong with the child and that it was sexual in nature, then a therapist will have a better chance to explore in depth the sexual assault, his personal history, and his sexual behavior. Although such admissions may occur within the family, usually admissions of sexual intent occur when the offender has seen a counselor skilled in the field of sexual abuse. Admitting sexual attraction to children is so frightening to the child molester that it normally occurs only during therapy and with the support of offenders in treatment who have already admitted their sexual attraction to children and now want to change. By reaching this stage, whether talking to the wife, a police detective, a probation officer, or a therapist, at least he has opened the door to possible evaluation and treatment.

Partial disclosure most often happens when the offender recognizes that the evidence against him is overwhelming and that his denials and distortions are falling on deaf ears. Despite his denials, his alibis, and his tactics to coerce the victim and her mother, the greater part of the evidence is weighted against him. Under this weight, he may admit a fairly significant aspect of the allegation against him.

The offender, however, will still minimize the full extent of his behavior. He will still deny much of what his victim alleges. He may deny that there were other victims when there really were others. He will deny the extent of the sexual abuse by, for example, minimizing how long it took place, claiming there was no resistance by the victim when there really was, and claiming that it occurred far less frequently than it really did. Partial admissions are simply that: only part of the truth.

It is important at this stage to remember the offender's state of mind and why he is afraid to admit the full truth. Certainly, the offender wants to escape legal punishment. Also, he knows that no one but he and the victim know what really happened. It's his word against hers. Also, he fears that his family and acquaintances will ostracize him completely, that they will never have any personal or social contact with him again. What's more, the offender fears his own self-loathing. He may wonder whether he will ever be able to accept himself if he deals honestly with what he has done. The preponderance of offenders I have talked to believe that they are the worst of all offenders, and they are afraid to plumb the depths of their own personality, their own "psychological illness." They also believe everyone else will feel the same way about them once they reveal their true history. It is not surprising, then, that they give only partial disclosure and try to conceal a great deal more from everyone. Nevertheless, admitting to at least some sexual motivation sets the stage for professional evaluation and treatment to begin.

Partial disclosure can serve the child molester's purpose of minimizing family change. Understandably, he wants the relationships within the family to stay pretty much the way they are. After all, he has spent years structuring family relationships to his liking. As they stand, these relationships have served him well. In addition, he still may be planning future sexual assaults, particularly if he senses that he will be successful in sweeping this episode under the rug. He may also fear that he will be unable to control his own sexual urges and reoffend in the future. He knows how many times in the past he promised he would never repeat the sexual assaults, only to fail repeatedly. In the event that he does reoffend, the current family relationships are the ones that he created to reduce his chances of being caught. He may still believe that these relationships will work to his advantage in the future. Recognizing this, he struggles and fights to maintain things just as they have always been.

As always, the offender is still extremely sensitive to what others may be thinking about him. He continues to make decisions to protect himself from both legal and social repercussions. Above all, he wants to avoid a public trial in which the victim and a variety of others testify in open court, and where his ability to manipulate and intimidate is undermined by the prosecuting attorney and the judge. Basically, the child molester knows that a trial brings something he fears: the truth about his behavior into the light of day.

Once he has admitted the sexual abuse at least partially, the offender will often enter a plea bargain agreement. Research covering tens of thousands of sexual abuse cases has shown that sex offenders plead guilty 9 times out of 10 to avoid a trial (Champion, 1988). In plea bargains, the offender agrees to admit certain essential facts necessary for a specific crime with the understanding that the prosecuting attorney will make a more lenient recommendation to the court than if he demanded a trial. Such agreements are one reason why most sex offenders plead guilty; that way they receive reduced sentences while still making only a "partial disclosure." The offender has not been required to admit to anything but the bare elements essential to a crime. As a result, he still maintains a great deal of secrecy about his sexual assault on his victim(s). Under such circumstances, he will continue to deny as much as possible, conceal any secrets that he believes he can successfully hide, and distort further allegations of the victim if she dares to bring up any further issues.

Ironically, his plea bargain often sets the stage for further manipulation. To friends, family, and acquaintances, he may explain that he is not "really" guilty but, rather, that he was willing to plead guilty to "spare" the family the trauma of a court trial and negative public exposure. He is willing to "sacrifice himself to save the family." He may still present himself as a martyr. He may admit that he went "a little farther than he should have," but he will claim that the discovery of what he was doing was more than enough of a shock to his system to "knock some sense into him." After all, he will say, his only intention was to give the girl some affection. He points to her obvious emotional trauma, claims she has been known to lie before, and is now exaggerating or even grossly distorting a single experience, but he will "generously" offer to get the whole matter over with by pleading guilty to the criminal charges. All of this distorts the truth. Even to this point he has disclosed only a part, at best, of what he actually did to his victim.

The circumstances of pleading guilty easily lend themselves to ongoing secrecy. Often, because the family is spared the criminal trial, the wife feels a tremendous relief. She usually does not know the full truth herself, just the conflicting stories of what her child says and what her husband claims. Her typical and understandable hope is that counselors can "fix" all of the problems. "Well, let's just get some counseling and look at what has been going on in this family," she thinks to herself. The mother usually knows that there have been an number of problems in the family so this is at least a chance to start making some progress. (For a discussion of the incest family's inclination for "magical expectations" see Sgroi, 1982.)

A variety of reactions may occur among the others who know the sex offender. Family and acquaintances hope that a court conviction, probation supervision, or counseling will offer a "cure" and that all will return to normal soon. Some who know the convicted offender will believe that the offender simply got mixed up in a horrible family situation. There is usually ample evidence to support this belief, ranging from problems with children (as previously noted, victims often act out their victimization in a variety of ways), to marital problems (as a part of the setup, offenders commonly discuss the wife's "problem" with others behind her back), to alcohol or drug abuse. Family and acquaintances are easily inclined to agree that the offender did the "right" thing by admitting guilt because they too fear the prospect of a public trial. They also are spared the unvarnished truth. Employers are often simply happy and relieved to have the offender return to work after his release from jail. Employers are also burdened with what they should tell co-workers, if anything at all, and with gauging the co-workers' reactions. Knowing the details of the offense is usually the last thing that the boss wants. Co-workers may resent working next to a child molester, but if they must, it is easier for them to believe that the convicted child molester, their friend, was "railroaded." Often, too, as a part of "setting up" his employer and co-workers, the child molester maintains exemplary attendance and performance records, making himself an indispensable part of the company. Everyone at work is usually anxious to get the offender back on the job and put whatever this "ugly" thing was behind them all.

The tendency to ignore the full truth about the child molester can potentially cause problems for everyone. Some problems are more significant than others. If the offender works in new construction and rarely or never has access to children during working hours, less risk is posed than if the offender is a salesclerk in a department store where children may frequently come to shop unattended by parents. In the latter instance, the employer's lack of knowledge about the offender's sexual history can prove critical. A sex offender working in telephone sales may be safe unless he can use this job for making lewd phone calls. Depending on the circumstances, such an employer may well benefit from knowing the details of the offender's history. It is usually better for the employer to be sure, by getting the information from a knowledgeable source other than the offender himself, than to risk the company's reputation and business. Relatives, friends, and neighbors who have children and who socialize with the offender without knowing the details of his sexual history make a critical mistake. The specifics friends and acquaintances need to know about the sex offender for the safety of children are found in later chapters of this book. Simply pleading guilty (or being convicted) does not end the risk that an offender poses to children, especially when so much remains unknown about him.

Full Disclosure

For the purposes of this book, full disclosure means that a trained professional in the field of sexual abuse has attempted to evaluate the child molester's full history and has expressed satisfaction that as much as is possible has been revealed by the offender about himself. This requires that to the extent that is possible, what the offender says about himself is verified through whatever legal means are available to ensure that he has given complete admission of all sexual crimes and a complete personal and sexual history covering his entire life. Full disclosure is important because only through full disclosure can the family expect to make decisions that ensure its own safety, and only through full disclosure can the offender participate in meaningful sexual deviance therapy.

The term *full disclosure* is a relative, rather than an absolute, term. The "full" truth about any individual can probably never be known. Many factors influence what we can discover about ourselves or others. Memory is one of the most important of these factors. For example, an offender undergoing a rigorous evaluation may tell the counselor with utter and complete truth everything he remembers about himself, only to discover later that he forgot about significant events in his childhood. It is not uncommon for offenders in treatment to make such revelations. But these are different from deliberate attempts by the offender to conceal significant information. Full disclosure implies the offender's cooperation in revealing his past behavior, along with the interviewer's efforts to verify by all reasonably available means what the offender has to say about himself.

Full disclosure seldom, if ever, comes easily. After his legal conviction, the sex offender begins to assess his chances against the criminal justice system. He watches to see how much secrecy he can still maintain. He begins gauging whether he can avoid any further disclosures. One way he maintains such secrecy is through the plea bargain agreement as discussed above. A major threat to this plan, however, is the court requirement, or the family's insistence, that specialized counseling take place.

In some localities, the sex offender may choose his own counselor, who may or may not have any expertise in the specialized area of sex offender treatment. Similarly, the family as a whole may enter counseling that places no emphasis on the fact that sexual abuse has taken place. Such counseling programs will typically deal with whatever problems the offender or the family bring forward. In other treatment programs, although families may be identified as victims of sexual abuse, the sexual abuse itself is not identified as the principal problem and, as a result, reducing risk to the child or children does not become a guiding principle of the treatment.

In such "generic" family counseling programs, no special effort is made to deal directly with issues of sexual abuse. Typically, they do not require or even attempt to arrive at full disclosure of the offender's sexual history. They often view the sexual offense and the offender's true deviance as only a part, and sometimes only a minor part, of a larger treatment plan. Counseling that ignores the sexual abuse runs counter to the best professional standards in the field of child sexual abuse whether for treatment of the child molester, the victim, or the family as a whole. As noted clinician Nicholas Groth and his colleagues indicate,

> Some agencies are willing to treat the offender, but do so in traditional ways which are often inappropriate and/or ineffective for this client. They may avoid discussing the actual offense, for example, because they are uncomfortable with the subject, whereas we feel that it is necessary to discuss and directly confront the behavior [of sexual abuse] early on in treatment. (Groth, Hobson, & Gary, 1982, p. 142)

Similarly, noted authors and researchers Gene Able and Joanne-L. Rouleau (1990) write,

> Therapists evaluating and/or treating sexual assaulters need valid, reliable information from the sex offender. Without this, the therapist is less able to identify the precise treatment needs of the patient, to evaluate precisely the impact of treatment interventions, and to quantify treatment's long-term effects. (p. 10)

In other words, failing to get full disclosure can have serious results. If the offender admits that he molested the daughter in the current marriage but fails to disclose that he molested a son in a previous marriage (and the son never disclosed the abuse), the current treatment program may fail to treat the offender's sexual arousal to boys. Furthermore, such a treatment program may fail to recognize the risk the offender poses for boys in the current home and may take precautionary measures to protect only the girls, thereby leaving the boys at risk. There are many such serious errors that can occur when counseling programs fail to address the full scope of the problems related to sexual abuse.

When these programs fail to heed the warnings of such experts as Groth, Abel, and Rouleau, they may also be overlooking the child's trauma as a result of the abuse. As noted clinicians and child advocates Lucy Berliner and Doris Stevens (1982) write,

> Treatment plans . . . have addressed marital discord, alcoholism, stress, family conflict, and child behavior problems instead of the sexual abuse, with the assumption that the abuse will disappear if these other problems are cured. All these responses fail to validate the child's experience. (p. 94)

In those situations where full disclosure is not obtained, the offender is essentially in charge of his own fate. He can maintain as much secrecy as he desires. He is in the position of revealing secrets in his own time, in his own way, and at his own convenience, because he is fully aware that no one will ever know his full sexual history unless he tells it to them. Simply put, it is his word against the child's. The offender can continue to lie virtually unchecked. When the counselors do not aim for full disclosure, the offender usually knows that "the heat is off." The wife, understandably, dearly hopes that there is no more sexual abuse to be revealed, especially if she has decided to stay with the offender to try to restore the family through counseling. She may also be anxious to focus her attention away from the pain the family has experienced. To discover additional acts of molestation by the husband would only cause more pain and trauma. Without the support of a knowledgeable counselor, the wife is no longer a threat to the offender's secrecy.

Counselors can generally find many family conflicts to "treat" in therapy without discussing the sexual abuse directly. A child is withdrawn and communicates poorly with her mother. The siblings fight. Father plays favorites. Discipline is inconsistent. Self-esteem is low. Anger and resentment persist and interfere with family harmony. Family members do not recognize their own feelings or express them openly. Family members to not listen to one another. The generic family counselor can quickly focus treatment on any one of dozens of issues without having made an adequate diagnosis of the family situation, and yet family members may feel that effective therapy is taking place. Therapy may indeed be taking place, but the problems of sexual abuse are not being resolved. Members can feel that the family is making some progress because the members are communicating in ways they may never have before. The offender himself typically experiences a sharp decline in his sexual libido but this is caused simply from having his sexual assaults exposed. The decline in libido may be absolutely real for the offender and it may alter his disposition markedly, making him feel and act far more concerned and sincere than ever before. This decline in sexual libido is called by some professionals "the monastic effect" (based on the myth that monks do not have significant sexual libido and therefore do not engage in sexual activity). The monastic effect is, however, short lived. Inexperienced counselors, or counselors who do not deal directly with sexual issues, may take the monastic effect (as may the wife) to be a sign of progress. This is a mistake. Unless the sexual arousal pattern and other issues directly related to the offender's sexual abuse in the family are addressed, the father's sexual arousal to children invariably returns.

Ignoring the full scope of an offender's sexual abuse history is a serious mistake. The offender's veil of secrecy is restored. If more sexual assaults are uncovered, those who learn of them may mistakenly take refuge in the fact that he is in counseling and a therapist will take care of the problem. Even older children, who may have been abused but never revealed it, may be reluctant to make disclosures now because they saw how difficult it was on the "identified victim" (the younger sibling who blew the whistle on the offender).

Without full disclosure being required as a part of sexual deviance counseling, the sex offender sees clearly that he has won the battle for secrecy.

Fortunately, some therapists will not allow this to happen. These therapists confront the offender directly with the sexual assaults. Their primary goal initially is full disclosure. They are aware of the damage that can result from allowing secrecy to persist. Professionally, they are aware that failure to evaluate and treat the child molester properly would be a breach of professional, and sometimes even legal, standards. Furthermore, they face sanctions and legal action by future victims if the offender commits new sexual assaults that were preventable by reasonable, prudent, and cautious procedures in their evaluation and treatment of the offender. Most important, therapists are aware of the tremendous benefit to all parties, including the offender himself, when they aim for full disclosure on the part of the offender.

One important tool for achieving full disclosure is the polygraph examination. The lie detector test has become widely accepted in the Pacific Northwest both by private therapists who treat sex offenders and by the Washington State Legislature. In fact, the legislature authorizes funds to pay for sex offenders to take the test if they are indigent, so that no offender can escape, even for reasons of poverty, taking the polygraph examination. This policy has also been formally recognized in Washington State's legal code governing the certification of sex offender therapists.

The lie detector test was first used routinely by a small group of therapists in the Seattle area during the 1970s and, gradually, the benefits of the polygraph examination became recognized by most therapists who treated sex offenders because of its remarkable ability to convince the offender to be more open about himself, including his sexual history. Initially, there was widespread resistance by many therapists against the use of the polygraph. This resistance was due, in part, to a reluctance to use new technology in an clearly innovative way. Lack of familiarity with polygraph procedures led some therapists to believe that the test could be detrimental to the therapeutic relationship with the offender. A few therapists even claimed that their interviewing skills were so good that they could get as much information out of the offender without a polygraph examination as anyone could using the test. Others resisted the use of the polygraph, they said, because they felt it would reduce their profession to a series of impartial and dispassionate tests equivalent to "big brother" intruding into every aspect of the offender's life. Each of these concerns raised important issues to be considered to avoid some of the problems that can result from the misapplication of technology. After two decades, the use of polygraph examination has become so routine and widely accepted that it is frequently required by courts in Washington State as a condition of sex offender treatment.

The question of whether the polygraph examination is a scientifically valid tool is a serious one that deserves consideration. A large amount of scientific research, and a large number of books and articles, have addressed questions about the polygraph examination's scientific reliability and validity. Perhaps the most comprehensive review of these issues was conducted by the U.S. Congress's Office of Technology Assessment (1983) and reported in *Scientific Validity of Polygraph Testing: A Research Review and Evaluation.* Although the report clearly states that there is no justifiable basis for polygraph examinations as part of a preemployment screening process, it does find that their use in criminal investigations has definite practical applications. Another authoritative statement regarding polygraph examinations is found in the *Journal of the American Medical Association* (1986), which states,

> It is well established that the polygraph can recognize guilty suspects with an accuracy (60% to 95%) that is better than chance. . . . Criminal investigation has often benefited from polygraph usage because the investigator can focus on the incident in question. . . . Sometimes the simple threat of a "lie detector test" may facilitate the obtaining of a confession. (p. 1175)

As previously stated, full disclosure does not come easily with the convicted child molester. His arguments against a polygraph examination are usually manipulations designed to cause a lot of emotional turmoil, anxiety, and debate. His purpose is not to decide logically whether lie detector tests are scientifically accurate or legal.[1] Seldom, if ever, has he read any scientific articles on which to base his arguments. His intention is simply to avoid taking the test. The only thing that makes him change his mind is pressure from members of his community. Specialists in treating sexual deviance routinely use them in evaluating child molesters. Judges and prosecutors know the limitations of the examinations and they know their value as much as therapists do. With few exceptions, polygraph examinations are not used to convict men in court (Burns, 1975).

Therapists who specialize in evaluating and treating convicted child molesters ordinarily use a wide variety of sources of information. They gather all of the written reports that may be available, including police reports, victim and witness statements, the offender's own written statement, reports from school teachers, other counselors, and the Presentence Investigation Report (which is the focus of Chapter 7), and they conduct interviews with as many parties as they feel is necessary to obtain a clear picture of events. Then they spend considerable time cross-checking all of the information that they have gathered to look for inconsistencies and inaccuracies and to weigh the overall evidence gathered from a thorough evaluative process. During that evaluation process, therapists will ask the child molester to disclose the true extent of the molestation of his victim(s) and to disclose all other victims he has had at any time during his entire life. They ask him to give a full accounting of his sexual life from birth through the present. And if other circumstances indicate that it is appropriate, then they ask him to take a polygraph examination to demonstrate that he has been truthful about the information he provided. This careful and objective data-gathering process, when coupled with a polygraph examination, provides what is probably the most powerful evaluation tool available, literally a counterassault on the child molester's life of secrecy.

Considering how powerful this approach is, it is no surprise that the offender will argue fervently against thorough evaluations, especially when backed by polygraph examinations. Once it becomes clear that there is no way to avoid one, he either submits to the evaluation process or claims that the evaluation process is flawed, unprofessional, or biased in some way. He may even argue that it is a violation of his constitutional rights if a polygraph examination is required, and that he would rather face jail or prison than give up his constitutional rights.

The offender who agrees to submit to a polygraph examination may still attempt deception, as will be discussed later. It is often during this stage, though, that the offender becomes far more candid, hoping that by doing so he can get help for his problems, atone for his criminal behavior, and salvage and rebuild the relationships in his family.

The purpose of the polygraph examination in a sexual deviance evaluation is simply to try to ensure that the offender is telling the truth about himself so that he can be properly evaluated and treated. Used in this manner, polygraph examinations increase the safety of the children, the family, and the community because they help the therapist evaluate how dangerous or how far out of control the offender really is. The evaluation process described here is the most effective means known for achieving, once and for all, full disclosure by the child molester. (For a description of the use of the polygraph in investigations prior to conviction see Knefelkamp, 1988.)

Breaking the barrier of secrecy is painful for the child molester who is being evaluated and receiving counseling for his sexual problems. He is confronted by a counselor who is trained to see through his facade of deceit and distortion. He is confronted with demands that he talk about parts of his life than make him terribly ashamed. His therapist will require that he make more and more disclosures about himself as he grows throughout the treatment process. The demands for honesty never cease in therapy. He is usually required to continue this process in group therapy with other child molesters, who will demand that his honesty continue. Child molesters themselves often have the same feelings toward child molesters as the rest of the public. In other words, they despise them. The fact that he must spend time being confronted by a group of men he himself finds repulsive is another source of personal pain for the child molester. These fellow offenders can often see through his lies and deceit. They will challenge his manipulations and excuses. These men know about his reliance on secrecy from their own personal experience. They will make demands that he start being completely honest.

Breaking down the sex offender's secrecy helps expose him to the light of day. This is necessary to ensure the safety of the community, the victim, and other children. It is also essential for effective therapy because effective therapy must be directed at all of the offender's real, known sexual problems, not just the few that he may be willing to talk about voluntarily. Breaking the child molester's pattern of secrecy is necessary to shift control away from the offender to others who are responsible, mature, and truly concerned about the welfare of others. Others must now be in charge.

Note

1. The aforementioned report by the Office of Technology Assessment presents an extensive discussion of the scientific findings regarding polygraph examinations. The report concludes that the use of lie detector tests in preemployment interviews cannot be supported. However, the report is careful to indicate throughout that these findings do not apply to criminal investigations. For further discussion of the polygraph examination see Ansley and Garwood (1984).

Blaming

Blaming refers to the child molester's attempts to hold others partly or fully responsible for his own behavior, to lessen his own responsibility for his sexual assaults, or both. The child molester commonly tries to blame the victim. Sometimes an offender will even blame a very young child. The wife is also often a target for blame. Another favorite target for blame is alcohol. If others will agree with the molester that alcohol is "to blame" then he can escape responsibility, to some degree, for the molestation. Neither the wife, the victim, nor alcohol are to blame for the offender's actions. He alone is to blame.

❖   ❖   ❖

DOUG

Doug was convicted of molesting his 8-year-old niece, Wendy. Doug was single, in his twenties, and a high school dropout who worked at a variety of casual-labor jobs. All of his brothers and sisters were also blue-collar workers struggling to survive. Several of them were divorced. All except he had children and times had been pretty tough on them all recently. They kept in touch with each other on an "as needed" basis. When they needed something, they would call around and find out who was available to help.

Doug was skilled at working on cars, but his social skills—making small talk, keeping commitments, and keeping sober—left much to be desired. The mother of his niece was divorced and wanted to get off welfare, so she took a job working evenings as a clerk in a convenience store and she was able to get a neighbor to baby-sit Wendy until she came home. Then her boss asked her to work the late shift and the neighbor couldn't continue to baby-sit. So Wendy's mother called around and Doug was the only one available to baby-sit. Doug didn't act happy about doing it but he agreed, "So long as you leave a six-pack in the fridge."

Six weeks after Doug started molesting Wendy, she told her mother about what had been going on. When the probation officer interviewed Doug, he asked him about molesting Wendy. Doug explained that he'd gotten drunk and that he knew a lot of stuff like that went on even in his own family. "And besides," he said, "why blame me? She wanted it. Wendy was only 8, but she looked and acted like she was 13! She's gotta also be to blame. At least partly to blame, anyway. Anyone can see that I didn't do this completely alone!"

❖   ❖   ❖

We have looked at the setup, denial, and the offender's use of secrecy in this book. Even after denial and secrecy have been broken down, there are still other characteristics of the child molester that predominate his interaction with others. One of these is his desire to blame someone else or at least to share responsibility for his deviance.

Blaming the Victim

From the moment the sex offender begins to groom the victim, he has been planning some way to blame the victim if he is caught. Some examples of blaming the victim are "I was asleep . . . only half awake . . . intoxicated, when the child came into my room; I didn't know what was happening, I was totally exhausted and before I realized what was going on, she was in bed with me and had her hand in my pajamas." "I didn't start it. I never would have been involved. I didn't know what was happening. I barely remember any of it now." "Man, she was all over me. This wasn't my fault, she did the whole thing. Oh, I didn't resist well enough, but I didn't know what was going on. I didn't even know who it was. I thought it was my wife." "She's acted this way before with her brother, her cousins, too. Everyone knows she's been acting out sexually. She's totally out of control. Even the neighbors complained about her hustling their little boys!"

Blaming even young children is an effort by the offender to test the gullibility of anyone he may be talking to, whether it is the victim's mother, a relative, a police officer, a therapist, or a probation officer. If the offender can convince the listener to blame the victim to any degree, he has achieved a significant goal. He often believes after that point that he will not be held fully accountable for the sexual assault. He also begins to think he can escape accountability for his other still undisclosed, deviant behaviors and can escape responsibility for future behaviors as well. Most of all, he gains a foothold in his effort to persuade the other person to trust him so that they will lower their guard and loosen their controls over him. It is a mistake for anyone to join in this complicity to blame the victim. Such blaming reduces the offender's willingness to admit his sexual past and his responsibility honestly and to participate in therapy in a meaningful way.

Blaming older children is easier than blaming younger children, especially in the child molester's own mind. Unfortunately, many persons who have regular contact with the offender are sometimes inclined to accept the offender's blaming of adolescents. Many people believe that teenagers are preoccupied with sex and predisposed to act out in sexual ways. The child molester capitalizes on such beliefs, whether they are true or not. Even in cases where the actual victim may be totally naive about sex, perhaps even frightened of sex, as some adolescents are, the offender will talk at great length with any listener who is inclined to place any blame on the victim. The offender's motivation here is to create an ally, someone he believes he can use for sympathy now and use in his defense at some point in the future.

The child molester finds many ways to blame adolescent victims. A common accusation is that the adolescent victim was promiscuous. The sex offender will claim that she was sexually involved with many others preceding the molestation. "She came on to me. I didn't seek her out. I didn't initiate anything with her. This was entirely her doing. I was completely passive. She's just a sexually aggressive lady." Therefore, the offender argues or implies that the victim is less worthy of the full protection of the law. In essence, the offender argues that he is not fully guilty, and therefore, his blame and his accountability (punishment) should be less because the victim was partly at fault.

Such arguments against an adolescent victim actually expose the sex offender's grossly distorted value system. If encouraged to explain further what happened, he will sometimes argue that the victim was not only promiscuous but also involved in drugs and alcohol, was a runaway, was disruptive in the family, a school dropout, hung out with the wrong crowd, and/or was a known liar. The offender's list of accusations against the victim is virtually endless. He offers long and derisive descriptions of the victim, hoping to trigger some responsive chord in the listener.

The perceptive listener will recognize the distorted views of the child molester. Even granting that his victim may have an alcohol or drug addiction and other emotional problems, these circumstances in truth prove that the victim was disadvantaged. These circumstances do not ever justify sexually molestation. In fact, they point to the offender's callous disregard for a child who was already suffering from a life often largely beyond her control. He chose to sexually molest the child on top of all that she may already have endured in life. The offender failed to bring responsible help to the victim. The offender failed to connect the victim with an agency that could provide effective counseling for the victim or her family. Instead, he took advantage of an already vulnerable human being. He sexually molested her without regard for her humanity and dignity, and he satisfied his own transitory sexual appetite.

A mature and empathic response to a troubled adolescent is not sexual molestation, even if the victim were to ask for sex but, rather, to recognize her difficulty and support positive, growth-enhancing solutions to her troubles. A mature and compassionate person with an acceptable set of values would encourage and help a troubled person enter a counseling program. That person would try to help her rebuild relationships with parents in a constructive way. That person would help her build trusting relationships with counselors, avoid drugs and alcohol, and establish goals leading to earned self-confidence, independence, and self-respect. That person would not enter into a secretive, exploitative relationship and then attempt, in any way, to blame the victim for his own actions. Those who know and work with convicted sex offenders recognize this. They view any attempt to blame the victim as evidence of a faulty value system. This value system is just one of many problems for which the offender will need specialized counseling.

If asked whether he tried to help his victim with her many problems and special vulnerability, the offender may respond that he did try to help, although it was without success. He may also claim that he thought sexual relations would "help" the victim by increasing her self-esteem or helping her understand that sex was one way that she could have a positive relationship. Or, he may argue that he wanted to help her overcome her sense of social isolation: "She was such a lonely kid. There was absolutely no one she could relate to." The undercurrent of such arguments is that if the victim had not been so bad and if he had not been so helpless, he would not have sexually molested the victim. Therefore, he will argue, he himself should be seen, at least in part, as a victim of the child/victim and a victim of his own good intentions. As a result, he feels that he should not be held fully accountable for the molestation.

Blaming the Mother

The offender often blames people other than the victim. Most often, the offender will try to blame his wife or the mother of the victim. He will blame her in as many different ways as he will blame the victim herself, because he knows that people are often more willing to accept blame against the mother or wife than against the child. He will accuse the mother in a variety of ways: "She's an alcoholic." "She's on drugs." "She is sexually frigid." "She was unfaithful." "She never showed any interest in me." "She's mentally ill." "She's always depressed." "She's always tired, she's too tired for anything." "She's violent. She battered me often." "She's hostile." "She's rejecting." "She's boring." "She's just angry because she was sexually abused." "She hates men." "She refused to satisfy me sexually. She left me with no choice, absolutely no sexual outlet!"

The purpose of listing these blaming strategies is to let the reader know that when the sex offender tries to blame someone (you or someone you know), he is following a typical pattern that has been used by thousands of sex offenders before him. The sex offender's attempts to blame others should be rejected. They are simply an effort to deflect attention and responsibility away from himself. Although the mother of the victim may indeed have one or even all of the problems mentioned above, they do not reduce the child molester's responsibility for the sexual abuse in any way. He is completely responsible for his acts of sexual abuse. It is important to remember that he always had other ways to handle the problems. Sexual abuse was not his only alternative. He, like anyone else, had professional help available in the community to aid him in resolving his own problems without resorting to the kinds of abuse that he chose.[1]

As noted earlier, some of the sex offender's accusations may be true, but he will distort them for his own personal benefit or gain. For example, the wife may suffer from alcoholism, but the offender will fail to mention that he frequently bought her alcohol so that she would pass out—during which times he would molest the daughter. The sex offender was making it easier for, in fact enabling, the mother to abuse alcohol and he did it so that he could achieve his own deliberate goal of molesting the child. Often the term *enabling* refers to someone who is not aware of how he or she is encouraging unwanted behavior in another person. In the case of child molestation such enabling is often, if not always, conscious and deliberate. Ironically, it can be the mother herself who is unaware that the offender was nudging her toward alcoholism.

The offender may claim that his wife was unresponsive to him sexually, but he will not reveal other important pieces of the puzzle. For example, the offender will not mention that he has never tried to satisfy his wife emotionally or sexually. Instead, he will attempt to isolate sexuality from all of the other important aspects of a wholesome sexual relationship, such as mutual tenderness, sensitivity, and caring. Similarly, an offender will not reveal to others that his sexual arousal to children may be considerably greater than his arousal to adult women, or that he has virtually no personal interest in his wife. In other words, the child molester is arguing that his wife is responsible because she bores him, leads a drab life, or is too emotionally needy for him to care for or love her. Sometimes an offender will reveal that he married his wife only because she had children by a previous marriage whom he was planning to victimize. Others will purposefully marry women to have children they can sexually abuse (Lanning, 1986).

Blaming Alcohol

At times the sex offender may blame alcohol for his own sexual deviance and at other times he may deny the importance of alcohol, depending upon how badly he wishes to be able to keep on drinking. As always, he considers the circumstances of his offense and how blaming alcohol might suit his purposes at the moment, depending upon whom he is talking with. If the listener reveals a belief that alcohol explains many of society's problems, the offender will be inclined to blame alcohol. In his mind, if he can persuade the listener that alcohol is to blame, the solution to his sexual deviance is really quite simple: quit drinking. He may simultaneously be trying to convince the listener that he has great willpower and that quitting alcohol will be no problem for him. The offender knows that admitting an alcohol problem is far easier than admitting he is sexually aroused by children. Admitting an alcohol problem, difficult though it may be, is also far easier than facing a trained counselor who will probe him about his personal sexual habits and his sexual assaults. If alcohol is to blame, he can also argue that it is pointless to punish him with jail or prison. If alcohol is to blame, he will argue that all he needs is sobriety to keep from molesting again.

Occasionally, the offender will claim that alcohol had no part to play in his sexual offenses even though it really did. This is especially true of the offender who is seriously alcoholic and is determined to keep on drinking. He knows that if he admits alcohol's role in the molestation, a judge, counselor, or probation officer will require that he quit drinking alcohol. To avoid this possibility, he will deny any relation between alcohol and his sexual behavior and even risk jail if he believes that he can then continue to drink once he is released.

Researchers and specialists who treat sex offenders virtually never view alcohol as the cause of a sexual assault. As David Finkelhor (1986) writes,

> Although most researchers disclaim the idea that such conditions [impairment from alcohol] explain most molesting, they are seen as contributing factors or as the essential elements in at least some individuals. The presumed mechanism at work in all these conditions is the lowering or disappearance of inhibitions against acting on pedophilic impulses. (p. 112)

Alcohol is considered a "disinhibitor." This means that under the influence of alcohol, the child molester is more likely to act out sexually than he would if he were sober, because he exercises less self-control. The risk of abuse of drugs other than alcohol is generally considered a concern as well, especially for illicit drugs, because their use is another indicator of lack of self-control. Prescribed medications are considered safe only when taken with the knowledge of the therapist and attending physician who knows about the offender's sexual history. It must be noted, however, that although the use of alcohol or drugs is not a cause of sexual assaults, when inhibitions are lowered most people, including child molesters, have less self-control. Their sexual urges may become stronger and more difficult to resist, resulting in a greater likelihood for sexual abuse to occur.

Alcohol does frequently appear to be correlated with sexual abuse (Finkelhor, 1986, p. 115; see also Lilies & Childs, 1986). Correlation means that they occur at the same time but one (alcohol) does not necessarily cause the other (child molesting.) As Judith Herman (1981) writes,

> although sex offenders who are alcoholic often commit their crimes while drunk, it is naive to attribute the offense to demon alcohol. The sexual assault, more often than not, is planned in advance. On careful questioning, offenders often admit that they drink in order to gather courage for the approach. (p. 76)

The offender who claims that alcohol caused his sexual deviance typically relies on his secret wager that the interviewer (whether a probation officer, wife, or therapist) will not question him extensively about his drinking nor investigate carefully how it relates to his sexual deviance. It is extremely difficult to investigate a sex offender's history of alcohol consumption and determine the exact pattern of drinking as it relates to his sexual history. To do so requires a very time-consuming, carefully structured, complex interview. Professionals skilled in the area are usually the only persons who interview in such depth. The child molester often understands this and believes that he can get away with blaming alcohol when talking to the nonprofessional (the wife or parent) or the naive or careless professional.

For these reasons, in cases of child molestation it is wise to rely on a substance abuse evaluation by a certified counselor who is familiar with the dynamics of this kind of sex offender. If the facts are not gathered very carefully, and if the offender in essence "wins" his gamble that the person interviewing him will accept his history in whatever fashion he chooses to reveal it, his chances are improved for convincing the listener that alcohol was either (a) the cause of his sexual offending or (b) not related to the assault at all. This is another way that the sex offender can blame something outside of himself for his crime and lower his chances for harsh punishment and/or effective, safe monitoring and control.

If the sex offender thinks he can make others believe he is less guilty through blame sharing, he is then more inclined to believe that he can manipulate, break and bend rules, violate court requirements, and still gain support, understanding, and leniency from others, including his wife, the probation officer, friends, his employer, and other family members. To put it simply, he may then believe that he can avoid the full consequences of the law. This sets the stage, potentially, for reoffending. Such an attitude exposes both the family and the community to increased risk.

For these reasons, the offender's spouse, relatives, friends, employers, minister, and other acquaintances who are informed of his crimes should convey to the sex offender the very clear message that they will act firmly, not accept his excuses, hold him to his commitments, confront him in his deceptions, and insist that honesty and openness form the basis of their relationship. They will insist that the cause and the solution to his sexual deviance lie within himself. He is to blame for what he did, no one else.

Note

1. The author is aware that for many families, especially impoverished ones, such help is often difficult, if not impossible, to find. Given the reality of the lack of societal resources at a level truly demanded by the problem of child sexual abuse, the idea of mothers taking charge of sex offenders as suggested by this book is even more important than ever.

Manipulation

Manipulation by child molesters includes everything they do to try to control others without being open, honest, and direct about their true intentions. They particularly try to manipulate their wives or the guardians and parents of their victims, their probation officers, and the court. The fullest communication possible among all parties who know the offender is the best defense, although a child molester can sometimes outwit even the greatest efforts of those involved. Ultimately, full communication among everyone serves not only the safety of the children and the community but also the interests of the offender himself, because once he recognizes that full communication is taking place, he will more likely adopt a positive and constructive attitude about changing his life and gaining the true benefits of a treatment program.

❖　❖　❖

JERRY

Jerry was a tall, blond, bearded young man, with piercing blue eyes, always well dressed and charming. He usually wore a coat and tie when drumming up clients for his business. People seemed naturally attracted to him and opportunities came knocking at his door. When they didn't knock, he knew how to cook them up. His first criminal convictions were not sexual crimes; they were burglaries. He approached a new day care center that Martha had opened in the neighborhood in an old home that she had bought after divorcing her husband. She was struggling financially, but she was conscientious and there was quite a demand for good day care, ensuring her enough clients to establish business in the first year. Jerry watched as business grew and one day he approached her with the proposition that he would paint the entire day care center at half his usual fee in exchange for her referring her customers to him for home improvements and painting services. She was delighted and soon Jerry was busy painting, magically turning the old gray dwelling into an attractive sanctuary for children whose parents worked. To avoid disturbing the infants and toddlers sleeping during the day, Martha gave Jerry the keys to the center so that he could come in during the evenings. Raised in an orphanage himself, he loved children.

Martha appreciated the sensitivity that Jerry showed in protecting the older children outdoors as he painstakingly painted his way around the outside of the building. He even took time to carefully scrape the eaves and brighten the formerly dim reaches at the roofline of the structure. Changing empty buckets of paint for full, he cavorted with the children occasionally and he proved to be a lively addition to the scheduled activities that Martha had planned for them.

During the evenings, Jerry not only painted the interior rooms but also entered Martha's computer system, gathering the information that she had studiously entered on her customers, such as their residences, phone numbers, and their vacation plans. Behind her back, Jerry showed some of the older children "his badge" and told them he was a reserve county sheriff's deputy (the badge was fake, of course, but children seldom know the difference). He was investigating a rash of burglaries near the children's homes. They could help with the investigations by letting him know where their parents kept spare keys to the homes, where they would go on vacation, and when. Many of the children had no idea but others told him where to locate hidden keys: under doormats, flower pots, and on nails hung behind bushes. Others told him "Oh, we never lock the doors." He reassured the children that he was talking with their parents and he knew enough about the parents by now, such as where they worked, who to contact in emergencies, the children's physicians, and so on, that he had little difficulty convincing the children that he was a real undercover detective. Of course, because he was "working undercover" he persuaded the children to say nothing about these conversations until the case was solved. He told them that it would be "our little secret" until the burglars were caught and then he would let them and everybody else know, telling them that "their names might even be in the newspapers."

Knowing the family's vacation plans made burgling their homes the easiest part of Jerry's work. The parents were heartbroken upon returning from their vacations to discover that their homes had been burglarized, and they were frightened, as most burglary victims are. They had virtually no suspicion that there might be any connection to their children's day care center until one child, although sworn to secrecy by Jerry, reassured his parents not to worry because "Detective Jerry's already working on the case." A little detective work of their own led the parents and real sheriff's detectives to Jerry's home where much of the stolen property was recovered. The case was solved but, as a result, Martha's day care center closed. Her reputation was ruined: She was guilty by association with Jerry.

Jerry served 6 months in jail and was released on probation. He persuaded his new girlfriend, Connie, that he had nothing to do with the burglaries at all; he had only given a little information to an acquaintance about a couple of the center's families and he had no idea that the property the acquaintance had given him was really stolen property. "Why didn't you tell this to the police?" his girlfriend asked. "I'm not a snitch! I'd get killed if I did that. You know how criminals are, don't you? They're ruthless. I couldn't tell. What are you suggesting, anyway? Is that all the concern you have for my hide? Besides, Connie, I got a plea bargain based on cooperating with the sheriff's office to crack a burglary ring in town. I found out about it when I did my jail time. I've talked to the police about it. I want to turn it around and straighten things out now. I can't change the past, and I can't snitch on the guy who stole from the day care center parents, but I want to make amends, so I'm actually working for the police now. So that's the end of it. I can't tell you any more about it, it's confidential. If I did tell you information, it could even put you in danger. There's an awful lot that you just can't, you just should not know. I'm only concerned about you."

Jerry's aggressive response persuaded Connie not to pursue the questioning any further. After all, despite his brush with the law, he was otherwise courteous, well liked, and he had supported her better than anyone else had during her whole life. She had a home with heat during the winter, new clothing for her two children and as far as she knew, Jerry was telling the truth. She decided "to stick by her man." She had been involved with other men before and each of them had been abusive toward her. At least Jerry had never abused her or her children.

While on probation, Jerry violated several of the conditions of his court order. First, he stood at the exit of the downtown parking garage and collected fares to pick up pocket money. He had purchased a blue jumpsuit at a thrift store with an official looking "Karl" emblazoned over the left pocket. When departing customers asked him why they couldn't continue leaving their fares in the bucket as they exited, Jerry told them that the honor system for payments had recently been abused too much. Either that, he said, or the proprietor suspected that juvenile delinquents were stealing the proceeds, so for a while Jerry would be monitoring and collecting some fares. The new "system" worked well for Jerry until the proprietor himself drove out one day and listened patiently to Jerry's story about why he was collecting parking fares. Then he drove directly to the police station. This was Jerry's first probation violation, second-degree theft.

The second violation was assaulting Connie. At a party one evening, Connie met another woman who was swooning over her new boyfriend. Comparing notes, Connie soon learned that this was none other than her own Jerry. Connie was working Saturday evenings in a small stationery store and the other woman told her that this boyfriend had invited her to his home for a lovers' tryst this coming Saturday. Slowly, a light went on and Connie's eyes began to open. She excused herself from work that Saturday, hid herself in the bedroom closet and listened as Jerry entered the house with the other woman. Gradually, they made their way to the bedroom and during their amorous embrace, Connie made a deliberately suspicious noise of her own in the clothes closet. Jerry leaped to the closet and drew back the hangers of clothes only to be surprised by Connie's swift knee striking him squarely in the groin. Writhing in pain, Jerry grabbed Connie, struck her several times, and threw her to the bedroom floor where she landed on a footstool, seriously injuring her back. An ambulance was called, and then the police were called when it became clear that the injuries resulted from domestic violence.

At the trial for probation violations, the judge listened carefully to Jerry's explanations of all these events. Jerry said he had planned to return the parking garage fares to the proprietor because he really had seen juveniles taking the money from the fare bucket and everyone knew that there were a lot of customers who drove out without putting anything in the bucket at all. He felt that if he did a good volunteer job, he could assess the situation and take everything to the owner and make a full report. He hoped that this might even lead to a job, which he sorely needed. He was extremely sorry for what had happened to Connie, especially because her injuries had disabled her, and especially now that she needed someone to help her on a daily basis during her rehabilitation. He was the only one available to help her and if he were sent to jail or prison, Connie would have to be put in a nursing home. If that happened, her two young children would be placed in foster homes not only to their detriment but at great expense to the state. "The reasonable thing to do," Jerry explained, "and I know that I'm at least partially at fault, is to give me a work release. I've got bona fide work all lined up installing fences with Fine & Fancy Fences, Inc., and that way I can get passes to go home and help Connie, to make up for what I did, the part that I'm responsible for, of course. That way, at least the children won't be made to suffer too. That just wouldn't be fair. None of this was their fault, after all." It was a tough position for the judge to be put in, but, ultimately, Jerry's sense of fairness and the judge's did not match. The judge revoked Jerry's probation and sentenced him to prison. In the judge's opinion, he wouldn't be helping Connie by encouraging her relationship with Jerry.

When Jerry was released on parole 2 years later, he decided to make a fresh start. He took the bus to a completely different part of the state where an uncle lived. He got a job as an apprentice carpenter, found his own apartment, and met Bobbi. Bobbi had just started a day care center and Jerry obviously knew a lot about the business, including business computer software and marketing. He offered to help her make a go of it. Her parents had put up most of the money and Jerry's help and knowledge of computers gave the business a really professional touch. Jerry said he would help out because he really preferred indoor work to carpentry, now that winter was coming on, and he enjoyed working with the kids a lot, but he really didn't want to be employed in any official capacity. He knew that with a criminal record, the state licensing authority would not allow him to work there. Also, his parole officer would refuse to allow it if she knew that Jerry were working in a capacity related to his past criminal conduct. Eventually, Jerry was working full-time "under the table" for Bobbi at the day care center while he collected unemployment compensation, and Bobbi's business was on solid footing. A year later it was discovered that Jerry had been sexually molesting many of the children at the center. Jerry was prosecuted and sent to prison. Bobbi's reputation, like Martha's, was ruined.

❖   ❖   ❖

This chapter will discuss various strategies that offenders use to manipulate others and will identify special times when these manipulations are most likely to occur. This chapter will also provide suggestions for how to respond to the offender both before and after the manipulations have occurred.

As many authors have noted, the convicted child molester is exposed not only to severe social censure but, at least potentially, to rather severe punishment. As Nicholas Groth and his colleagues have written, "the child molester is the recipient of the strongest societal anger and disapproval" (Groth et al., 1982, p. 131), so it is natural to expect that offenders would attempt to manipulate others with a sense of acute desperation. Some sexual offenders are quite successful at manipulating others. They do not get caught or are caught when it is difficult to hold them accountable for their behavior. Jerry knew he had at least some chance of escaping the judge's wrath because of the situation he had placed himself in through a series of manipulations. Other offenders are extremely poor manipulators. Those offenders are clumsy, childish, and they give their plans away to anyone who pays reasonable attention. Most offenders fall somewhere in between on this continuum. Sometimes they get caught manipulating, other times they do not. Virtually all child molesters manipulate in some way at some time. They especially try to manipulate those who have power over them, those who have the authority to influence their lives, such as their wives and relatives, their probation officers, and their therapists.

The wife (and children's mother) is potentially the most important and powerful figure in the child molester's life for many reasons. She usually has the best day-to-day working knowledge of how the offender is doing. She is most likely to detect any violations of court orders. She also represents good community support and, in this way, plays a significant role in the court's decision to allow the offender to remain in the community. The therapist often views the wife as instrumental for similar reasons and will invite the wife into therapy sessions to inform her about the nature and goals of the therapy and to get feedback from her regarding how things are going at home. The wife is a vital link to spotting the offender's manipulations. She can often communicate problems that she discovers to the therapist and the probation officer before those problems become too serious or get out of control.

Typical Offender Manipulations

The broad range of manipulations that the offender uses reveals that he is both imaginative and innovative, if at times malicious, toward other people. This chapter can only introduce the reader to a few of the common manipulations. The offender's manipulations range from the most subtle, almost artful, tactics to direct attempts to force his own will on others. Whether subtle or not, manipulations are by their very nature planned so that the offender can take advantage of others, even to reoffend against his original victim or other children. For that reason, all manipulations should be taken seriously. The child molester that you know will likely use his personal set of circumstances to manipulate in unique ways. However, with vigilance, such manipulations can often be identified and stopped before serious harm is done.

   A common manipulation involves an offender asking someone for approval to do something that is actually a cover for doing something else. For example, Slim asked his probation officer for permission to spend the Thanksgiving holidays with his wife Shari and his stepdaughter Bernice, whom he had molested. He had no violations on probation so far and due to his cooperation, and the cooperation of Shari, contact among all three of them was gradually being restored. Slim knew that the probation officer liked Shari and believed her to be highly responsible and reliable because she has been consistently helpful throughout probation. She had communicated openly with the probation officer, asked insightful questions, and indicated her desire to be firm but also fair with Slim. She told both Slim and the probation officer that she would give Slim a chance to prove himself but that she would tell on him if Slim ever stepped out of line.

However, neither Shari nor Slim ever told the officer a significant fact: Shari was a recovering alcoholic. Also, she had "fallen off the wagon" every Thanksgiving for the past 5 years, partly because Shari had lost her first daughter to a rare disease on Thanksgiving Day several years before. Shari had never told the probation officer about her drinking problem because her second daughter, Bernice, was a ward of juvenile court. Before she had begun her successful recovery, Shari had left Bernice alone often and juvenile court authorities determined that Bernice's welfare should be monitored to make sure that no similar neglect occurred in the future. Furthermore, if Shari were to drink any alcohol at all, Bernice could be removed from her care and put in a foster home permanently.

Slim knew that he would have no difficulty provoking Shari to drink alcohol this Thanksgiving. Then, while she was passed out, he would be able to force Bernice to have sex with him again. This time, Slim thought, young Bernice would not disclose the abuse because the last time she had been put in a foster home she said that it had been the worst experience of her life. This time, Slim thought he could get away with it completely, no one would ever know, even though he was on probation. Even if Bernice told her mother, Shari would not report the assault for fear of losing Bernice permanently for repeated neglect. He calculated that Bernice would tolerate the sexual abuse more readily than she would foster care placement. Fortunately there was something dramatically different and important about Shari that Slim had not yet discovered.

On Thanksgiving, Slim tried to provoke Shari. He "inadvertently" mentioned how badly he was feeling about the first daughter's death. He quickly apologized for bringing the subject up, and immediately began to awkwardly console Shari, doing an intentionally miserable job. "If we'd only gotten her to the doctor sooner, we might have saved her," he said. "If you'd only demanded that the doctors run those special medical tests when the problem first appeared. She might have been saved!" While Shari sobbed, Slim said he had brought something to console her because he knew that she was feeling miserable and would need some cheering up: a bottle of Shari's favorite apricot brandy.

To Slim's surprise, Shari refused the bottle. She walked to a telephone, dialed, and began talking desperately to a party on the other end. She sobbed, related what had happened, asked questions, listened intently, agreed, and gradually made a plan to meet the other person. Shari had joined Alcoholics Anonymous and the person she had telephoned was her "sponsor" from the group. Because of her sponsor's support, Slim's plan failed. This year, Shari could not be manipulated into drinking alcohol. Bernice was safe.

This case example illustrates how manipulative child molesters can be. The case also illustrates a key element for any person hoping to foil an offender's manipulations, that is, getting help and support from others who know about the offender. Without the reliable support of her Alcoholics Anonymous sponsor, Shari might have succumbed to alcohol as she had so many times before.

Another offender on probation illustrates a second method of subtle manipulation, which is speaking in vague, rambling, and unclear language. Bob, a plumber, requested permission from his probation officer to visit his aunt and uncle, Betsy and Jim, in another county. He failed to say that his daughter, Janet, who had been his victim in the past, might be visiting them. The judge prohibited Bob from having any contact with Janet for the time being. Bob hoped that he could meet her and persuade her to retract her accusation of sexual abuse. If the probation officer found out about the contact, Bob could claim that meeting her there was entirely coincidental and so he could not be blamed for the contact with Janet. Although it was technically a violation of the rules of probation, he could claim that it was a situation totally beyond his control. He could say how sorry and remorseful he was and that he hoped the probation officer would remember and understand what he had said so many times before.

"I have been trying hard to follow all the rules on probation. And after all," he would declare if he got caught, "I did request your permission to visit my aunt and uncle, I wasn't trying to hide anything from you." He had planned his defense well in advance, in case he got caught in his scheme.

As it turned out, the probation officer telephoned Aunt Betsy in advance. He explained to Betsy what the rules of probation were, including no contact with Janet. Betsy said that the daughter would probably be coming by and she thought Bob knew this. Betsy wasn't certain, but she thought she had mentioned this to Bob some time ago when they first talked about him coming for a visit. Permission to travel to the other county was denied. Bob's manipulation was foiled because those who knew him communicated with each other.

Typically, a judge will prohibit all contact between the child molester and any minor children unless the visit is supervised by a "chaperone." The chaperone must be an adult who knows about the child molester's sexual assaults and knows what the rules and restrictions are governing the molester's behavior. The chaperone can be trusted fully with the responsibility to ensure that during any contact between the child molester and children, the children will be safe. Chaperoned visits must usually be approved in advance by all of the responsible parties, including the probation officer, the children's parents, the offender's therapist, and perhaps even the child's own therapist if she has one. Even so, the offender will frequently attempt to manipulate the chaperone for any number of reasons, whether to bribe or groom a child, intimidate a potential victim or witness, or even to molest another victim. In some cases, the offender may find persons who are simply inappropriate to be chaperones. Offenders have been known to try to use mentally retarded adults and individuals suffering from severe alcoholism or other mental health disorders as chaperones. Such circumstances pose a high risk for children.

Ideally, the chaperone should be informed explicitly about the offender. The chaperone should be told about the exact nature of the offender's sexual offense and relevant personal history, the requirements of probation, the rules of the therapy program, and the procedures that must be followed when the chaperone supervises any contact between the offender and minor children.

Steve requested that his grandmother be approved to be the chaperone during weekend visits with his daughter. Steve said he had told his grandmother what he was on probation for and that she knew all the details. On the surface, this appeared appropriate. However, it turned out that the grandmother was in poor physical health, had cataracts, and was unable to leave her house. She had a swing, a teeter-totter, and a large sandbox in her backyard for her grandchildren, but the yard was well screened by bushes and shrubbery from both the grandmother's windows and from the adjoining houses. The yard was totally secluded and Steve knew this.

To Steve's surprise, the officer called the grandmother immediately, while Steve sat in his office, to arrange an appointment to meet and talk with her in his office. The grandmother agreed to the interview, but she asked the probation officer if he could come out to her home. That way he could see the nice play area she had for her grandchildren. She also indicated that, owing to her blindness due to cataracts, she could not drive. A few follow-up questions alerted the probation officer to the other serious pitfalls in this chaperone arrangement. The grandmother was not approved as a chaperone. (Actually, she was relieved when advised of this decision. People are often persuaded to do things for manipulative sex offenders even when they are uncomfortable with the situation.) Steve's manipulation was prevented because the probation officer and grandmother talked to each other clearly regarding the visit in advance.

Steve's case illustrates the importance not only of giving others such as chaperones information about the sex offender but also of gathering information and ideas from others who know the offender. Information should travel freely among all parties involved to reduce offender manipulations. In the case of chaperones, for example, a personal visit among the probation officer, therapist, and chaperone is always advisable. This provides the opportunity to see where the visits will take place and avoid problems that could come up later. All interested parties, including chaperones, parents, and the victim's mother, among others, should discuss the plans and any potential problems with each other in advance. If the child is involved in counseling, the child's therapist should also be consulted. Usually, when the information flows freely, everyone discovers that they have important information to contribute.

Face-to-face meetings also help erase any doubts that others may have about the probation officer or therapist. It is common for offenders to tell their wives, relatives, and employers that the probation officer or therapist is unreasonable, demanding, and untrustworthy. Face-to-face meetings usually erase such misperceptions. Such meetings also help those parties understand exactly why strict rules are necessary because, in most cases, those people have heard about the offender's crimes only from the offender himself, if at all. They usually have only a vague impression of what the offender did and, as has been previously discussed, the offender invariably minimizes the seriousness of his own history. When everyone has the same information about the offender, when they have met and spoken in person, it is far more difficult for the offender to manipulate because everyone has a common understanding about how dangerous the offender is. Face-to-face meetings usually result in clearer communication.

In one instance, after 2 years of good progress in therapy Carl returned home to live with his wife Carol and their daughter Julie, whom he had molested. Things went well for several months. Carl did not yet have permission to be alone with his daughter, but Carol still was very pleased with his progress. Carl, however, "forgot" that Carol told him never to pick Julie up at school. One day, Carol had a doctor's appointment at the time she normally picked Julie up at school. Carl "forgot" she had made arrangements for someone else to pick Julie up. He went to school early and got Julie. The school had not been notified that Carl should never be allowed to pick up Julie, unless specifically instructed by Carol. He then took her out for ice cream and bought her a present, as he later rationalized, "Just to show her I still loved her even though she turned me in. I wanted her to know it was the right thing to do." He arrived home a few moments after Carol returned from the doctor's appointment. When confronted, Carl claimed, "I simply forgot! And this seemed like an emergency. You were on your way to the doctor's! I couldn't reach you and I thought you might have forgotten too. I only thought I was helping out, and besides, what could happen in the car?"

Experience shows that grooming and actual sexual offenses against children do occur in cars. Even while offenders are driving through traffic, they have been known to simultaneously molest children. Carl had recognized that his wife was pleased and surprised at how well he had been doing for over 2 years. He knew he could claim he forgot the instruction never to pick the daughter up because so many things had changed since his return to the home, and he felt he would probably pay only a small penalty for the violation. He knew he might get caught, but he had a strong urge to spend some time alone with his daughter, and he took a chance that he could get away with it. He hadn't been alone with Julie for over 3 years, he missed her so much and he wanted to prove to himself that he could be "safe" around her. In his own mind, he did not believe this small violation would lead down the path to reoffense. He sincerely believed he would be proving it was at last safe for him to be alone with Julie. His "proof" came from manipulation, rather than from a direct request and discussion with all of the significant parties involved in his case about whether this was the right time to begin unsupervised contact. Luckily, those parties—Carol, their therapist, and the probation officer—recognized how dangerous Carl's manipulative behavior was. Through counseling, Carol had learned that such manipulations were her husband's effort to see whether he could return to his old ways without resistance from her once he was off probation, when the probation officer and therapist would no longer be around to back Carol up. As it turned out, the judge was equally concerned, and he gave Carl 60 days in jail. He also extended probation for another year.

Transition Points

Family members should be aware that offender manipulations often occur at transition points in the offender's life. These are periods when things are changing in significant ways. A new job, the release from jail, the end of probation, and other moments add significantly to the offender's potential adjustment problems and demand particular vigilance. The following are times of special concern:

1. Upon disclosure of the original sexual offense
2. Upon being sentenced in court to probation
3. Upon release from jail or prison
4. Upon first permission to have chaperoned visits
5. Near the end or upon completion of therapy
6. Upon discharge from probation or parole
7. Upon separation or divorce
8. After discharge from probation, parole, or therapy

William Pithers, a noted therapist and expert on sex offenders, refers in his 1988 chapter on preventing relapse to offender's inclination to revert to keeping secrets during times of particular stress, highlighting times when he was in danger of reoffending. For example, when the offender is first placed on probation, he will often test the rules to see how much freedom he can gain for himself. He tests how closely the probation officer, the therapist, and his wife will be watching him. Typically, when the offender finishes his jail sentence and knows that he must attend therapy, he fails to begin his counseling program until the probation officer contacts him and tells him to report to therapy immediately. Because court orders rarely are so precise that they tell the offender he must report to a counseling program immediately upon his release from jail, he may rationalize his waiting for as long as possible to avoid counseling. Typically the offender will claim, "I was waiting for you [the probation officer] to tell me when I needed to go."

The completion of therapy and probation are significant transition points. At the end of therapy, the offender will sometimes break rules, which presents a number of dilemmas for all parties involved. At this time, for example, it is difficult for therapists to admit that their treatment was less successful than they had hoped. Probation officers have new cases to start supervising and often want an offender to "succeed," to be discharged from probation, and for the caseload to be reduced as well. The offender may try to capitalize on these attitudes. If, for example, the offender has done well throughout probation and therapy, he is often allowed to spend time alone with his daughter through very carefully planned visits involving the offender, his therapist, the mother, the daughter, and the daughter's therapist. His manipulation may be to allow him to spend a longer period of time alone with his daughter than was agreed. He often feels confident that at this point he will only be warned, not punished, and he wants to see what the mother's resolve is going to be once probationary controls are lifted.

Other writers have discussed the warning signs of reoffense, which in many ways present similar problems. One writer, Nancy Steele (1988), suggests that if an offender is on the verge of committing another offense, he is probably displaying many signs. Although her writing refers specifically to the problems of treating men who are in therapy programs in prison, the areas she identifies should also be useful regarding offenders out in the community, living with their families. These signs include problems in treatment; becoming emotionally distant; and emotional changes such as belligerence, hostility, and unwillingness to cooperate with others. Similarly, special stresses may occur when there has been a significant change, even an improvement, in employment, because the offender may have increased anxiety about failing. Steele (1988) writes, "It is a bad sign if the offender, or any of the family members, begins to minimize or downplay the original conviction" (p. 118).

Confronting Manipulation

Setting the Tone

Many researchers and sex offender therapists have pointed out that sex offenders seem to seek out children because they have never learned how to interact positively and successfully with adults (Groth et al., 1982). As one writer observes,

> A pedophile may experience difficulty, but cope with the phase of initiating a relationship, and fail utterly at the phase of friendship requiring a capacity for expressing and receiving intimacy and for making self-disclosures . . . pedophiles tend to view adults in terms of dominance and submissiveness and find adults overbearing, whereas children are viewed as nonthreatening and easy to relate to because of their submissive status. (Howells, 1981, pp. 73-74)

This suggests that sex offenders gravitate to children because they are more successful in carrying on conversations and interacting at a child's level. Sex offenders often have poor verbal skills for conversing with adults about important, especially intimate, topics affecting their lives. They overlook many sensible solutions to interpersonal problems. For example, Carl, who picked his daughter up at school, could have phoned his wife at the doctor's office to see what arrangements had been made and phoned the school to be sure their daughter was not left alone. He could also have arranged for another adult to pick Julie up. Better still, he could have arranged in advanced for an approved adult to pick Julie up and discussed the whole plan openly with Carol ahead of time. Professional experience with sex offenders shows that, without careful therapy and learning new social skills, they fail to discuss such solutions in advance and they show noticeable difficulty in thinking up solutions to problems on their own.

If handled properly, confronting the offender about his manipulations can show the offender that someone cares about him. Such confrontations, when conducted in a caring but firm manner, also show that someone wants to help him. Virtually all adults can help teach the offender how to talk openly with adults, and they can demonstrate to him that interaction with adults can be enjoyable and personally rewarding. Finally, even when confronted about manipulations, the offender can learn the important skills necessary to relate to adults successfully. Direct, caring confrontation can teach the offender that problems can have solutions that satisfy everyone.

There is no simple formula for how to confront an offender who has been caught manipulating. However, there are basic principles that can increase the likelihood that such confrontations will be successful. These principles pertain to (a) a humane approach that maintains the dignity of all persons, including the offender; (b) consulting with professionals who may be involved in the offender's case; and (c) using specific agreements with the offender to clarify expectations.

A Humanistic Approach

The first and perhaps the most difficult principal in confronting the offender's manipulation is to be mindful of maintaining the dignity of the offender. Stanley Brodsky and Donald J. West discuss this humane aspect of confrontation in a description of their design for a therapeutic community to treat sex offenders. Their design emphasizes the importance of open discussion in an optimistic atmosphere that is geared toward improvement of the quality of visible social interactions. Not only are the offender's sexual problems a matter of attention, but *all* aspects of his behavior are viewed through his interactions with others (Brodsky & West, 1981). This means that when Carol discovers Carl manipulating her to be with Julie, she must confront him, even showing her own anger, but without belittling or denigrating him. Confronting him for what he did is important because he can change the things he does through relatively clear, achievable agreements.

Criticizing the offender's personality or moral character is not likely to be productive. The sex offender cannot have much hope of realistically changing his basic personality or moral character quickly, easily, or in the immediate future. While criticism of the offender's moral character may be justified in some minds, personal criticisms only push the offender farther away from adults, leaving children the most viable source of social interaction and satisfaction, which obviously is a dangerous situation for everyone.

Instead of criticism, identifying specific behaviors can prove beneficial. For example, an offender may repeatedly come home late from work without letting his wife know or he may spend money outside of the planned budget. An offender may interrupt while others are speaking or not listen when others are speaking to him. He may dismiss the importance of what someone else says and refuse to discuss the issue, even when it is extremely important to the other person. Each of these are specific behaviors that can be addressed without attacking the offender's personality and that can, at the same time, identify more acceptable behaviors. Each of them also identifies areas of common courtesy, an area in which child molesters may be grossly negligent. Such confrontations lay the groundwork for improvement in the child molester's behavior.

Avoiding the tendency to criticize or scoff at the offender is not an easy task. This is another reason that the wife should seek professional counseling for herself. Jon Conte and Lucy Berliner, two noted therapists and educators, write in their 1981 article,

> In many incest cases, the nonoffending parent, usually the mother, will require counseling to handle her own reactions to the discovery of the abuse, to assist her in her dealing with the offender, and to assist her in being a protective and supportive parent to the child victim. (p. 606)

Consulting With Others

The second important principle in confronting the offender's manipulations involves talking with other people, especially other professionals, who know the sex offender's history. These discussions can be of great help. Such communication from the beginning will help to establish consistency among all persons dealing with the offender, so that everyone gives clear and consistent messages regarding manipulations or any other unacceptable behavior. Talking frequently with others will also help prevent isolation, the sense of loneliness and helplessness, that often accompanies those interacting with child molesters. The risk of making a miscalculation is much greater when made without consulting others. Even therapists must deal with these persistent problems and rely on each other for mutual support. As noted therapist and researcher Gene Able and his colleagues have written,

> If the therapist is looking for reinforcement [personal satisfaction] from the patient [i.e., sex offender] for having helped him with symptoms, such reinforcement is usually not forthcoming [at least not immediately]. For this reason, it is helpful for the therapy to be done by two therapists . . . so that support can come from fellow therapists involved in the treatment program. (Abel et al., 1986, pp. 8-9)

It is often very difficult to tell whether your confrontation of an offender is entirely appropriate, whether the confrontation is being received sincerely and appropriately by the offender, or whether the offender's response is another manipulation. Therefore, consulting with others who know the offender will help resolve such doubts. Talking to everyone about manipulation when it occurs is important for several reasons. First, it reduces risk. Second, it reinforces in the offender's mind that his chances of manipulating successfully are dwindling and he would do better to quit his struggle to control others and instead invest his energies fully in his treatment program.

Specific Agreements

If the offender is discovered in a manipulation or in violating requirements, even in some minor way, certain steps can encourage the offender to avoid this "forgetting" in the future. Probation officers often send a formal violation report to the court for even minor violations. Although the report may recommend no official court action, the offender gets the message that such violation behavior is serious and does not escape the judge's attention.

In a similar way, if the offender is caught breaking rules or attempting to manipulate, the offender and family members can benefit from specific agreements. Anyone else involved with the offender, including relatives, friends, or an employer, can also use such written agreements effectively. Clear agreements can be beneficial because they serve notice to the offender that particular behaviors are considered serious by all parties. Also, agreements can erase ambiguity. Actually writing and signing agreements can provide a visible record, and if a written record exists, it is more difficult for the offender to claim that he did not understand. If it turns out that the written agreement was ambiguous, it can be revised. Having clear understandings, after all, is only fair to everyone involved.

One can take the time to review with the offender all legal requirements, rules of therapy, and other personal requirements that may pertain to the offender's case. While discussions of this nature may initially seem awkward, such actions can strengthen relationships in many ways. The reader should recall that many prominent therapists describe the offender as, among other things, grossly immature (Groth et al., 1982). As such, offenders need clear reminders about rules and requirements. A necessary condition for maturation to occur with child molesters includes open discussion, learning to talk and to listen, and a true exchange of ideas in a caring, supportive environment. Reviewing rules is also a firm reminder that this is serious business.

It is sometimes perplexing to the wife, family members, and others such as employers that probation officers must take a strong, directive, controlling stance with the sex offender, in essence establishing a relationship in which building the offender's trust plays only a minor part. They sometimes comment that controlling the offender appears to be causing more problems than it solves. While this may be true in some (rare) cases, experience shows that a strong, controlling stance at the beginning more often results in a successful probation, whereas a less controlling attitude more often results in the offender having serious problems later.

One notable result of this firm, no-nonsense approach is that once the child molester realizes that he will be held accountable, he will often become noticeably more compliant and cooperative. This does not mean that he is "cured" or that his problems are solved. It does not mean that his rehabilitation is guaranteed or that the work of counseling him is done. Instead, it means that counseling can move on to a new and more important set of problems: changing his deviant behaviors and personal lifestyle on a long-term basis.

Those working with child molesters should remember that the offender thrives in an environment of secrecy. Secrecy allows the offender to manipulate others. Understanding this and not allowing secrecy in the offender's life should help protect children from further abuse. Furthermore, ending secrecy will contribute significantly to the offender's involvement in a successful therapy program.

A firm, vigilant, controlling role does not, however, suggest a demeaning or belittling attitude toward the offender. Firmness, while essential, should not replace but should, instead, complement the goal of a positive, supportive responsible relationship that encourages increasingly mature behavior by the offender. This kind of relationship should help the sex offender himself in that he will be more likely to make requests directly and honestly rather than to try to get what he wants through manipulation.

The Presentence
Investigation Report

The primary purpose of the presentence report is to provide the sentencing court with relevant and accurate data so it may select the most appropriate sentencing alternative and correctional disposition. Although use of the report for sentencing decisions is paramount, its potential use for probation supervision and/or by other agencies within and outside the correctional system should be recognized. (Crim, 1978, p. 15)

The Presentence Investigation Report or PSI (or sometimes PSR) commonly refers to the investigation and report completed by a probation officer after an investigation has been conducted of a person convicted of a crime. The investigation and report are completed before the judge decides the sentence the defendant will receive. The format and content vary from state to state and even from county to county within the United States. There has been some effort to standardize the PSI but with varying degrees of success. In the most general sense, the PSI contains all significant information discovered from the investigation of the defendant from the moment he was born to the day the report was written.

The PSI helps the judge decide whether an offender should receive a long-term prison sentence or a jail sentence and/or probation. If the offender is sentenced to prison, the PSI helps prison officials select the best programs for the offender during his term of imprisonment. If the judge grants probation, the PSI then helps the judge decide what rules should be required of the offender while on probation.

The PSI can also help many other persons understand and work more effectively with the child molester in several different ways. First, it can provide a concise description of the offender's crime and other related criminal activity for which the offender may have been charged but not convicted due to plea bargain agreements. This information is important in assessing how serious a threat the offender may be to his family and the community. Second, the PSI includes documentation of other criminal convictions, which is equally important in understanding the offender. On the other hand, the PSI can help rule out the existence of other known criminal convictions. It can be just as important for an offender's wife to know that the offender does not, in fact, have other criminal convictions. Third, the PSI may also contain the probation officer's observations made from an experienced professional's point of view, clarifying such important areas as whether the offender was cooperative during the investigation and interviews that took place. If, for example, an offender tried to deceive the probation officer during a presentence investigation or if he refused to answer particular questions, anyone who reads the report gains important information about the offender's desire to continue his pattern of secrecy.

Disclosure

Before discussing the report itself, it is important to discuss ways to obtain the information contained in the PSI. Historically, corrections agencies (probation and parole offices) have not always been willing to release PSIs to anyone but the judge. The first presentence investigations were conducted in 1910 in Chicago and were strictly for the judge's use (Crim, 1978, p. 3). Since then, the PSI has gone through various stages of development as theories for understanding and responding to criminal behavior have changed. For many years, the PSI was not considered to be "disclosable." In the United States, each state is free to determine its own approach to handling criminal sentencing procedures. As a result, there is wide variation in how the Presentence Investigation Report is handled from state to state and from county to county. Recent federal law states that defendants in federal crimes not only have a right to know what is in the PSI report but also have a right to have their attorney present during the investigative interviews. The trend in state laws continues in that direction. Many states now have laws to protect the public through warning citizens about the presence of convicted child molesters who live in their neighborhoods, their history of sexual crimes, and the risk they present to the public. At present, the clear trend is toward disclosure, or opening the files up, on child molesters and other sex offenders.

U.S. District Court Judge James B. Parsons wrote some of the arguments against releasing PSI information in a 1964 article saying that, in his view, federal cases should continue to be confidential documents as they had been up to that point in time for several reasons. He believed that, first, releasing the report to the defendant would cause many sources of important information to "dry up," second, that probation would be granted less often, and third, disclosure would be damaging to the defendant and particularly to the defendant's relationship to the probation officer. However, because there were no specific rules prohibiting the release or disclosure, some federal courts allowed the PSI to be released to the defendant's attorney.

Seven years after Judge Parsons's writing, the chief U.S. Probation Officer for the Milwaukee District, William G. Zastrow, reviewed the problems identified by Judge Parsons after his district had adopted the practice of releasing the PSI information. He wrote that the problems Judge Parsons was concerned about never materialized.

In his article in *Federal Probation,* Zastrow (1971) came to the following conclusions:

> Release of the presentence report to the defense attorney has not resulted in the problems we at first anticipated. Sources of information have not dried up. In many instances we have observed a more helpful and cooperative attitude on the part of the defendant and his counsel. There is less "sparring" between the client and officer at the outset of probation. The probationer is aware that we have knowledge of many of the facets of his life—his problems, his strengths, his weaknesses, his potential. The probation officer becomes a better and more objective investigator, carefully screening fact from hearsay. Presentence summaries are less judgmental and more analytical. The presentence investigation is a basic working document in the judicial and correctional process. Fairness to the defendant should require its release to the defendant and his defense attorney. (p. 22)

At present, in the federal system (and the same is true of the individual states and U.S. territories) "each district court is . . . free to use its discretion in this matter. . . . The practice varies between making the reports public in some districts and treating them as confidential in others" (Chandler, 1987, p. 14).

The federal system illustrates what is true in a general sense at the state level of the criminal justice system. The laws governing the disclosure of the PSI vary from one state to another, so it is impossible to categorize or group states' practices in meaningful ways. Furthermore, the laws governing the handling of the PSI are also changing at a very rapid pace. During the decade of the 1980s, for example, every state and all of the U.S. territories passed new laws or regulations controlling how official criminal records would be maintained and whether those records should be open to the public (U.S. Department of Justice, 1989). These changes are important to understand because it is at the state level (under state felony laws) that most sex offenders are prosecuted and sentenced. The trend is clearly toward more openness about offender's criminal records and history.

Although there is still no universal (federal) law requiring states to allow public access to criminal records, a report published by the U.S. Department of Justice (1989) stated,

> Criminal history record information is increasingly becoming available outside of the criminal justice agencies. Thirty states have adopted open record or freedom of information statutes which cover some types of criminal history record data. . . . This does not mean that criminal history data are publicly available in these states in all circumstances, but it does mean that the data are more available than they previously were. . . . For example, special access rights are increasingly accorded to *those involving public safety, supervision of children* or custody of valuable property. . . . Several states . . . require that the record subject [convicted offender] must consent in writing to any release of his criminal history record for non-criminal justice purposes. . . . The absence of federal legislation or regulations establishing a uniform nationwide dissemination policy for state criminal record systems has permitted the states to develop and implement their own approaches to the release of criminal records for non-criminal justice purposes. This has had the laudable effect of leaving the states free to establish their own privacy and confidentiality laws and policies to strike a proper balance between the rights of record subject and the public interest. (p. 6, emphasis added)

Although differences exist among the states, the reader is encouraged to obtain the PSI whenever possible because the information in it can be valuable in planning a relationship with the child molester in a way that will enhance the safety of children and others in the community. However, because there has been some resistance to releasing it to the defendant in the past, the reader should not anticipate that the PSI will necessarily be released in all instances, even when the sex offender has provided his written permission for its release. In some states and counties, the PSI may be easy to obtain. In others, it may be impossible. Where it can be obtained, it can provide a wealth of information vital to anyone wishing to make the safest, most informed decisions possible.

Even if the probation officer is unable to release the PSI despite being given written permission by the offender, the probation officer is nearly always able to discuss that information with the offender's permission. In most instances, the probation officer will want to do so to help avoid reoffenses and to provide for the safety of children and other members of the community. Experience shows that in nearly all instances, a strong working relationship between the probation officer and those who know the offender lead to greater chances of success for everyone involved.

How can the PSI be useful to those who know a convicted sex offender? The following are three examples of how the PSI information can be valuable. First, if the sex offender refused to answer certain questions or was otherwise uncooperative during the presentence interviews, his lack of cooperation is usually described in the report. As a result, the wife would have this information and may have a strong basis for believing that the offender is continuing to maintain secrecy about his sexual deviance. Second, information describing the offender's overall sexual history can be useful for parents who may wish to provide an adult son who is a convicted child molester with a place to live, but who also want a realistic understanding of how serious his problems have been and what precautions they should take to be sure he does not get into deeper trouble. If they learn from the PSI that he molested not only his own children but those of neighbors, they will want to make provisions for the safety of any children in their neighborhood. Third, an offender's minister or pastoral counselor will want to have clear knowledge about whether an offender was predatory (i.e., offended against children outside of his own home) to make plans for when the offender attends religious services. The pastoral counselor will want to be sure that the children in the congregation are safe and possibly arrange for responsible members to keep a knowledgeable eye on his activities.

Releasing information to wives and pastoral counselors, among others, can be beneficial to the offender himself. Experience shows that a full and honest disclosure is often a great relief to the offender. Child molesters often feel that their sexual deviance is the blackest part of their spiritual life and they want to keep it secret from everyone. They are relieved to find they are still accepted by those around them even when the truth is known. Also, they no longer live in the constant dread of someone else finding out about their past behavior.

Obtaining the Presentence Investigation Report

The following examples suggest several ways that an individual can obtain the PSI report. It is strongly recommended that the report be obtained with the knowledge, consent, and cooperation of the offender. Dealing with him in an open, honest, and forthright manner provides an example for him about how mature adults who truly care about other people behave.

The most successful way to obtain information about the child molester you know is with the assistance of your own therapist. If you are involved in your own therapy program, you can have your therapist request the PSI from the probation officer for purposes of your own (or your child's) treatment program. Your therapist can clarify whether providing the document is allowed and can share with you the information that you need in planning for the safety of yourself and your children. In nearly every instance where it is possible, the probation officer will be happy to share this information with your therapist.

Other ways to obtain the PSI include asking the offender or his attorney for a copy. In many localities it is common that he was given a copy of the report to review for errors before he was sentenced. Or you can ask the offender to give permission for his probation officer to release a copy to you. He can do this by signing a "Consent to Release Confidential Information" form for the probation officer. The PSI can also be obtained from the defendant's attorney if the offender asks his attorney to release the report. Here, it is important to distinguish between the report prepared by the probation officer and another report prepared by the attorney, which typically does not have the same thoroughness or objectivity of the probation officer's report. Finally, the PSI report can sometimes be obtained in the offender's file at the county court clerk's office. It may be helpful to bring the court number under which the offender was sentenced. This can usually be found at the top of any court orders pertaining to the offender's case. The clerk's staff can often provide assistance in determining the correct court number and proper file.

When the Offender Refuses Disclosure of the PSI

At times, the offender may refuse to allow his PSI or other informa-tion about his background to be released, claiming his right to confidentiality. Confidentiality refers to the criminal offender's right to privacy, whether it regards his criminal record, information in his case file, and/or his adjustment on probation. In the author's 25 years of working with sex offenders, it was extremely rare for an offender to refuse to sign for the release of information about himself. More often, people simply did not know how to ask about where to get information about the offender. Nearly all offenders are willing to allow disclosure of sensitive information, so long as they understand that it is intended for legitimate and appropriate purposes.

If the offender insists on preserving his right to confidentiality and he is not willing to allow the release of the PSI, great caution should be used in all further contacts with the offender. The safest assumption is that the offender is dangerous to you and any children he may have contact with. The child molester's refusal to allow an open, honest discussion of his true history based on the PSI demon-strates his continuing effort to maintain secrecy. Information may exist about the offender that would show he is a serious threat right now. Benefit of the doubt does not go to the child molester, it goes to children and to the public.

Many authors have written about the matter of sex offenders and confidentiality. In virtually all instances, they agree that an offender's refusal to have information about him shared with those who have a legitimate need to know is a bad sign. As noted therapist and author Nicholas Groth and his colleagues have written,

> Although confidentiality may be appropriate when treating non-criminal behavior, it is not appropriate when dealing with the child sex offender because it perpetuates the secrecy which is so much a part of the offense itself. The therapist must assume professional responsibility to protect any potential victims of this client. (Groth et al., 1982, p. 143)

An even higher degree of responsibility generally falls on the shoulders of the probation officer. "Protection of the community" is usually understood as the probation officer's primary responsibility. Certainly in the case of crimes of violence such as child sexual abuse, protection of the community is of the highest importance.

No one's responsibility, however, is equal to the mother's responsibility to protect her children from a known, convicted child molester. No one can ever have the interests of her children as close to heart and as constantly in mind as the children's mother. Probation officers will do everything that they can to help protect children, but they sometimes supervise as many as 500 to 1,000 cases, including all varieties of offenders, from burglars and drug offenders to child molesters and murderers. (The probation officer's duties will be discussed thoroughly in Chapter 9.) Although the probation officer may have professional judgment and experience of great value, the officer can spend only a small fraction of her or his time on any individual case. Similarly, the offender's therapist may have unsurpassed training in diagnosing mental health disorders and a superb ability to recognize potential problems, but again, the therapist will be able to dedicate only a small amount of time to any one offender's case. The professional can never replace the final authority, responsibility, and role played by the children's mother. No one will ever be able to do as conscientious a job as the children's mother, provided she is able to obtain the necessary information herself, along with the assistance and full cooperation of the other professionals who know and work with the child molester.

How can the offender's refusal to allow disclosure of the PSI be dangerous? In many ways, keeping the PSI secret enables the sex offender to minimize his sexual abuse, distort or deny the seriousness of his criminal history, and shroud himself in a cloak of secrecy. He is more able to blame others and to manipulate others to his own selfish ends. Such secrecy and manipulation can lead to his reoffending against children. The reader is reminded that although agency policies may not allow the release of the PSI report itself, the probation officer can nearly always discuss relevant information about the child molester based on file material with the offender's consent.

The Presentence Investigation Report

As previously noted, the PSI is a written report that helps the judge sentence the criminal offender.[1] It is usually based on a careful investigation of the offender, and it is most often prepared by a probation officer whose job it is to give fair and impartial but factually correct information to the judge. Sometimes, the sex offender's attorney will prepare a report for the judge to consider at sentencing, and the attorney will title it "Presentence Report" or give it some similar sounding name. However, any report prepared by a defense attorney should not be considered equivalent to a PSI prepared by a probation officer. The goal of the defense attorney in most instances is to try to reduce the offender's punishment. It is *not* to give an unbiased, thorough account of the offender. In the interests of justice, it is vital that someone give a truthful but favorable picture of the offender at the time of sentencing and defense attorneys may do so through their own presentence report. It is important to remember, though, that this report is not the same as the PSI prepared by the probation officer whose goal is to give complete and impartial information, to let the facts speak for themselves, even when they speak negatively of the offender.

The PSI prepared by the probation officer generally includes information on an offender's prior criminal history, a summary of the crime(s) for which he is being sentenced, and the offender's own statement or explanation about the sexual offense(s). The report also includes detailed information about the offender's personal history, from the day he was born to the present time. This includes family history, education and training, military service, employment history, marital history, mental health history, drug and alcohol history, and medical history. Most PSIs include the probation officer's recommendation for sentencing. The probation officer is often in an excellent position to give such recommendations because the officer not only has the experience of investigating large numbers of other offenders but also has had immediate, usually intense, and in-depth communication with the offender. The probation officer is in the best position to present a nonbiased report on the offender because the probation officer's duty is to be impartial. She or he does not work for the prosecuting attorney or the defense attorney. The probation officer's report is intended to let the facts speak for themselves, so that the judge can make a good decision.

Qualities of a Good Presentence Report

Thoroughness

A thorough investigation means looking under every stone and exploring every corner of the offender's life as is reasonably possible. To do so, the investigation should also rely on a wide variety of good sources of information, not just on what the offender himself claims or what the police reports allege. There are many sources that can potentially be used in gathering information about the offender, and some sources will obviously be better than others. Probation officers typically will request information from the following sources: the offender's parents, brothers, and sisters; current and past spouses; schools and training programs; criminal justice agencies (police departments, the FBI; county sheriff's departments, etc.); current and past employers; current and past mental health counselors; doctors, neighbors, or personal references; ministers and pastoral counselors; previous probation officers; juvenile court services; polygraphers; caseworkers; the victim's therapist(s); the victim's mother; the investigating detective or police officer; U.S. military records; state departments of motor vehicles; drug and alcohol counselors; previous victims (when they are adults); and relatives.

These are only the major sources that are typically contacted for information. There are other sources of information who can be contacted as well, depending upon the circumstances in each case. Each of these persons may be able to shed light on the offender, his overall adjustment in society, his ability to get along with others, his willingness to follow rules, his willingness to keep his word, and his general honesty. The fewer the sources used in any PSI, the more limited its thoroughness. Reports that use fewer sources are also less reliable, although they should not be discarded, because they do add additional information and the more information one knows about the convicted child molester, the better. If, for example, the PSI states that an offender has been employed as a shoe salesman for 10 years, the report should tell whether the information was verified by writing or telephoning the offender's employer or whether the offender only claimed such employment with no further verification or proof.

Objectivity

The next important requirement for a good PSI is objectivity. Objectivity means that the PSI should not be conducted and written for the purpose of supporting the prosecution of the defendant or for the purpose of supporting the defense. Furthermore, the PSI should not be designed to represent exclusively the wishes of the victim or any other interested parties. The purpose of the PSI is to present the basic facts pertaining to all aspects of the accused offender's crime and his personal history because those facts speak for themselves. Furthermore, objectivity means that facts take precedence over opinions. The probation officer may feel that an offender has many convictions (an opinion), but the most important thing for the reader is the actual number of convictions (a fact). This approach allows the reader to reach her or his own opinion.

Contents of the Presentence Report

Now let us look at the PSI and how it is written. Generally, the PSI is divided into various sections that include prior criminal history, the crime (including a victim impact statement), the defendant's statement about the offense, family history, educational history, employment history, marital history, military history, substance abuse history, mental health history, medical history, reference letters, and recommendations. By understanding what should be included in each section and how the information is gathered, the reader will be able to tell whether significant gaps in information exist in any report. Each section of the PSI will be discussed here because each section has aspects that are relevant to understanding and making plans to work with the sex offender.

Prior Criminal History

In a reliable PSI, records checks on sex offenders should have been completed in every city, county, and state in which an offender has lived throughout his adult life. This is particularly true for those offenders who are not undergoing a thorough sexual deviance evaluation completed by an experienced evaluator/therapist who will verify findings through a polygraph examination. Furthermore, police reports for every arrest and/or conviction should be requested from the agency involved if the nature of the arrest seems to have any bearing on the current charges against the offender. Finally, conviction data from the courts in each arrest should be requested and included in the report.

The importance of thorough records checks cannot be overstated. A probation or parole agency is, for the most part, the best equipped agency for gathering criminal history on offenders. Gathering prior criminal history has been one of the traditional tasks assigned by courts to probation officers. They have the legal authority to request such information and other criminal justice agencies usually respond promptly to requests because those agencies recognize the importance of sharing this vital information.

The reader may ask why it is necessary to write to each police and sheriff's office, each court, and every other law enforcement agency that might have information. Some might ask whether complete records on all criminal convictions are kept with some central agency such as the FBI? The answer is, unfortunately, no. In 1991, the Attorney General of the United States, who is the chief law enforcement officer in the nation, drew the problem of accurate criminal records to the public's attention by declaring that "improving the quality of the Nation's criminal history records is one of the most important challenges facing the criminal justice system today" (Thornburgh, 1991, p. 224). Federal laws have been passed requiring background (records) checks on those wishing to buy firearms, but a battle between federal and local governments has emerged because of the complexity and staggering costs of such checks. There is no simple solution to this problem despite the strong desire by many parties for effective legislation in this area. Records checks in the United States are difficult and time-consuming, whether for firearms checks or for sex offenders.

Little has improved since 1991 when the U.S. Attorney General addressed the issue of obtaining criminal history records. Eventually, advances in computer technology will bring about vast improvements in our ability to track individual criminal histories. But for the present, exhaustive city-by-city, county-by-county, and state-by-state checks are the only reliable way to try to obtain complete criminal history information. In the United States (unlike in Canada), there is no effective and centralized national repository for all criminal history records.

Child molesters often attempt to conceal prior arrests because they have a bearing on the charges against them. For example, records checks were made in every state Brad had ever lived in, and it was learned that he was cited for "public urination" years before in a distant state. The officer requested reports and conviction data to find out what happened in the incident. Initially, Brad denied ever having been convicted of any crime. When the probation officer confronted him with information about the incident, Brad claimed he was just caught urinating in public but that nothing more was involved. He said that he paid a $75.00 fine but that he forgot about the incident because it was so many years ago. The police reports that the probation officer obtained showed that Brad was in fact exposing his genitals from a parking lot to school girls passing by on the sidewalk. After the third day of exposing himself, the girls told the police, who then caught and arrested Brad in the act of exposing himself. The girls were afraid to testify because they thought Brad knew where they lived. Without forcing the girls to testify, the prosecutor felt they would have no case and agreed to accept a plea of guilty to public urination.

If the information about this incident had not been obtained, important facts would have been absent from the PSI. In this case, the information was important because it indicated that Brad had a proven sexual interest in minor girls many years before his most recent crime of indecent liberties. Initially, Brad had tried to argue that his most recent sex crime, molesting his 7-year-old daughter, was a "one-time thing" and everyone could be sure that it would never happen again. The thorough records check revealed Brad's attempt to conceal his lifelong sexual interest in young girls. This information dramatically altered the requirements of Brad's probation and the nature of the treatment program required of him.

The Offense and the
Victim Impact Statement

The offense (or offenses if the offender is being sentenced for more than one separate crime) should be described in clear, specific detail, including exactly what occurred, where it occurred, and over what period of time it occurred. The PSI should also provide basic information such as the age, sex, and maturity of the victim(s), and it should describe any special circumstances bearing on the crime. The reader should have a clear understanding of the entire scope of the crime(s) sufficient to begin making plans to keep the offender from taking advantage of others in the future.

The report should also include an assessment of the physical and psychological harm caused to the victim(s), based preferably on the written evaluation by a physician or therapist who specializes in treating victims of sexual abuse. Statements from the victim's parents can also provide significant information, not only in understanding the impact that the crime had on the victim but also in understanding the extent of the offender's deviousness as well.

In one case, a college professor was convicted of molesting his 14-year-old daughter. His wife was reluctant to give any information but suggested that the probation officer contact the victim's 22-year-old sister. After contacting all three of the older sisters, the probation officer learned that the offender had molested each of his four daughters over a period of 14 years. Until then, none of them had ever disclosed that they had been sexually abused by their father. Each assumed that when she left home her stern warning to her father would be enough to make the father stop molesting the younger sisters. Each warning, however, failed. This important information would not have been known if the probation officer had not diligently probed to gather information about the offender beyond the facts of the known crime against the youngest daughter.

The PSI should indicate clearly when any charges were dismissed due to plea bargaining. It is not uncommon, for example, for many charges to be reduced to only a few charges or possibly a single charge through plea bargain agreements. For example, one man whose wife ran a day care home molested nearly every child that had ever been in the home. The offender, 60 years old, agreed to plead guilty to only three counts of indecent liberties in exchange for the prosecutor recommending only 7 years in prison to avoid 36 counts of indecent liberties, which could have resulted in his being sentenced to prison for the rest of his natural life. The prosecutor judged that with a 7-year sentence, justice could be served considering the man's age, and the community would be spared the enormous expense of a very costly and potentially traumatic trial involving so many child victims. In this case, it is clearly important that the person reading the PSI understand that this child molester did not have just three victims but actually several more.

The Defendant's
Version of the Offense

The PSI includes the offender's statement about the crime, if he chooses to give one, because there are often aspects of the crime that might be overlooked by others. The PSI allows the offender an opportunity, in the interest of justice, to "put his best foot forward," to be sure that significant aspects of his case are not overlooked or that any bias in the PSI can be countered through his statement about the crime.

Initially, Henry, a school bus driver, was asked by the probation officer conducting the presentence interview to describe how he made preparations to molest one of the children on his bus. He claimed that his offense was spontaneous. He told the probation officer that, "It just happened! I didn't plan it at all. I didn't even think about it. It just happened and it was over." The probation officer looked Henry calmly in the eyes and said, "In that case, I will have to recommend a long prison term. If you have absolutely no control and can just suddenly rape a child, you are truly dangerous." Within minutes, Henry changed his story and revealed that he had been planning the molestation for months, watching the children to see which one was most vulnerable, planning how he could "fake" a bus breakdown on a rural road and bribe his young victim with candy not to tell.

Through this revelation by Henry and similar information on other child molesters, the reader can evaluate, for example, whether the offender was still strongly denying all problems of sexual deviancy or attempting to blame others for what happened. It can also show whether he appeared at the time of the investigation to have any realistic remorse for his offense and any appreciation for the harm he had done to his victim. It can show how extensively he has manipulated others, groomed victims and other adults, and planned his alibis.

The offender's version of the offense is, by and large, a yardstick against which the reader can at some future date measure how far the offender has come. If the offender completely denied the offense during the investigation but at a later date acknowledges the offense in its entirety, the change may indicate that the offender is abandoning his attitude of denial. Under such conditions, he is more apt to do better in a therapy program because he can begin to look at himself more honestly.

Family History

Family history includes questions regarding where the offender was born and raised and as much biographical information as possible regarding his family. Of particular importance is whether the offender was exposed to any abusive experiences, including child physical abuse or neglect, child sexual abuse, and family violence, alcoholism, or drug abuse. Here, corroboration (verifying information the offender gives about himself with others) is extremely important.

Osmond, a sex offender in his sixties, resisted having anyone in his family contacted regarding his background. He claimed that his ailing mother might have a heart attack. His father was deceased. Osmond's brother was contacted by the probation officer despite Osmond's objections. The brother responded with a lengthy letter that indicated he was surprised that Osmond had "again" gotten in trouble with sexual problems. "We thought we had licked him of this problem when he was 13, when we kept finding him fondling the younger sister, Anna Mae, out behind the chicken coop. We (the older brothers) gave him a few good lickins and thought that had done the trick. Told him to stay clear away from Anna Mae. Sure hope he gets the right help this time. By the way, don't tell Ma about this, if you can help it. She's been pretty sick recently, heart attacks and all, and this could just be too much for her to take. Sincerely . . ."

Education and Training

Education and training may or may not be crucial to understanding a sex offender, depending upon the circumstances of the case, what has already been gathered from the family history, and whether there are any obvious deficits that would preclude the offender from participating in specialized treatment for sexual deviance. In some instances, the offender makes claims about being able to get work, arrange counseling, and pay for restitution to the victims because he has superb training in some field. Verification will at times corroborate such claims. In some cases, such claims by the offender are proved to be untrue. These exaggerated claims about employment potential are simply the offender's ongoing desire to manipulate all whom he comes in contact.

Employment History

Employment history is relevant, especially if the offense took place at work or if the job somehow allowed the sexual abuse to occur. An offender may have used his employment as a base for offending by grooming the employer and other employees as well as children. This is typical in the case of teachers, clergy, counselors, and others. Gathering information from current employers can be especially instructive if the offender is going to continue working in any place where offenses could conceivably occur. Prudence would suggest that in any case where employment might contribute to or enable sex offending to occur, the employer should be notified and the offender should be prohibited from any situations that might contribute to reoffense. Both spouses and future employers benefit from learning the details of how the offender used his job to enable his sexual offenses. Employers usually want to know this. Furthermore, the wife should know, for example, whether her husband had been able to drink alcohol while working at a certain job, in case he planned on working there in the future. She and the employer might wish to communicate about the situation to be sure that the offender is not allowed to drink alcohol.

In one case, two friends had sexually abused a mentally retarded woman in a nursing home where they worked. By contacting a previous employer at a similar institution in another state it was discovered that years before, the friends had sexually abused other mentally disabled women and had been fired from their jobs because of it, although due to evidentiary problems they were not prosecuted. The victims were too mentally disabled to provide convincing testimony in court, so the men were simply fired.

Marital History

A sex offender's marital history is usually of particular significance because it reveals so much about his past sexual functioning. Offenders often hide or distort the details of past marriages from present spouses. The PSI can help set the record straight. Current wives can make better decisions when they read the PSI and become aware of the details of past marriages. As previously noted, verification such as telephone calls or letters from former spouses can be extremely valuable. An offender's self-report (what he says about himself) is usually distorted to make him seem better than he really is, especially regarding past marriages.

Mack was a smooth-talking, self-employed construction contractor convicted of molesting the young daughter of his girlfriend. He claimed that he was drunk and couldn't deny the crime but insisted that he couldn't remember a thing about it. "Must have been the alcohol," he told the probation officer during the presentence investigation interview.

Mack had been married several times and claimed that he divorced all his previous wives because his wives were spending too much of his hard-earned money, making it difficult for him to succeed in business. Two former spouses responded to letters from the probation officer stating that they left Mack because their daughters disliked him so much and didn't want to be around him.

The daughters were developing emotional problems and the wives got tired of Mack's constant demands for attention. A third wife indicated that she broke up with him because Mack began asking her to perform unusual sexual acts.

In his effort to manipulate the probation officer, Mack told the probation officer during the presentence interview that he knew only the address of his last wife and said he could not help locate the other wives. When the last wife was contacted she provided the names and addresses of the two other wives, all of whom had communicated numerous times over the years. She said that Mack did have their addresses because he would frequently show up on their doorsteps, late at night, drunk. All three wives admitted to spending large amounts of his money on cosmetics, clothing, and expensive perfume, but they did so because Mack encouraged them to. One wrote, "I didn't care that much about buying new clothes. It was as if Mack had a fetish for how me and my daughter looked." They also mentioned that he was always willing to look after their daughters whenever he sent the wives out shopping. Obviously, Mack was attempting to keep his marital history secret from the probation officer. Any women involved with Mack in the future would benefit from knowing about his tendency to deceive and use others for his personal, selfish ends.

Military History

Military service is sometimes a period when a sex offender was exposed to significant sexual activities through the use of prostitutes and other unusual sexual liaisons. Such experiences may have played an important role in shaping the offender's attitudes about sex and about women in general. Also, military service may reveal important information about how the offender handles his relationships with those in authority over him.

Substance Abuse History

Substance abuse includes both the abuse of alcohol and the abuse of drugs. The abuse of drugs includes abuse of prescribed medication

and illegal (street) drugs. Research suggests a very special relationship between alcoholism and some sexual offending (Finkelhor,
1986; Herman, 1981). Professionals generally state that alcohol
itself does not cause a child molester to offend. However, it is
sometimes present when molesting takes place and appears to have
negative effects on the offender's ability to control his impulses. Sex
offender treatment programs nearly always prohibit alcohol consumption by the offender because of this effect. Also, chronic alcohol
use may cause serious damage to the offender's ability to think and
make good, moral decisions. Therefore, the PSI usually looks carefully at the role alcohol and other drugs may have played in the
offender's pattern of molestation.

Mental Health History

Research tends to confirm that, except in a small number of cases,
child molesters do not suffer from major mental illness (Schwartz,
1988a). Sexual offenses generally take place in secret and persons
suffering from major mental illnesses, it would seem, have difficulty
hiding such symptoms as hallucinations, delusions, and incoherent
thinking, making it hard to maintain any kind of secrecy.

Medical History

Medical history can play an important part in evaluating the
child molester during the PSI process. Some medical problems may,
in the physician's view, prevent participation in specialized treatment
for sexual deviance. By its very nature, therapy with child molesters
usually includes frank discussions and the graphic details of sexual
activities. Also, therapy usually includes confronting the offender's
dishonesty, denial, minimization, and faulty value system. In those
cases where an offender has suffered a stroke or has heart problems,
it is essential to gather the most current medical information available to be sure that he can withstand the emotional reactions that
often occur in sex offender treatment. In some cases, a medical
condition or prescribed medication may affect the offender's sexual

libido or ability to achieve an erection. Knowing about such conditions are essential in understanding and providing effective psychological treatment. Such information also will help those living with the offender understand his needs and the overall situation.

Reference Letters

Reference letters are often cited in the PSI. Usually, reference letters are written on behalf of and in support of the offender. It is difficult, if not impossible, to tell whether the writer of the reference letter has full knowledge of the offender's sexual deviance. The reader will recall the description of the school teacher, Dan, who amassed over 75 reference letters. None of those letters showed any understanding of the true nature of Dan's sexual assaults, nearly all thought he was innocent. None of those writers knew that Dan had already admitted his guilt. Such letters must be analyzed carefully for their true meaning(s). What character reference letters can reveal is the extent to which those who know the offender are aware of his sexual problems and whether they understand the need to shift control away from the offender and toward responsible adults. The more persons in an offender's life who know about his deviance and who support controls, the better. Dan's situation underscores the importance of getting as much information as possible, even from biased friends. Ironically, due to their distorted value systems, child molesters often misjudge what will work for them. Dan thought that 100 letters of support would work in his favor. The probation officer was very pleased to get the letters but analyzed them differently than Dan had anticipated. They illustrated not what a wonderful man Dan was (as he had hoped) but, rather, how effectively Dan had manipulated and groomed the entire community.

Recommendations

Often the PSI contains a recommendation by the probation officer. This recommendation can be very useful in gaining a professional's opinion and perspective of how serious the offender may be and what controls or requirements should be imposed by the judge. However, a recommendation alone will never substitute for the complete, thorough, and verified PSI. Ideally, the report will provide all of the significant information about an offender and that information will support the recommendation in a logical way. However, it is often possible to argue for different recommendations based on the same facts. This is especially true when the PSI contains both favorable and damaging information. When the PSI does contain both the positives and the negatives, the reader can usually presume that the probation officer has successfully maintained his stance of impartiality. The reader will recall that the purpose of the PSI is not to make sentencing by the judge easier but, rather, to make the sentencing more appropriate.

For example, in the case of a young man who committed a very serious sexual assault and homicide, the presentence investigation uncovered witnesses who said the offender had been physically assaulted by his father from the time he was 6 weeks old. Relatives stated that they had observed the offender during infancy with bruises on his back from his head to his heels. Throughout his childhood he had been mistreated, chained to wood stoves, beaten, denied food, and left to suffer the worst kinds of physical and emotional abuse imaginable. Everyone was distraught over the tragic facts of his crime, but they still were compassionate about the young man's plight, even though he had raped and murdered an elderly (male) friend and neighbor whom they had also known for years. Over time, these witnesses had contacted a variety of social service agencies as well as police to attempt to stop the family from abusing the offender. Despite their efforts, the system failed to stop the abuse until the offender committed the crime at age 16.

When he was interviewed in jail, it became apparent that the offender had a keen intelligence. He was widely read and had definite plans about what he had wanted for himself in life, before his crime brought all of his plans to an end. He candidly admitted he must have committed his offense, although he explained that he had no memory of it. He explained that at times, he would "black out" and discover later that he had done things he could neither remember nor explain. He expressed deep remorse for his offense. There never was a trial. He admitted his guilt from the beginning based on the evidence against him. He never maintained in any way that he was innocent. He even agreed that he had been so psychologically damaged that it was clear to him he was not safe to be free in the community.

Certainly, without knowing how abuse had mentally crippled this young man, it would have been far easier for the judge to sentence this offender to prison, where he would no longer pose a risk to innocent persons in the community. The case illustrates, however, that the purpose of the PSI is not to make anyone's job easier. Instead, the PSI should provide a wealth of unbiased information to help everyone make better decisions.

Summary

When one relies on the PSI for information about the offender, several points should be kept in mind. First, the PSI should be thorough and based on many sources of information. Second, the PSI should be objective. That is, it should be largely based on verified facts and direct observations by the probation officer or eyewitness sources. The facts should speak for themselves and as much of the known factual history about an offender should be included as possible so that the reader can come to his or her own conclusions about the offender. Any report that relies principally on the offender's self-report, without verifying his statements with independent sources of information, is of doubtful value because of the known fact that sex offenders distort, minimize, and lie. Opinions and impressions of the probation officer may be useful as well, but they should not substitute for objective, factual information. Judges, prosecutors, and defense attorneys at times disagree with the probation officer's recommendation. Those who read the probation officer's recommendation should view it as only a suggestion and should not feel compelled to agree or to limit their own thoughts and plans to those expressed by the probation officer. By obtaining the PSI and evaluating whether it is based on objective and verified information, those working with the sex offender will be far more able to make plans that will minimize the offender's chances to manipulate and to reoffend.

Note

1. The description of the basic elements of the presentence report can be found in Crim (1978). The discussion of the reasons for those elements and why they are essential is based largely on the experience of the author, who has completed literally hundreds of PSIs on sex offenders.

You and the Offender

Confidentiality and trust are necessarily different when dealing with a child molester than when dealing with most other people. Clear communication is essential between all parties. Each person's role with the child molester should be as clear as possible. All persons should tell him that the rules must be followed and that any violations will be reported appropriately. At the same time, those persons' care and emotional support are essential for the offender to learn an acceptable, law-abiding, nonabusive way of living. Discipline and long-term vigilance over the child molester for years (not simply months) will be necessary, and confrontation—a clear discussion of any rule violations— is essential.

❖　❖　❖

JEB

Sex offenders will go to extreme lengths to offend against children. Jeb, 74 years old, was literally willing to "go the extra mile" so that he could molest a family's two daughters. He described himself to others as an avid biker and lover of the outdoors and long country roads. He rode his bicycle for miles through the woodlands he called home. One day, on a short trip, he saw that a new family had moved into an old ramshackle house. The family included two girls, Robin and Randi, who were 3 and 4 years old. There was also 8-year-old Bobby and the children's mother, Wanda.

Jeb looked and sounded like everybody's favorite grandfather. "My wife works in town," he said to Wanda as he mopped his sweating brow with a large red handkerchief. He told Wanda about his biking and other hobbies and activities. "So I guess you oughta expect ta see me passing by. Maybe I could trouble you for a splash of water from your hose occasionally. It surely gets hot on these warm spring and summer days. I sure would appreciate it! If it's no trouble, of course," he told her.

Before long, a stop at Wanda's home was a regular part of his daily trip in the country. As winter approached, he saw Wanda struggling with heavy firewood and he offered to chop and carry some. Soon he was making repairs to the old house that Wanda and her children were living in. He said he prided himself in his health and strength, and he considered such chores an opportunity to keep himself young and strong. He also showed a playful interest in the children, he wrestled and rough-housed with Bobby. Before long, he was spending hours with the children, laughing and playing, entertaining them, while, grateful for his help, Wanda went about her daily mountain of chores and shopping trips. He delighted the children by whittling whistles from tree branches and bought some balsa wood airplanes to throw in the fields around their home. Because Jeb's wife worked 5 days a week and he was retired, his wife had no objections or concerns about how he spent his daytime hours. He had no problems maintaining their own home in perfect condition with plenty of time to spare.

Jeb began to baby-sit occasionally while Wanda drove into town to visit her ailing mother, who was confined to her home. One day, Jeb offered to watch the children all day while Wanda took her mother to the hospital for extensive medical tests. "Just let me know if you won't get back before five, so I can let the wife know," he advised her. This was a great relief to Wanda. It had become a challenge to manage her three children, and she was very conscientious about her children. She knew it was unfair to expect them to endure the long days she sometimes spent in town. A hospital trip would be out of the question. Her own mother, whom she often saw in town, said Wanda was "conscientious to a fault." Out of appreciation, Wanda asked Jeb if there were anything she could do to repay him, but he said "playing with the children is reward enough for me."

In the fall, Bobby started leaving on the country school bus at 7:30 a.m. He was gone the whole day, until the school bus dropped him off at 4:00 p.m. Jeb, however, had no objections to Wanda dropping Robin and Randi off to be baby-sat at his house occasionally. He said he'd miss seeing Bobby and had even said he'd like to show Bobby about gun safety and teach him to shoot an old single shot .22 sometime. But he was willing to baby-sit the two girls anyway, and maybe teach Bobby about guns on the weekends when he was home from school. Jeb was careful to ask Wanda what he should fix the girls for lunch and whether it were okay to give them cookies and candy for dessert if they behaved. "Some parents are pretty strict about what they let their children eat, you know. Wouldn't help you if I spoilt them here, would it? I don't wanna cause them no cavities."

As time passed, Wanda became busier and busier. Jeb's help had opened up opportunities that she had only dreamed of before now. She began to look for work in town. She also checked into an adult education program to find out about earning her high school diploma. She had always wanted to take secretarial training. Now, she might really be able to do it. Jeb's help with the children allowed her, for the first time in her life, to see a realistic chance to get training, a good job, and freedom from the welfare cycle.

Then came Wanda's good luck! She completed her G.E.D. program, passed the diploma test, and was approved for classes at a local business school. All expenses, even child care, would be covered. The school would be opening a child care center in 2 months. In the meantime, with school 2½ days a week, Wanda asked whether Jeb would be willing to baby-sit the two girls and Bobby when he got home from school. Jeb seemed delighted to help promote Wanda's career, and he was even willing to watch the girls for free because Jeb knew Wanda could use the money she saved to buy books and supplies. He suggested that she might start thinking about buying her own computer, too. Because it was only for a couple months, Jeb's wife had no objections. She felt it would be a worthwhile community service and there were fewer chores for Jeb to do around the house at this time of year, anyway.

After Bobby caught the bus to school in the morning, Jeb came by to watch the girls. Wanda was on the road to success! She was earning straight As by the end of her first quarter of classes. She had never done well in school before, but her teachers were impressed with her aptitude and encouraged her along the way.

Jeb and the girls had great fun playing each day after they watched Wanda go out the door to her classes in town. He read to them, saw that they watched good television programs, helped them learn their ABCs, and taught them how to count. He even took them to the library. He introduced them to a variety of games to further their education in ways appropriate to each child. Their affection for each other developed warmly, and each day the girls would tell their mother what they had learned that day. They would sing the new songs Jeb had taught them as he conducted them with his finger like a symphony maestro.

One game Jeb taught the girls required that they find which pocket of his coveralls he had hidden candy in. Later, Jeb wore trousers, but the game otherwise remained the same. The girls looked forward to the game every day. One day, the girls discovered that Jeb's pockets were different. They were very, very deep. In fact, Jeb had cut the pockets out of these trousers and he helped the girls by lifting them up so that they could reach far into his pockets to find the candy. Before long, he began molesting the girls by lifting them up to reach into his pockets while "inadvertently" slipping his hand inside their underpants. Later, he fondled them nude while they took showers together after getting dirty in the sandbox. He never forced the girls to do anything they didn't want to and he was able to persuade Robin to play with his genitals, although Randi was hesitant about doing so. For doing it, he gave Robin an ice cream cone on the way home from the library and he gave one to Randi, too, for "not telling anyone about our special game."

Eventually, the girls became more uncomfortable and described the game to their brother. Bobby had heard about child sexual abuse in a class at school and told his mother. By the time the investigation was completed, Jeb confessed to molesting not only Robin and Randi but also his niece's granddaughter and several of her friends.

※   ※   ※

Basic Principles

Those who know a convicted child molester will find themselves confronted by a unique set of circumstances that places demands on them unlike those of any other relationship. What are those demands? What are the concerns and the approaches that the mother should have if she decides to try to restore her relationship with her husband, for example? What can others do to help make sure the offender is not lapsing into old and dangerous patterns? Is there a role for employers and other acquaintances to play? This chapter will define some of the unique aspects of the relationship between the child molester and those he knows and will discuss establishing a relationship that both helps the offender maximize his use of therapy and reduce the risk to any children. Whether the child molester is a young man, a middle-aged man, or a retiree such as Jeb, these principles remain basically the same.

Confidentiality

Historically, counseling relationships have been based on an abiding trust between the counselor and the person counseled. Whatever was disclosed to the counselor was felt to be confidential and the counselor, traditionally a psychiatrist, psychologist, church leaders, or social worker, could be trusted to keep that information strictly confidential. The person in counseling could trust the counselor not to reveal "hidden secrets" to others and to spare the person any potential embarrassment, personal trauma, or legal problems. Based on this trust, the counselor and the person receiving counseling could talk honestly and openly.

Therapists who specialize in the psychological treatment of child molesters today, those counselors who deal with convicted sex offenders on an intensive and long-term basis, for the most part agree that the traditional agreement of confidentiality works to the detriment of the sex offender's ability to solve problems, as well as increases the risk to potential victims (Groth et al., 1982, p. 143). Generally, the therapist treating a convicted sex offender does not base the therapeutic relationship on the traditional concepts of trust and confidentiality. Instead, the therapist informs the sex offender that while he does retain his legal right to confidentiality, the therapist is usually only willing to provide treatment if the offender gives his permission for the therapist to talk freely to anyone in the offender's life that the therapist feels is necessary. As a result, the trust that the offender feels in the therapist is every bit as important, perhaps even more so, because the offender must trust the therapist's good judgment about who will be informed and what the therapist may be telling them. The therapeutic relationship is based on the therapist determining the pace and manner in which information will be shared with others. Similarly, the therapist informs the sex offender that, as a condition of treatment, the therapist will be requiring that the offender inform certain individuals about his history of sexual deviance and his participation in counseling. The therapist is clear regarding these conditions and emphasizes the manner in which confidentiality is handled differently in this special kind of counseling. The therapist likewise notifies the offender that the offender may at any point withdraw from therapy and cancel this agreement. Under those circumstances, the therapist would notify the probation officer, the judge, and the other interested parties such as the defense attorney. Then, the offender would face potentially severe consequences from the court. Therapy cannot be effective without this special handling of confidentiality.

In most cases, the sex offender is under some form of court order to participate in counseling, and often he has been informed directly that he must abide by any special requirements or conditions imposed by the therapist. So, confidentiality is clearly handled in a different manner than in traditional forms of counseling. Under this arrangement, the therapist, not the patient, decides what must be disclosed, when, and to whom.

There are many reasons for therapists imposing this requirement. Some therapists use this approach because of the view that the child molester, by and large, is compulsively addicted to sex in much the way that an alcoholic is addicted to alcohol. Under certain circumstances he is virtually unable to control his impulses and in the case of sex offenders, "slips" may mean committing further acts of sexual assault. As a consequence, extra precautions must be established to try to reduce further trauma to innocent children. One precaution is making sure that those around the offender know of his risk to children. Another reason is that the child molester has demonstrated that he lacks the judgment to know what is healthy and safe for other human beings. He needs the help of mature individuals around him to maintain safe conditions. One way to do this is informing those in his life about his sexual assaults and risk to reoffend. This special treatment of confidentiality also breaks down the barriers of secrecy that the offender used to set up, groom, and molest.

Skepticism

While trust is a cornerstone of traditional forms of therapy, skepticism takes on much greater importance here. Even when sex offenders have been in a treatment program for a long time, they are known to have difficulty stopping their old pattern of lies and deception (Pithers, 1988, p. 129). Specialists who deal professionally with convicted child molesters know that "most, if not all, offenders have been hiding or covering up their sexual deviancy problems for a long time and are well-practiced in lying about their lives" (Freeman-Longo & Wall, 1986, p. 60). Simply put, child molesters must learn how to be truthful. Therapists, and others as well, must be skeptical of many things that the child molester says about himself. A very important way to tell whether the offender is learning to be truthful is by talking freely with those who know him and those who know about him. Skepticism also establishes a precautionary tone. That is, rather than trusting that the offender will tell his wife, family, and friends the truth about himself, the therapist needs to hear from those individuals directly to be sure that the offender is being honest with them. This approach puts the offender on notice: Those who know him will be contacted.

While sex offenders often resist disclosing the truth about themselves, they also acknowledge that they have a competing desire to let people know. When they find that they are still accepted by those who know about them, sharing the truth makes their own lives more secure because they are less likely to be able to manipulate others. The greater the number of child molesters' personal acquaintances who know about their history of child molesting, the less likely the molesters are to reoffend. Being "found out" is often a major concern of the sex offender, even after he has been convicted. Despite the anxiety and public humiliation of appearing in open court, the offender quickly discovers that most people do not know about his conviction. Although it is a relief that most people do not know, the offender is then left with the fear that each new person he meets might find out about his conviction. Multiplied by the number of people an offender may know in all of his social circumstances, the burden of this fear looms quite large. Disclosing his history of abuse to his friends and acquaintances clearly dissipates his fear, and helps him focus on treatment issues.

Nonprofessionals Relating to the Child Molester

These two aspects of the therapist-patient relationship, confidentiality and trust/skepticism, are important for the wife to remember when she is attempting to reestablish her relationship with the husband who has molested. The wife can never successfully place herself in the role of therapist to the offender, but she can learn from how therapists handle confidentiality and trust. Wives of offenders are often devastated by the discovery that their husbands have committed incest within their home against their own children. Nevertheless, when they look at the scope of the crime, the limited options available to the family, and the choices that they face, they often choose to try to stay with their husbands and reconstruct their marriages to put their families back together.

Even then, the most caring approach to the offender is as that of a therapist, which means no secrets, no confidentiality, and skepticism. The wife will share information openly and honestly, particularly with the therapist and probation officer and anyone else for whom the offender presents a risk. The offender needs to know this policy because it motivates him to be honest with his therapist, which increases the chances that therapy will be effective. It also motivates him to avoid situations where his presence would even remotely jeopardize any children. The harsh reality is that the risk of further harm to children through new incidents of sexual molestation is too great for unilateral trust to be the cornerstone of relationships with him. Trust should only be restored through years (not months) of rebuilding family relationships. Any offender who has trouble accepting this idea has, in all probability, failed to reckon with the seriousness of his own violation of the trust that others placed in him. The offender who objects to an approach characterized by skepticism, for example, should be viewed with even greater caution.

If he thinks his crime wasn't so serious after all, what is to prevent him from repeating his crime?

Four Principles for Relating to the Child Molester

The author's experience working with child molesters on probation and parole shows that they have lied for more years than they have molested. Many others who work with offenders on a professional basis have written and spoken about the sex offender's willingness to be dishonest and to lie (see, e.g., Freeman-Longo & Wall, 1986; Groth et al., 1982; Pithers, 1988). As we have seen, the offender has deliberately hidden the truth about himself from others. He has also deliberately revealed parts of his life that would decrease suspicion. He has learned to read others' reactions and gauge when others might be suspicious. Simply put, the sex offender has often become an extremely skillful deceiver. For these reasons, persons who know and continue to interact with a sex offender on a personal basis need to take special steps to recognize and prevent this pattern of deliberate deception.

Relating to the convicted offender can be demanding work. The current wisdom of most sex offender treatment programs is that, as with alcoholics, a sex offender is never "cured." If we accept this assumption, as most therapists do, the relationship with the child molester should be based on confidentiality and skepticism in the way discussed above. There are four other basic principles necessary to provide a positive and constructive foundation for relating to the convicted sex offender:

1. Being clear in communication
2. Clarifying roles and expectations
3. Maintaining self-discipline and vigilance
4. Being confrontive

When used, these principles should reduce the offender's opportunities to manipulate others and to molest children. They should also help guard against the offender's use of secrecy, denial, blaming, and manipulation in general. Overall, they will contribute to his effective and successful use of therapy and increase the chances that the offender, the wife, and the family can again live together in relative safety.

Being Clear in Communication

For practical reasons, most of us rely on a certain amount of ambiguity in our daily lives, and we necessarily use vague messages when communicating with others. We rely on unwritten rules, implicit (unstated but commonly agreed upon) expectations and understandings to help us structure how we get along with others. Where the child molester is concerned, however, something as simple as a trip to the grocery store may conceal a wide variety of possibilities for manipulation, grooming, and reoffending. For example, an offender might leave to go to the store but stop next door to groom or abuse the neighbor's child. While claiming to go to the local grocery store, he may in fact travel several miles out of his way to groom or molest a relative's child. He may go to the store to buy groceries but also to buy candy to groom children, or he may stop at a bookstore to buy pornography. He may stop at a tavern to have a beer and be gone long enough for the smell of alcohol to dissipate. The simple errand of going to the store takes on completely new meaning when communicating with the sex offender.

While every contingency cannot be anticipated, clear communication with the offender means feeling free to ask the offender whether he is making any side trips and whether he is buying anything besides what is on the shopping list. When he returns from the store, clear, explicit communication means not hesitating to ask (when any suspicions or uneasy feelings exist) whether or not he made any side trips, what else he bought, and whether he talked to anyone along the way. Just as the offender's ability to molest a child resulted from granting too much trust (even though he deliberately abused that trust), working with him after his conviction means looking closely at any situations in which he might be returning to old, dangerous, or high-risk behaviors.

Following your intuition is similar to the therapist's attitude of skepticism. Whereas in most mature relationships such skepticism would have a negative impact on the relationship, in the case of the child molester such skepticism is essential both for the protection of children and to provide an added safeguard for the offender (McDonald, 1982).

Giving Clear Messages

How probation officers communicate the rules of probation to child molesters provides a good illustration for how others can favorably shape their communication with the offender. For the probation officer, clear, explicit communication means that rules, requirements, and instructions are discussed *explicitly* during interviews. Legal documents are read aloud to be sure that the probationer has heard every word. Plenty of opportunity is provided for the offender to ask what the documents mean, and a give-and-take discussion assures both the probation officer and the offender that their meaning is understood. Copies of legal documents and all rules are given to the offender so he cannot later claim that he was not informed, he forgot, or he did not understand.

The probation officer can usually expect that the sex offender will resist the rules (at least initially) by arguing with the officer about whether they are fair or whether they are absolutely necessary, or he will attempt to modify any rules he dislikes. The offender will try to bend the rules if he cannot get them dismissed altogether. He will test the willpower of the probation officer by repeatedly raising new arguments about rules so long as he has some hope that he might be able to get the rule changed or reinterpreted to his own liking.

Unfortunately, clear, firm rules are usually not enough. They must be repeated many times over. Because convicted child molesters have been talking to themselves for years, preparing their defense in case they got caught, they can easily transfer their fallacious arguments and distorted thinking to new situations. Generally, there are few other kinds of criminal offenders, such as drug offenders and burglars, who are as capable of putting up a good argument as the sex offender. And few, in the author's experience, are generally as persistent in their desire to argue against and fight the rules. This is not a habit that will disappear quickly. Learning that he cannot cajole, intimidate, trick, confuse, guilt-trip, or stimulate undeserved sympathy in the probation officer may prove a difficult learning process for some child molesters. Only slowly, sometimes very slowly, does he finally give up his efforts to fight the rules and get down to the business of changing his habits, his behavior, and his life.

Jeff had a long history of child molestation. As a condition of probation he was required to maintain a stable residence and to change residence only with the advance written approval of the probation officer. During the first interview, he said he was living in a trailer on his mother's property and hoped that this would satisfy the probation officer. Initially, it did. To his surprise, however, the probation officer made an unannounced visit to his home. There the officer met Jeff and his mother in the driveway of the mother's house. When asked to be shown the trailer where he was living, Jeff resisted, saying that he had a job interview, the trailer was pretty dirty, and it was cold because the heater was broken. The officer insisted. Jeff then turned to his mother and asked her for the key, which she took off a keychain and handed to Jeff. The mother, who had been protecting Jeff from authorities all his life, said she had to leave and departed immediately. Jeff and the officer walked around to the back of the house to where the trailer sat. At the trailer, the probation officer stopped Jeff from putting the key in the lock. Instead, he observed out loud to Jeff, "Moss seems to be growing over the key hole, Jeff. How long has it been since you've stayed here?" Jeff insisted that he stayed there all the time, claiming that the moss must grow fast in the humid area beneath the trees. After Jeff unlocked the trailer, exposing the bright shiny metal of the lock, they entered. It was clear from a cursory review of the trailer that Jeff had not lived there in a long time.

When asked about this, Jeff responded, "This is my *official* residence. I need to have an established residence and this is it. But

I stay a lot of other places, depending on what I'm doing." The probation officer suspected that Jeff was concealing a large number of violations and, as a result, imposed the requirement that he keep a log of every place that he slept, the date, and who could verify this. It eventually became apparent that Jeff was actually staying with his wife and their children, a serious violation of probation. The officer investigated Jeff's log and found that he was lying, so he arrested Jeff.

Jeff's story illustrates how an offender will interpret a simple word such as *residence* to meet his own devious ends. Simply repeating the special condition about his residence was not enough. In the end, the probation officer had to tell Jeff, "Jeff, keep a diary telling where you sleep every night, and include the name and phone number of someone who will vouch for you."

Even the most clearly written instructions from a probation officer will generally need some clarification or explanation. For example, an offender is often required to secure the probation officer's advance written permission to change residence. However, to one offender, staying with a girlfriend 3 weeks out of 4 is not changing residence. To another, living with a woman full-time is not changing residence if he simply maintains an address, as in Jeff's case, or pays rent on a room or an apartment whether he occupies the room or not.

Just as the probation officer must communicate repeatedly, verbally and in writing, to clarify expectations many times, so too, may the wife, his parents, and his friends find that they need to give clear messages many times over, in many different ways, to be sure that the offender has gotten the message. This is not to say they should badger, criticize, or cajole the offender by constantly reminding him that he has lost the trust of others by his offending. Rather, a businesslike approach is needed, much like the probation officer's, in which everyone recognizes that clear communication can help the offender stay out of further trouble and help keep any children in the offender's life safe.

With help from a professional counselor, the probation officer or the offender's therapist, the wife can develop the special rules that she will need to require the offender to follow. She can then communicate these to him in the same way as the probation officer. Such rules may be the same as the rules required in court orders, by therapists, or by probation officers. They typically include rules such as "You shall never have any contact, written or verbal, or through any other means (letters, cards, telephone, or through third parties) with your victim (our daughter) without my express permission in advance," "You shall not consume or possess alcohol," and "You shall not have any contact with any minor children until your therapist, your probation officer, and I all agree in writing in advance." Many more examples of rules are discussed in Chapter 10.

There may be a variety of concerns or requirements that the wife will have, for which she will want to make special rules of her own that go beyond the probation officer's or the therapist's rules. For example, the wife may wish to require that the husband not use any threats or intimidation of any sort under any circumstances. Defining threats or intimidation may be extremely difficult except through examples given over time. Therefore, the wife may tell her husband, "If you wish to rebuild our relationship and help restore our family, I am willing to try but only on the condition that you no longer use threats and intimidation." The husband may ask, "What do you mean by intimidation?" The wife can then respond, "What I mean is no raised voices giving orders and no threats, even quiet ones, that bad things will happen, if someone doesn't obey you. *But also—as time goes by—if I notice anything that I consider unacceptable, anything that seems intimidating but is in a gray area that I find unacceptable, I will let you know by pointing out what you did as an example.* The point is that we lived under your heavy hand and verbal abuse for years. Now, I am no longer willing to tolerate heavy-handedness. I will let you know if any examples come up, and I hope that they do not. I would like the relationship to work, but I must be able to say what is acceptable and what is not. The safety of my children is my responsibility. I must now be the one to make the rules for their safety. The choice is yours. The rules are mine."

It should be noted here that the wife can change the rules she makes as time goes by. It is her family and she, more than the probation officer and therapist, will be most sensitive to conditions in the home, new developments in relationships, and ultimately, her children's safety. It is her full prerogative to take charge, which means that she is not limited to just one chance to establish rules. She may, and should at times, based on her best judgment, create and modify rules as conditions warrant. An offender who expects her to get the rules "right" the first time is being unreasonable and expecting far more of her than he showed about his own integrity when he committed the sexual assault. If his wife changes the rules several times and he objects, the relevant question for him to ask is whether this is the kind of relationship he wants to remain in. No one is forcing him to stay in the relationship. To object or to criticize the wife for changing the rules is simply intimidation. There is always the far more constructive approach that he could take by sharing with her his ideas about how to make the rules successful. That way, if the rules do not work, he can blame himself for not being more successful in participating in the creation of rules that really solved the problems they were meant to.

Although the wife should be open to his ideas about making the rules to solve the intended problems, she should be very leery of negotiating those rules with the offender. First, the rules are not a business deal in which one party agrees to do something to get something from another party. The rules are constructed to make life safe for children and the wife, and to be sure the offender does not reoffend. Also, it should be recalled that the sex offender is often a very skillful negotiator. He has spent years thinking about how to argue (negotiate) his way out of getting caught. Although many child molesters lack basic social skills, many are very skillful with words, especially if they have spent much time in therapy where they have abundant opportunities to watch and learn from other offenders how to sharpen their verbal skills. It is not unusual for the offender going through treatment to quickly surpass his wife's ability to argue and debate, especially when she is not in her own therapy program. This is particularly true when the offender has spent years undermining his wife's self-confidence and intimidating her in arguments rather than helping her develop a strong sense of identity.

Finally, the offender has a proven track record showing that he cannot follow rules that respect the rights, privacy, and safety of others. Rules have simply been tools for his abuse of others, or at best, inconveniences to his selfish whim. For these reasons, the wife should decide, with a counselor's help, what the rules should be. If the offender has difficulty accepting those rules, he can work with his own counselor to try to understand why he has trouble accepting an assertive wife who is willing to make clear, reasonable requirements for her own children's safety.

It is important to remember that establishing rules can become a means of simply intimidating and punishing the offender. Despite the understandable human reaction to want to punish the abuser, it probably does not serve the children's interests to create rules that simply fulfill this understandable and entirely human impulse. The rules should have the primary purposes of, first, protecting children, and second, helping the offender succeed at legitimate goals such as completing counseling and living a law-abiding life that respects and nurtures other human beings. There may be personal habits or patterns of social behavior that would contribute positively to the personal happiness of everyone involved, but trying to use rules to reshape the offender's entire personality probably will not work. At some point, one would hope, generosity and goodwill would shape human relations in the family. Rules should be specifically designed to promote the safety of the family members.

As noted, the mother should not feel that she must limit rules to those laid down by authorities such as the judge, the probation officer, or the therapist. Despite their experience and best intentions, judges, probation officers, and therapists sometimes overlook important problems and circumstances. Also, circumstances change in unpredictable ways. Moreover, those authorities may bear legal responsibility for attempting to define and control the offender's behavior, but they may also be constrained by laws that limit how they deal with the offender. The mother is not bound by such limits. She may decide that there are many more rules and requirements needed to assure the protection of her children, not to mention her own peace of mind.

More than anyone else, the children's mother has final and critical responsibility for making sure her children are safe from the offender. No one is as likely to pay more attention than she is to her children's safety. No one can be as sensitive to the family's changing dynamics on a daily basis and respond with the speed that may be necessary. No one can sense the mood shifts of the children or the offender and take those as carefully into account as can the mother. In other words, the judge, probation officer, and therapist do their best and have a wealth of practical experience and training in working with sex offenders, but they have only limited time to spend on any single offender. The mother, however, is on duty full-time, 24 hours a day. More than anyone, she should know whether there are additional rules that should be applied in her husband's situation.

Each child molester is unique, just as each family is unique. Each will require an individualized plan. One offender may be intimidating, while another may be too acquiescent and afraid to express his own needs and preferences. One offender may use guilt to try to manipulate others and another may use self-pity. Some offenders try to use "forgetting" to excuse their behavior, while others concoct a never-ending stream of excuses (freeway traffic, flat tires, no phone money, etc.). Each family may have unique circumstances such as nonstandard work schedules or special family financial problems (e.g., a combined home-business setting). Moody reactions by the offender, lack of personal hygiene, a demanding or critical tone around the home, and failing to listen carefully are only a few of the characteristics that may require unique rules.

While a probationary sentence of 3 to 5 years may seem like a long time, it will pass quickly, in part because the process of treating the sex offender and reuniting the family involve so many major readjustments in the family. Ultimately, at some future date, the authorities will no longer be available to hold the offender accountable. At that time, the wife will need to be prepared to exercise control and monitor the rules for the family's safety and welfare. There is seldom a better time to begin than while the offender is still under court supervision, when help and support to the mother are most often available.

Gathering Information From the Offender

Giving clear and explicit messages is the first part of good communication with the offender. Listening to and being sure to understand the offender is equally important. For the wife who chooses to remain with her husband, there will be many challenges in understanding what he says and what he means. Here, one principle stands above all others: The wife should always feel free to expect and require that all information received from him be clear and understood. Otherwise, gathering information from the offender can be pointless or a waste of time, and possibly dangerous.

Gathering information begins with asking the offender what all of the rules of the treatment program are and what the requirements of the probation are. The wife and others should expect that his responses be clear, explicit, and unambiguous. If any of the sex offender's responses are not clear, she should ask him to explain them until she has a clear understanding. It is possible that the offender truly will not understand some of the rules, especially during the early part of treatment. It should not be assumed that the offender is deliberately concealing or distorting any information. Rather, he may need help and encouragement to find out the exact meaning of certain rules. The wife can certainly ask him to talk with the therapist to gain a clearer understanding of a rule. For example, a treatment rule may prohibit all contact with children, yet the couple wants to attend church. Is this prohibited? If the offender does not know the answer, he needs to find out, and the wife can help by asking him to get a clarification from the therapist. In such cases, the wife should take note of any questions that remain in her own mind about the rules and consult with the therapist directly to learn the exact meanings of specific rules. The rules, after all, exist for a purpose and if they are not understood, their purpose may not be fulfilled.

The wife should expect the offender to be equally clear about probation rules and court requirements. Virtually all corrections agencies (i.e., probation offices) have the rules and requirements printed and signed by the offender. Usually there are two documents, the court order and the probation department rules. In nearly all cases, the offender is given copies of both documents after the first interview with the probation officer. Nothing prevents him from showing these documents to others. If the offender cannot explain the rules of probation and the court requirements, the wife can simply ask to see the rules of probation and the court order. If the offender indicates that he does not have them, the wife should telephone the probation officer to discuss the situation.

Gathering Information About the Offender

There are two areas that should always be covered when consulting with the offender's therapist or probation officer: (a) the requirements imposed by the therapist and/or court, and (b) the high-risk situations for the sex offender and how to intervene if any high-risk situations arise. High-risk situations are those in which the offender's probability of reoffending is increased.

Numerous specialists who deal with child molesters have described the mother's special role in watching the offender and protecting against his lapsing into critical situations that place children at risk. William Pithers, a noted educator and therapist, writes that not only the wife but all those who know a child molester have an important role to play (Pithers, 1988, p. 130). The therapist is usually happy to work with the spouse and others because it increases the chances for successful therapy and decreases the chances for relapse, or reoffending. Also, such communication increases the therapist's understanding of the offender and whether there are any treatment needs that have been overlooked.

If the offender shows any resistance to explaining the rules clearly and in a forthright manner (i.e., if he shows resistance other than honestly not understanding them), the wife should promptly contact the therapist and explain that the offender has shown resistance in discussing the rules. It is a bad sign whenever the offender resists an open and clear discussion of the rules because it usually indicates that he dislikes one or more of them and wants to conceal the requirements that he dislikes. This is clearly manipulation. The wife should assume that his resistance signals the potential to reoffend.

In this case, after the offender has explained the rules, the wife should contact the therapist directly to see if the offender's account of the rules was complete and accurate. The therapist can clarify any misunderstandings or areas that were not clear. This can also help the therapist assess the offender's ability to learn rules, and in so doing, provide added insight into the offender's own ability to benefit appropriately from therapy. The therapist will also inform the wife if there are any important rules the offender failed to mention and probably will take the opportunity to clarify any misunderstanding about treatment in general.

The rules of treatment and probation are not simply ideas that are worthwhile, recommended, or advisable. They are vital. Therapists spend considerable effort designing rules to fit the individual offender because they help the offender change his past unsuccessful ways of dealing with others. If he does not follow the rules, the offender is not learning the new behaviors that are an essential part of a successful treatment program. The wife must know what the rules are so that she can monitor the offender and report rule violations to the therapist or probation officer.

If the rules require, for example, that the offender not be nude outside the bedroom, and with the bedroom door always closed (to avoid inadvertently exposing himself to the children), but the wife discovers that he left the door ajar, potentially exposing himself to the children, the offender may be backsliding and reverting to a potentially serious pattern of reoffense. If the wife does not know this is a rule, she cannot report the matter to the therapist. The offender, furthermore, is not learning to close the door to the bedroom. Moreover, he may be testing to see whether he can weaken his wife's resolve. He may be attempting to return to old behaviors of pressure and intimidation. When the wife reports violations of the rules, the therapist or probation officer can deal with problems before they get out of hand. This increases the chances for successful treatment. It also reduces the chance that the offender will go back to jail or prison.

A second reason for reporting violations pertains to the offender's use of secrecy and manipulation. Vague communication and ambiguous answers are a part of the offender's manner of grooming and controlling others, manipulating them so that he can molest a child without being detected. From one perspective, all opportunities for secrecy and manipulation contribute to potential opportunities to molest. Discussing all of the rules of treatment and probation lays a solid foundation for the wife and the offender to understand one another. The offender can begin to learn how to discuss matters openly. Gradually, the offender usually becomes more comfortable with admitting that rules are necessary, even though he may resist them at first. After reporting violations, particularly minor ones, communication among all parties generally becomes more honest and reliable. One therapist recently related that after an offender was caught violating a rule after a full year in treatment and was given a short jail term as punishment, the offender expressed sincere and deep appreciation for having been held accountable. Until that point, the offender said, he was still "playing games" and had not recognized how dishonesty was continuing to harm him, not to mention jeopardizing others around him.

In summary, expecting clear communication is critical to everyone's safety. There is no question about the harm caused by child sexual abuse (Finkelhor, 1986). Ambiguous messages are often one way for the offender to set up a family and manipulate them so that he can molest one of the children. Although most people can be trusted, so that ambiguity and unclear messages pose no threat of harm, for the sex offender, any ambiguous communication may be a return to old, unacceptable behaviors that potentially pave the way for further incidents of molesting children. Inevitably, some ambiguity is necessary in all human communication. In any instance that the wife wishes a clearer answer, however, the husband should be expected to provide it. Children's well-being may be at stake.

Clarifying Roles and Expectations

We have looked at the importance of clear communication among all parties involved, including communication with the offender himself. In addition, clear roles and expectations need to be set. Clarifying roles means that the child molester knows what is expected of him and what he can expect from others. For those watching the child molester, there are basically two roles: *the cop* and *the social worker.*

The Cop

The role of the cop refers to taking steps to reduce the offender's chances to reoffend or break the rules of probation or treatment. The term *cop* is used in its most favorable sense, referring to the officer who is eminently firm in expectations but also fair and never abusive. This role is exemplified first and foremost, as described above, by explicit communication in telling to the offender what the rules are. The probation officer's job is a good illustration. During the initial interview, the probation officer will typically read the rules to the offender from the court order and the standard rules of the term of probation set by the agency. As if directing traffic, the probation officer makes clear to the offender what actions will result in arrest and what typically can result in a new jail or prison term. The probation officer will answer the many questions that will arise in the offender's mind and will specify suggested courses of action should problems arise. When a question arises that the probation officer cannot answer, the officer will typically indicate that she or he will consult with others and get back to the offender with the answer.

There is value for the wife, and others as well, to incorporate the cop into their role when relating to the offender. Although it may be somewhat unfamiliar and uncomfortable at first, most wives develop strong motivation in this area when the sexual abuse is first disclosed. Because it can be an awkward and unfamiliar role, it is advisable that this role be developed with the help of a therapist or in consultation with the probation officer.

The wife's primary duty is to protect her children. From this standpoint, her role is nearly identical to that of a real cop. This means giving her husband the clear message that if he ever abuses her child or children again, she will not hesitate to cooperate fully in his prosecution, and she will not attempt in any way to protect him from the full consequences of the law, even if that means a prison term. Similarly, it means telling the offender that she expects him to comply with each and every rule and requirement of treatment, of the court order, and of the probation department. She should tell him that she will report any violations to the appropriate authorities and that she will also be watching for any violations. She will be mindful of the harm that he caused her and all of her children, not just the victim(s), and she will spare no effort to protect herself and her children, as well as others' children. Just as society needs policemen, the child molester needs a wife and relatives who will be sure he follows the rules, persons who will call a halt to any of his efforts to bend or break the rules.

Therapists report that the offender who finds himself under such control is often relieved because he knows what to expect, and he knows that the pressure of others can deter him from entering any high-risk situations. Although he may initially dislike others taking charge of his life in this way, he has a competing desire for someone to do just that: to take charge.

Sometimes, the sex offender will resist such efforts to exert control over him, especially in the beginning when he is still inclined to blame others for what has happened. He does this because he still has not examined his own faulty value system and distorted thinking. The task of self-examination and the resulting self-awareness has not yet happened for him in his therapy program. He usually believes, often sincerely and especially just after he has been caught, that he can control his own behavior himself, without being policed by others. The reader is reminded that the child molester's sexual arousal often decreases significantly or disappears altogether after disclosure of the sexual abuse. He may have absolutely no sexual arousal to anything. The result of this *monastic effect* is that he sincerely and profoundly believes that he is cured. Regrettably, he is not. The monastic effect is only temporary. Without therapy, his old arousal patterns will return as time passes.

Because of the loss of his old sexual impulses at first, he has reduced motivation to control himself at a time when he actually needs more control. Because his sexual arousal around his daughter, for example, is now reduced or has completely disappeared, he may very sincerely believe that he no longer presents any risk to her or other children. But he does not know when the monastic effect will wear off and the old impulses will return. He needs the control agent, a person who plays the cop in his life, even though he cannot understand why. Later he will recognize that external control was not only necessary but in fact a kindness shown to him by others, and he will usually appreciate such controls in the long run.

William Pithers (1988) refers to those in the offender's life who watch over and monitor his behavior (the wife, the employer, relatives, etc.) as the *collateral network*.

> All members of the collateral network are informed about . . . high risk situations, lapses, . . . and offense precursors. They learn that assisting the offender's identification of factors involved in his relapse process will increase the likelihood of avoiding a reoffense. In the offender's presence, network members are encouraged to report lapses to the parole officer or therapist. (p. 130)

The Social Worker

A second and equally important role for the wife and others is that of the social worker. The probation officer's duties illustrate this role as well. In this capacity, the probation officer typically provides encouragement and guidance to the offender to help him succeed on probation and in treatment. While the probation officer may feel the same anger and resentment toward an offender that others feel because of the nature of his criminal activity, he must put aside those feelings to accomplish this role. Once the basic rules have been set, the probation officer spends considerable time listening to the offender to understand which areas of his life may be most problematic. Without condemning the offender's feelings, the officer helps the offender figure out which course of action is most likely to succeed. Rather than withholding useful information, the probation officer will refer the offender to appropriate community resources, such as job placement services or substance abuse treatment, for example. A simple, nonthreatening reminder to the offender when his behavior and/or attitudes may be counterproductive is useful as well. This role may include discussions to solve problems confronting the offender in his day-to-day life through a supportive, responsible, mature, adult relationship. There have been many times when a child molester felt that the probation officer was the only person in his life who really understood and was willing to be with and support him during times of difficulty, loneliness, and depression. Simply being available to listen to the offender during times of trouble, hardship, and disillusionment is a significant aspect of the probation officer's social worker role. Others can do this too.

Being a good social worker does not mean simply being an encouraging friend. Being the social worker means being open to the most sensitive aspects of the offender's life and personality. It means responding in a caring fashion. It is like the best of friendships occurring with the knowledge that what you are doing for him can make a significant difference in his life and the lives of many other persons. It is friendship with a very special purpose.

When one considers the life of secrecy led in the past by the sex offender, it is not difficult to realize the importance of talking with the sex offender about his past. The probation officer is often the only person other than the therapist willing and able to take 30 minutes or sometimes longer to talk with the offender exclusively about himself, his fears and anxieties, his hopes, his failures, and his struggle to avoid reoffense. While the probation officer has a responsibility to advise and warn the sex offender about high-risk situations, these conversations occur within an atmosphere of accepting the offender as a human being, with the potential to improve, the capacity to feel, to care, to hurt, and to change.

The probation officer's role, especially because the probation officer is not a therapist, is an apt model for others to follow. What the probation officer needs to know, and what the wife and others need to know, does not rely on years of formal education, training, and supervised clinical experience. Much can be accomplished by understanding the offender's sexual history, the situations that present high risk to the offender and children, and a caring attitude that encourages the offender to share openly of himself. One must make clear a commitment to help prevent any incidents of reoffense, and also to support the offender's compliance with *all* court and therapy requirements. At the same time, the wife needs to communicate to him that positive support, encouragement, and problem-solving assistance are available. The wife's time and commitment will be offered in a manner and time convenient for and determined by herself, as she will have many new demands placed on her as a result of the child molester's criminal behavior. He cannot make a demand, at any time, about how she should help. It must be emphasized that her positive support is offered freely and voluntarily, it is not owed to the offender. He has violated a fundamental trust and he has no legitimate claim to demand support, concern, or affection from family members against whom he has offended.

This role presents unique problems for the wife as well as for others. She and her children have been victimized by the offender's betrayal of trust. As a victim herself, it is sometimes difficult for her to decide what role she wants to take toward the man who molested her children. Ambivalence and self-doubt are common reactions. She often has a difficult time deciding whether to stay in the relationship with her husband or not. Furthermore, in many cases she has been groomed by the offender to believe that she, not the offender, is responsible for letting the abuse happen. She has sometimes allowed herself to believe the offender's accusation that she is the person with the sexual problems, not him, and that she caused all the problems. The offender has often persuaded her that it is she, not he, who is unreasonable, unreliable, and an unworthy human being. These messages have been inflicted intentionally on the wife over the course of many years. These efforts to destroy her self-confidence were in fact the offender's deliberate attempts to reduce her suspicions and distract her attention while the sexual assaults were taking place. Accusations of this sort against the wife are sometimes a strongly ingrained habit in the offender, and they often persist even

after conviction. As a result, after the husband's conviction, the wife
only slowly emerges from the confusion surrounding all of the
family's relationships and her own role within the family.

Due to this confusing and volatile mixture of human chemistry,
it is advisable that the mother and the children find an ally to help
them combat the psychological brainwashing to which they have
been subjected. They should find the most knowledgeable and
capable counselor they can, one who understands how devious sex
offenders can be. They need a counselor who knows that whatever
claims the child molester made, he and he alone is responsible for
the sexual abuse. Through such support, the wife can learn to
recognize the full reality that the offender, not she, was responsible
for all of the pain and suffering from the sexual abuse. Neither she
nor the children are to blame. The children, too, can learn similar
and important lessons about themselves and each other. Finally, the
wife will become more able to maintain a role that will protect her
and her children, and ensure that her husband will get the help that
he needs.

There are other important steps she can take. To strengthen her
role as protector of her children, the mother should establish clear,
trusting, open, and supportive relationships with her children, reassuring her children that they can expect her protection. The children
will need much reassurance that they were not to blame in any way
for the family problems. They need reassurance that they can talk
openly at any time about the events that took place, now or in the
future, and that the mother will be available to listen, trust, and
comfort them. She will protect them from the offender's criticisms,
challenges, badgering, and manipulations. She will ensure that a
nurturing, positive atmosphere will replace that which they formerly
knew.

As the groundwork is laid down, the mother will gradually
develop more confidence in her relationship to her husband. She will
be more able to listen effectively to her husband and to hear more
clearly what his concerns are. By his progress in his own therapy
program, he should show more ability to listen with understanding
and to hear and meet his wife's emotional needs as well. As she grows

comfortable in discussing sexual matters, she may discover that her husband's understanding of sex was far more backward than she ever suspected but that they can restore a satisfying sexual relationship to their marriage. As he demonstrates by his behavior over time that he is capable of changing, her support, encouragement, and acceptance can, and hopefully will, become even more important than that of the probation officer and therapist.

The roles that the probation officer and the wife establish with the offender provide clues for others outside the family in guiding their relationship with the offender. The employer, for example, who knows about the offender's past will be helping him when he tells him privately that he both knows about his past and will continue to employ him so long as he follows all court rules as well as meeting all job expectations. The employer should steer the offender away from any jobs where children may be present. In these ways, the employer plays an important role in protecting children and in encouraging the offender in honest, open, adult relationships. Convicted offenders under court supervision can often be very valuable workers, especially when the employer has taken the opportunity to telephone or visit the probation officer. This contact will discourage any thought that the offender may have had about manipulating the employer, the probation officer, or the judge.

Parents of offenders, other relatives, pastoral counselors, neighbors and friends, employers, and others are helping the offender when they find out the rules that the offender is required to follow by his therapist, the court requirements and probationary rules, and some information about patterns of sexual offense. Like the wife, they can ask to see a copy of the court order, the conditions of probation or parole, and the written rules of the therapy program. They can also contact the probation officer and therapist, who usually welcome such contact because the more people who have a responsible understanding of the offender, the less likely he will be tempted to manipulate others and place himself in a position to reoffend. It is a truly caring attitude of the most profound kind for the collateral network to inform the offender that they will support him as much as they can and that they will help see that he follows all rules.

Maintaining Self-Discipline and Vigilance

A third characteristic that should define the role between the offender and others is self-discipline. Maintaining this sort of discipline and vigilance, or watchfulness, over the long term is especially important for the wife. She has already endured enormous stress at the discovery of the molestation. Furthermore, she has faced painful confrontation with a complex and baffling legal system, police, caseworkers, children's therapists, prosecuting attorneys, defense attorneys, offender therapists, probation officers, and judges, to name only the most obvious. Unfortunately, this complex web of social agencies has not always made her task as easy as it ought to be (U.S. Advisory Board on Child Abuse and Neglect, 1990, p. xii).

To expect long-term discipline from the wife would seem a very great demand indeed. Discipline is, nevertheless, required. She must not give in to the offender's sincere and superficially persuasive apologies and promises never to do it again or to his remorse or veiled threats about financial ruin. These are simply manipulations. Following rules for months is not likely to cause lasting change. Just as the offender developed his problem over a period of years, the recovery process will also take years.

It is rare for an offender never to show signs of lapsing back into old negative patterns of behavior. Rarely will he follow all rules absolutely, without a single violation or suspicious behavior. However, such lapses can prove beneficial if he is stopped in his tracks at once. To confront such behavior immediately can prevent more serious problems from developing. Such confrontations can remind the offender that he is not as "perfect" as he may appear to himself. They can remind him that he needs the help of others. The fact that they are willing to watch him so closely illustrates their commitment to helping him in the sincerest sense of the word.

Requiring clear answers from offenders will often test one's patience and endurance. Many child molesters have highly developed verbal skills. They can often talk incessantly, interspersing irrelevant information with provocative statements that confuse the listener. In fact, such confusion happens even with trained professionals. As a result, those who question them will find themselves at times wondering what they are talking about with the offender. They will have difficulty remembering what question they originally asked. They will wonder whether their question has been answered or whether they should quit trying to get an answer altogether. Whenever this sense of confusion occurs, the questioner should assume that the offender is trying to cover up some sensitive or important information. Despite the frustration of these experiences, this should not dampen the discipline or resolve of those who know him. The child molester needs to be watched, not for months but for years.

Strategies to Avoid Confusion

When talking with the offender, there are several strategies to maintain discipline and to deal with some of the confusing situations described in this chapter. One is to interrupt the offender and ask him to help figure out the original question. Another, if this occurs frequently, is to write down important questions on paper to focus the conversation and for future reference. It is also possible to ask the offender how his response pertains to the question when he begins to sidetrack the conversation. These strategies should help maintain a disciplined approach whenever talking to the offender about important topics. If such problems persist, it would be helpful to ask the therapist about attending a counseling session to learn other effective ways of communicating with the offender. Guidance can also come from victim and family therapists and from the probation officer as well.

Being Confrontive

It should be apparent by now that verbal communication with child molesters presents challenges not normally encountered in most day-to-day communication. Because the offender denies, distorts, minimizes, and manipulates (sometimes without even being aware he is doing it), those who communicate with him often need to confront him directly to get clear information. This does not mean that one must yell, scream, belittle, criticize, or harangue the offender. That kind of confrontation may play a role in some kinds of therapy, but such tactics usually do little to enhance communication between the nontherapist and the offender.

Confrontation means here that whenever the offender does not answer a question, acknowledge his behavior, or is unclear in his answer, the person asking the question should simply point out that the question has not been answered and that an answer is necessary. Sometimes the offender will talk some more but still not answer the question. In fact, this is not uncommon. In that case, one can point out that he still has not answered the question and repeat the question again. If this occurs a third time, the questioner should take special note of the question being asked and the circumstances and repeat in a businesslike manner that the communication can go no further until the question is answered. Usually this will prompt the offender to begin answering clearly and directly. If it does not, the questioner should be concerned that the sex offender (a) is keeping something important secret, (b) has something else extremely important on his mind that is causing him some significant confusion, or (3) has a problem that needs to be discussed with his therapist. It is possible, too, that the question being asked is vague or ambiguous, and this is something that the questioner can usually double check.

The questioner should also evaluate what implications the offender's unwillingness or inability to be clear may have for the relationship. For example, if the offender avoids the question about why he stayed out so late the previous evening, the wife may want to require that the offender and she meet individually with the therapist to get to the bottom of what the offender is hiding. If the offender is unwilling to answer the wife's question as to whether he is fantasizing about children during sexual intimacy, the wife should consult with the therapist as soon as possible. If the offender avoids answering questions about how he has been spending his income, she may wish to consult with the probation officer and choose to restrict the offender's travel to direct trips between work and home, consult with the therapist, or monitor his spending in some other way.

As the offender learns that people in his life require straight answers all of the time, he will gradually develop the habit of giving straight answers. It eventually becomes less embarrassing and painful for the offender to talk directly and honestly than to continue to lie and manipulate those around him. He does not, however, come to this point of view without considerable effort on the part of those around him. For that reason, self-discipline and vigilance go hand in hand with the willingness to be confrontive.

Summary

Structuring the relationship with a convicted child molester requires several basic principles. First, clear communication is essential, especially regarding therapy requirements and the conditions of the court and probation department. Second, roles should be clarified so the offender knows what is expected of him and what to expect of others. The offender must follow all rules; those who know him will report all rule violations to the appropriate parties. Under these circumstances, those who know him will accept him, listen to him, and try to help him with the special problems that confront him. The wife should make it clear that her willingness to try to restore the marriage is based on her own goodwill and that she may withdraw her commitment to the marriage anytime she feels it is merited, especially if he violates clearly stated expectations or requirements. Questions will need to be repeated, sometimes often, until the offender gives a clear, unambiguous answer. Third, maintaining self-discipline is necessary because by most experts' accounts, the child molester's deviance problem is a lifelong problem. Progress is measured not in terms of months but in terms of years. The offender may not like this but it is the reality he faces. Finally, confrontation is usually necessary and helpful. Some may find this uncomfortable at first. Confrontations are not normally a requirement for communication between most adults. One should perhaps consider sex offenders as having permanent "disabilities" that will last their entire lives. Following these four principles will enable those who know them to contribute to their improvement and to the safety of the children and families around them.

The Probation Officer
and the Corrections Agency

*This chapter describes the typical duties of a probation officer
and the role of the corrections agency in supervising convicted
child molesters. The probation officer is the primary contact
for someone wanting to know more about the convicted child
molester. The probation officer may work at any level of
government, from the federal level, through the state and
county level, to the municipal (city) level. Probation officers
have a vast array of responsibilities, and understanding these
responsibilities will help the reader effectively communicate
with the probation officer. The probation officer supervises
not only sex offenders but many other categories of offenders
and, as the reader will see, although a convicted child
molester you know may seem like the most important matter
to deal with, often there are other even more demanding
responsibilities. Furthermore, in the United States, the
Constitution and the Bill of Rights reserve for each state the
right to process its criminal offenders as it sees fit. The result
is that laws governing child molesters differ dramatically from
one state to another. Although one course of action may seem
the only reasonable one, often that very course of action is
not possible under a given state's laws. This chapter will
explain many of the differences in how criminals are*

sentenced so that the reader will know the limitations that may exist. Also, this chapter will provide information about the basic questions to ask the probation officer so that the reader can obtain the crucial information about the offender that is needed to ensure the safety of everyone involved.

❖   ❖   ❖

ONE PROBATION OFFICER'S DAY

After I arrested Burt, who was described in Chapter 1, the months passed by quickly. It was some time later before the chilling details of my colleague's murder were revealed to me in an off-the-cuff comment by a state parole board member while we chatted informally before a parole revocation hearing. It was a brutally violent murder offending all human decency. And it was years before I even hinted to my wife about the horrible details of his death. His murderers have never been apprehended.

Spring came and the crimson, lavender, and salmon colors of Washington's state flower covered the leathery foliage of the rhododendrons. Often I would hear tugboat horns in Elliott Bay on Puget Sound as I drove along the Seattle waterfront searching for parolees who had quit reporting and for witnesses whom I could persuade to testify, all the time wondering how long my luck would hold out. From every vantage point, my number was up. I had been too lucky too long. Catching Burt was pure luck. Before long, some offender I supervised (there was no way of telling which one) would commit a serious, violent crime and I would be called on to explain why I had not prevented it. I supervised over 100 felony offenders, the majority of whom were violent offenders and most of those were repeat offenders. I had files that had been assigned to me months before that I hadn't even read yet. I'd never met many of the men I supervised. Even though spring had come, the relentless pressure of the workload had not lessened and the heat of summer was not far off.

I kept a list of serious cases needing a lot of immediate attention on several sheets of yellow paper with "Things to Do" printed conspicuously at the top. Most of my 100 plus cases needed some kind of attention. I prioritized the cases as well as I could, keeping the most critical situations on the first page whenever possible. But as the reader will see, I often ended up handling some important matter from beginning to end without its even reaching the yellow list of things I needed to do.

One foggy morning I arrived at work before the office opened, which was the only way to avoid the usual barrage of telephone calls and other interruptions that began at 8:00 a.m. I sat down at my desk, stirring a cup of coffee, and looked at page one of "Things to Do." As has been explained earlier in this book, the offender's names and their descriptions are fictitious. These nicknames, however, convey an intuitive sense of who they were and what they were like. The list read

1. Bananas—mentally ill offender, get a warrant
2. Gator—investigate for abusing his daughter
3. Robin Hood—serve legal papers at jail by Thursday
4. Smitty—assaulted wife—get warrant
5. Chopper—investigate threats against landlord
6. Billy—investigate attempted child abduction
7. Mr. Berry—get him into treatment or court
8. Packer—arrest for assaulting girlfriend
9. Reb—paroled for murder, new assault
10. Rob—guns, drugs, violence, arrange treatment

I carried, of course, a more complete description of each of these men in my head and whenever I could, I wrote appropriate notes chronologically on long narrow-lined sheets of paper on the left-hand side of each offender's file. These case notes explained what I had done in each particular case, whom I had talked to, what the offender said and did, what reports had been dictated, and what other probation officers needed to know if an emergency arose while I was out of the office.

Bananas was a drug offender on probation. He also had mental health problems but refused mental health treatment. He was most recently arrested in a drugstore when the pharmacist saw him stumbling up and down the aisles in an obviously drug-induced stupor. When the druggist gingerly approached him and asked him if he needed some help, Bananas stumbled again, knocking over a pyramid of blue glass mouthwash bottles. When asked politely by the druggist to leave, Bananas seemed not to notice what the druggist had said and continued stumbling down the aisles of the store, knocking other products to the floor. The police were called. When Bananas was placed under arrest and searched, the police found a large knife concealed beneath his "Rambo" camouflage shirt. He was booked at the county jail. Later, the police found a bottle of cheap shampoo and a cheese-and-crackers snack in his truck, which he admitted he had shoplifted earlier from a different drugstore. Officers also found a loaded rifle in his truck. Drugs, mental illness, and now a loaded gun. A sure recipe for tragedy. More than one pharmacist had been murdered in the Seattle metropolitan area during the past year.

My job was to investigate Bananas' case and prepare a detailed report for the judge and prosecutor requesting a bench warrant for probation violations to hold him in jail. If he were released on the shoplifting charges, it appeared likely that he would continue stealing from drugstores, possibly using the gun in the process. Under the law, I had the legal authority to sign a probation warrant holding Bananas in custody, but, because the local jail was so crowded, it had recently begun refusing to honor such probation warrants, requiring instead a warrant signed by a Superior Court judge. So I needed to find a deputy prosecuting attorney willing to prepare and take a warrant directly to the judge for his signature. This was a reasonable course of action and would usually take no more than 2 or 3 hours, depending upon whether my secretary could drop every-thing she was doing and type my report, and whether I could find a prosecutor available to review the case and prepare the warrant immediately. Despite the relatively little time these warrants take, the prosecutors often face the same workload problems that probation officers do. And like the prosecutor, I actually had other problems that seemed more important—other problems that presented a much greater risk to the community than Bananas. Gator is an example.

Gator was on parole for assault and robbery. Gator had also recently physically abused his 8-year-old daughter and his case was transferred to me when the first probation officer took a leave of absence due to health problems. Gator had been ordered to enter a mental health counseling program. That was all I knew at the time. I hadn't had an opportunity to read the whole file through; in fact, I hadn't even met Gator yet. He hadn't reported regularly to the probation office and whenever he had reported, I had been out of the office. However, I had been in the office the day before when Gator's wife telephoned to say that Gator had just assaulted their daughter for the second time in 2 months. Later, Gator's counselor phoned to say Gator had just been terminated from counseling for refusing to cooperate.

My job was to investigate Gator's case and decide whether to arrest him or to develop an alternative plan. Gator's daughter refused to talk to police or caseworkers because the last time she did, things got worse for her. Gator's wife did not want him arrested because he had just gotten a good job and had quit abusing alcohol for the first time since they were married. She was convinced that he could be helped if someone would only take the time to work with him and try to understand him. "He's really a good man at heart," she told me. "He doesn't need more punishment, he needs help!" The caseworkers I talked to were unwilling to place the daughter in a foster home because neither the child nor the mother were willing to talk to authorities. My first inclination was to arrest Gator because this was the second time he had abused his daughter in 2 months, but my agency's policy required that I explore all alternatives prior to issuing a parole warrant because space at the nearest prison (where parolees had to be held in custody) was tight, just as it was at the county jail. Investigating this case meant talking to the daughter, the mother, Gator, Gator's counselor, the police, and the caseworkers. A few hours' work at the most conservative estimate, but days might pass before all the facts could be gathered and a plan formulated.

Robin Hood was on parole for dozens of property crimes but, unlike his namesake, he spent the profits from his crimes on drugs. He had just been arrested again for possessing stolen property, including a sawed-off shotgun. This was a violation not only of parole conditions but also of state and federal laws regarding felons in possession of firearms. I had already arrested Robin Hood for parole violations, so he was securely behind bars at the county jail, but I needed to go back to the jail soon and serve him with legal documents, informing him of the exact nature of the violations charged against him (in this instance there were 12), and interview him regarding his version or explanation of each violation. Then I needed to prepare a lengthy report (10 pages, possibly more) for the parole board. If I failed to serve him with those documents by the next day, his legal rights would be violated and the parole board would release him.

Smitty was on probation for assaulting police officers. The last assault occurred when police came to his home on a rainy night to break up a fight between Smitty and his wife. Neighbors heard the wife's screams and had called the police, fearing that she might be killed. The police had come many times before, but Mrs. Smith always refused to cooperate with them. When the police arrived this time, Smitty was more drunk than usual and he became violent with the police. Even though his wife refused to file a complaint against him, as she had so many times before, Smitty was convicted of assaulting three police officers.

Now, Mrs. Smith had telephoned me and claimed that Smitty assaulted her again and was threatening to leave the state. She said she was willing to file a sworn statement against him because he had stolen and pawned her mother's heirloom jewelry. "He also threatened to come back and make me pay if I talked to the police. I'm scared, so I don't mind letting you know," she stammered and hung up. If I acted quickly I might be able to get a deputy prosecutor to prepare a warrant for the judge's signature and arrest Smitty before he left the state. This, of course, would require jumping through the same hoops as in Bananas' case, but this was the first time that Mrs. Smith said she was willing to cooperate with authorities against her husband and it was, therefore, an opportunity not to be lost.

Chopper was on probation for assault. He had carved up his victim with a razor-sharp bayonet in a drug deal gone sour. He apparently had gotten a special deal from the judge (probation instead of prison) because he was a highly decorated war veteran. His landlord called to tell me that Chopper had been threatening him when he tried to collect the rent money. Chopper was also leaving his large motorcycle in a neighbor's driveway, but the neighbors were afraid to do anything about it and had approached the landlord. Chopper was in fact suffering from Post Traumatic Stress Disorder, a mental health problem in which a soldier sometimes bottles up the memories and emotions from his war experiences until they explode uncontrollably. He was also a martial arts expert. Unlike Bananas, who simply dressed in Rambo clothing, Chopper represented a true Rambo, both in terms of his background and in terms of the destruction he could cause to the community. My job was complicated because threats are difficult to prove in court and I had had little luck with judges finding such offenders guilty or punishing them for mere threats. Needless to say, witnesses are seldom anxious to testify against offenders such as Chopper for any reason, but they are particularly reluctant to testify in open court where they must answer questions with the offender looking on. Nevertheless, an investigation was needed, as was a plan to handle any problems between Chopper, the landlord, and the neighbors.

Billy was 23. He told me that he had been an alcoholic as long as he could remember, although he couldn't remember much before his 13th birthday when he started drinking heavily. Alcohol, when taken in large quantities over many years, impairs a person's mental abilities. Billy had drunk so much that most people who talked with him would have guessed he was insane. When he was sentenced in court, the judge made Billy spend a full year in the county jail until, gradually, with prolonged sobriety, Billy's sanity began to return.

Billy had been convicted of accosting several teenage girls in broad daylight on the street. He attempted to assault them sexually by tearing their clothing off as they stood at crosswalks waiting for the light to change, although he was so drunk he was unable to complete the assault and the girls had successfully escaped him in all cases. He was literally too drunk to stand up. The last girl tripped him and police found him lying in the gutter when they arrived. He was unable to pull himself up. Two days before, the police had telephoned me to report that someone matching his description had been seen trying to lure a 6-year-old boy into his car as the boy walked alone to school. Based on the witnesses who spoke to police, it appeared that Billy was now drinking again, but this time his interest had apparently turned from teenagers to young children. My job was to get police reports, talk to witnesses, investigate to determine if the facts were true, and arrange to arrest Billy if the facts were strong enough.

Mr. Berry was put on probation for attempting to rob a convenience store. He went into the store late at night conspicuously pointing a hard object in his coat pocket at the clerk. He held her hostage for half an hour and he apologized tearfully until, at last, he spontaneously freed the clerk. The frightened clerk watched him walk slowly away from the parking lot, and he was arrested 5 minutes after she telephoned police. No gun was found, but he had a desk stapler in his pocket that looked like a gun to the clerk.

Because he had harmed no one, Mr. Berry was given 6 months in jail and 3 years' probation. He was released from jail after serving 4 months because he earned 2 months' "good time" by following all the jail rules and causing no trouble. Mr. Berry was homeless at the time of his crime and he was homeless when he was released from jail. He had little money, nowhere to go, and he slept in his car.

The judge ordered Mr. Berry to enter an alcohol treatment program and Mr. Berry made numerous promises to enter one, but he never kept his promises. He argued that he couldn't go to a treatment program until he had a job and money to pay for his alcohol evaluation. He was always "on the verge" of getting both a job and some money, but he never got either. He was in violation of his court order requiring alcohol treatment, but there wasn't room in the county jail for "technical violators." These are offenders who violated court requirements but who had not been charged with new crimes. I needed to locate Mr. Berry, try to persuade him to enter an alcohol center, or prepare a violation report and arrange a court hearing.

Packer was released from prison after a string of auto thefts. Because he had never been convicted of a violent crime, he was classified by the corrections agency as a "low-risk" offender. He had just gotten work cleaning up an auto detail shop on swing shift. Then his girlfriend called me. She said Packer had been arrested the previous evening for assaulting her. She had separated from him a week before. He had come to her new apartment drunk and, holding a sharpened tire iron to her throat, he threatened to kill her if she wouldn't take him back. He demanded that she forgive him for the times he had as-saulted her or he would kill her. When she offered him a beer from the kitchen, he dropped his guard and she escaped, calling the police from the apartment manager's office. Packer sat drinking beer at her kitchen table and surrendered peacefully when police arrived at her door. He told police, "If I'm going back to the joint [prison], it may as well be for something worth it." The policewoman took this as a threat on the girlfriend's life.

Whenever I had spoken with his girlfriend before, she had claimed that Packer was doing well and had no problems. Now she admitted that he had been drinking heavily for months, but she hadn't wanted to tell me before for fear it would get him in trouble. Now that trouble was out in the open, I needed to serve a parole warrant on Packer to hold him in custody before he was released from jail on his personal recognizance on the new charges. This involved convincing my supervisor that even though Packer was a low-risk property offender, he posed a threat serious enough to justify our using one of the scarce prison beds to hold him before he had his parole hearing.

Reb was on parole from another state. He was released on parole after serving time for murder. In the murder, he had lured his victim into an abandoned building during a drug deal. After selling the drugs, he gunned down the victim to get the drugs back. He dumped the body in the bed of his pickup, covered it with lawn clippings, and later cut it up and buried it in a shallow grave in the country. He got caught because his girlfriend wasn't careful cleaning out the pickup with her garden hose. Someone noticed peculiar red stains in the driveway and called police. When detectives found traces of blood in the bed of the vehicle and in their garage, the girlfriend confessed.

After he was paroled, the state in which he was convicted allowed him to move to my state. Then it requested that my agency investigate his circumstances and provide "courtesy" supervision for him under an arrangement that exists among all the states, called the Interstate Compact Agreement. Shortly after arriving here, Reb assaulted a new victim. The police officer who investigated the new assault told me that when he first arrived at the pool hall where the assault took place, he walked through the crowd to the unconscious victim lying on the floor. It was a small town and the officer knew most of the locals, but he did not recognize the person lying on the floor and concluded he must be new in town or an out-of-towner. The victim was still unconscious when the medic unit arrived, and his face was battered and bruised, still covered with blood.

Later, the officer visited the victim in the hospital to take a statement and the victim's face had been cleaned and partially bandaged. The police officer was startled to recognize the victim as a prominent citizen. He hadn't recognized the victim at the scene because Reb had battered him beyond recognition. My job was to suspend Reb's parole and begin the long, complex, and time-consuming legal proceedings required to send Reb back to the other state for parole violations.

Rob was sent to prison for robbery and drug offenses. Once in prison, he surprised and overpowered a prison guard. He choked the guard into unconsciousness and continued to assault him so seriously that the guard was left permanently disabled. He then took the cell keys from the guard and released the other prisoners from their cells. A riot ensued.

Like many men on parole, Rob said he realized that he had made a mistake and wanted to mend his ways, but he also knew it would be difficult. He had recently come into my office and confessed that he had developed a serious drug problem. "I've started shooting speed balls [a mixture of cocaine and heroin] and I can't stop. Can't you help me? You've gotta do something." He was actually pleading and tears were forming in the corners of his eyes. ". . . or I'm gonna get in some serious trouble. . . . I'm selling stolen guns to buy drugs. You know I'm a lunatic when I have guns. Stop me, please! Help me get into a treatment program, or just arrest me or something!"

Pleas for help such as Rob's are not uncommon, even from hardened criminals. Life gets to them the same way it gets to us all. So I told Rob I would ask my supervisor for permission to arrest him, just to get him off the street and out of his dangerous downward spiral. I figured he was really sincere because when I agreed to try to arrest him he said, "Thank you," sitting back and showing relief as I went to talk to my supervisor about issuing a parole suspension warrant and taking him into custody.

Unfortunately, my supervisor denied the request to arrest Rob because of the significant lack of space in the state prison system for parole violators. Instead, supervisors and administrators who make the policies about who can be arrested would see Rob as a prime candidate for a treatment program. After all, Rob had motivation and was willing to discuss his drug problem openly and honestly. The entire prison system was in a state of crisis owing to overcrowding, and there was even the threat of federal court action looming to release large numbers of inmates regardless of their criminal histories, if the prison population was not brought down to acceptable levels. Men worse than Rob would be coming out unsupervised if something was not done.

When I went back to my office and told Rob I couldn't arrest him, he was astonished. During most of his criminal career, starting at age 9 when his mother died, he had spent his energy manipulating his parole officers trying to avoid getting caught and locked up. Now he was volunteering, only to be refused. He tried to argue with me, claiming that it was my public duty to arrest him. He was not only wise to the system but also intelligent and articulate. "Do I have to commit some crime? Can't you help me before I get deeper into trouble? Isn't there something you can do? Man, I'm sleeping under a bridge right now. My father kicked me out and said not to come back until I had an honest job. If you don't help me, I've got nowhere to go. I wanna work, I really do. But I need help first. I'm not joking. I'm gonna die. He knows I stole his shotgun, his stereo, and his Social Security check last week. He said if I come back, he'll report it to the police himself."

I contemplated encouraging Rob to do just that, to go to the police himself so the police might arrest him on weapons charges, but Rob already had two felony convictions and knew that if he picked up on another one, he could be convicted as "an habitual offender," which meant a long mandatory prison term. Not even the parole board could release him until he had served his mandatory term. Rob might sincerely want help, but he would not volunteer to be a habitual offender. I did my best to encourage him not to commit any more crimes and I advised him to go back to the drug program he had been at recently. "Maybe they can do something to help you this time," I said, although I knew there was a long waiting list for men such as Rob who wanted to enter the kind of residential drug rehabilitation program that he needed. My instincts told me that Rob was sincere about his problem and wanted help. He could probably adjust to a drug rehabilitation program after the difficult period of withdrawal. But was there any help available for him right now, when he needed it?

That was a week ago. I knew Rob was out on the streets somewhere. I was keeping my fingers crossed, hoping that he hadn't committed a new serious crime. At times, like all probation officers, I felt helpless: You can't arrest them and you can't get them into drug programs. One group of offenders really wants help, although treatment programs are becoming scarcer or are not available at all. Another group of offenders deserves being locked up but not enough places can be found for them in overcrowded prisons.

❖   ❖   ❖

SIR LANCELOT, PROTECTOR OF THE KINGDOM, FAR AND WIDE

Lance was not on my "Things to Do" list. Not yet. He was under the supervision of my agency after being found not guilty by reason of criminal insanity for an earlier offense. He was tall, lanky, and wore his blond hair in a pageboy cut that was by all appearances measured and trimmed with scissors under a bowl perched on his head. Physically, he looked remarkably similar to a blond Prince Valiant. On his overalls he wore badges and buttons he found in thrift stores and a gold drapery cord cinched tightly about his waist. Few would have argued about his mental illness. He heard voices and saw people invisible to those around him. His adjustment, however, had been good, once he began taking the proper medication. He was doing everything required of him. He was cheerful, reported every 2 weeks as required, asked me for advice (even took it at times), and he appeared to have some of his significant mental illness problems under control.

Lance was placed on supervision following a psychotic episode. Walking through a derelict section of the city, he heard the mumbling of a gray-whiskered old man who lay between garbage cans in an alley. Lancelot was in a state of active hallucination when he heard the old man's voice. Then, as he later recounted to the police and his psychiatrist, Lance heard more voices, these from the planet Pluto. The voices told him, "You are Sir Lancelot, Protector of the Kingdom, Far and Wide. You must help this man." Lance walked over to the alcoholic lying on the ground and said in his deep, booming voice, "I am Sir Lancelot, old man. How can I help you? That is my duty because I am Sir Lancelot, Protector of the Kingdom, Far and Wide!"

The alcoholic kept mumbling as he stared into a garbage can that had been overturned when he fell to the ground. Suddenly a loud voice echoed from the garbage can and rattled through the crevices of Lance's mind, declaring, "I have sinned. I must be punished." So Sir Lancelot, Protector of the Kingdom, Far and Wide, feeling now that he had a commission from both Pluto and the old man, drew himself up and pulled a broken carpenter's file from his blue denim overalls, brandishing it like a broadsword. He stabbed the man in the chest with the tine of the file, missing his heart by a centimeter. Witnesses called the police and when the police and medic unit arrived, Lance explained everything to the officers exactly as it happened, including the commands from Pluto. The old man, miraculously, lived.

When Lance returned from the state hospital to face serious criminal charges, his court-appointed attorney persuaded Lance to accept a plea bargain of criminal insanity. The conditions would include requiring Lance to return to his mental health treatment program; take medication as prescribed by a psychiatrist; abstain from all illegal drugs; possess no weapons; and report to the local Department of Corrections, follow its rules, and talk regularly with a probation officer.

When he took the medicine needed to control his hallucinations, Lance was able to get along fairly well, cooking for himself, bathing, and keeping appointments at the community mental health center. He was friendly, cooperative, and it was painfully apparent to me after our first few meetings that he not only wanted help for his mental problems but also sincerely wanted to follow the rules. Before I had known him very long, he asked whether kitchen knives were considered weapons. "I don't want to make a single solitary mistake!" he said in a loud and earnest voice as I pondered the motivation behind his question. I advised him against handling any knives with sharp points or blades, although I knew such issues were very complex if the matter came to a court hearing. In the wrong hands, forks and even spoons can be used as weapons.

A few days later, Lance's elderly uncle, with whom he lived, telephoned telling me that Lance was taking every knife out of the house, including a set of butter knives and the two fingernail files he had found in the bathroom. Lance was not taking any chances and was throwing out anything remotely resembling the point of a blade. I went immediately to talk with Lance and his uncle and I finally persuaded Lance that he would not be risking a violation of the court order by having butter knives and a nail file in his residence. "Just to be sure," he told me, "I promise not to ever touch them, ever. I'll even spread my butter with a spoon. I know, it works. I've done it before! Camping!" Lance smiled broadly as he made this pronouncement. Such pronouncements, I had learned, meant Lance was serious; he was not mocking me or his uncle.

Two weeks of tending to the routine of my job had passed. I stirred my coffee as I reviewed my list of things to do and began a new day. I decided I should begin with Billy's case of attempted child abduction. Billy was a sexual assaulter abusing alcohol and possibly attempting to abduct a child. That seemed pretty serious at the moment. The child might be safe, but what was Billy up to now? Were there other children in danger? Like other probation officers I had ever known, my highest priority was trying to stop an offender from harming a child. Just as I reached for the telephone to make a call, it rang before I lifted the receiver. "It's not 8 o'clock yet," I thought. "I can ignore it. Go get a refill for my coffee." Before it rang again, I lifted the receiver from its cradle. A police officer identified himself. He asked if I supervised Lance and when we were through with telephone formalities, he said that he had been out to Lance's house because his uncle was agitated. He claimed something was wrong with Lance, but as far as the officer could tell there was nothing unusual. He just appeared to be an overly concerned uncle. But all the same, the officer asked if I would drop by and take a look at the situation.

It is hard to say no when the police call regarding someone you supervise, especially someone who is criminally insane. I started weighing the call against my concern about Billy and thought about Gator assaulting his daughter. Perhaps I could drop by to talk with Lance and his 89-year-old uncle after spending a few hours trying to locate Billy and talking to people who had seen him last, including the police. When I put the phone down, it rang again, immediately. It was Lance's uncle, and he was pleading desperately that I come by to help him with Lance. "He's talking about knives, nothing but knives and I'm worried. He just ain't right. I don't know. He just ain't right. I wondered if he's took some drugs." In the background, I could hear his voice shouting incoherently and then ordering his uncle to put the phone down. I told him I'd come right away, but before I finished, he had hung up.

I swallowed half a cup of coffee, made plans for who else I should see that day, arranged a schedule, and checked out one of my department's cars. I told the receptionist that I'd be gone for a few hours, but I'd be back before lunch. I drove down to the apartment occupied by Lance and his uncle. The apartment was situated between a liquor store and a tattoo parlor that had an orange day-glo sign in the window reading: "IF YOU ARE DRUNK, DON'T COME IN HERE!" I had been there many times before. The apartment door stuck at the bottom when opened. You had to pull up and push on the handle in one motion to get in. Getting out was sometimes a little more difficult, depending on the weather.

Lance welcomed me into the small, crowded living room of the apartment he shared with his uncle. By now, the police had been gone for quite some time. Another shift had come on duty. Lance's uncle stood in a corner of the kitchen, beginning to speak, but Lance interrupted him. "Welcome, my good bud," he said. "You were just the person I wanted to talk to most of any person at all!" His deep voice was rising slightly. He wore a black baseball cap with the words "Final Dimension" emblazoned over the red bill. I tried to be discreet reading it but Lance noticed my eyes glance upward. "That's me!" he said loudly, proudly. "I am THE Final Dimension! The Last! The Final! The ultimate. The last you will find. Anywhere. EVERYwhere." He stretched the syllables of his words as he swatted his right arm through the air, in front of my chest. "That's why I'm so glad you came. I can't understand why my SQUEEZE rubbed me off! She rubbed me off and rubbed me out. There is no doubt. Now it's out! So you tell me why!? I can't. I won't. But I just gotta know! How she could do this to me, bro?!!"

Lance's uncle ignored his showy bantering and, looking at me, said he didn't think Lance was taking his medication. He thought Lance might have taken some LSD, because the people who brought him home early this morning looked like people who used drugs. "Have you taken any drugs, Lance?" I asked abruptly. At first, he ignored me, told his uncle to shut up, and turned to me with a tone of pleading respect. "Can you hear the beautiful women's voices singing, singing so beautifully? It is such a beautiful day. The kind of day every day should be. We all know it should be this way. Don't take any drugs and if done there is no fault because someone would have spiked the punch!" He burst out into sardonic laughter. The fog had begun to clear and sunlight broke through the apartment window. I looked around to see whether there were any knives or potential weapons within Lance's reach. The old black telephone, a handy weapon within easy reach, sat on a table behind Lance.

Lance had been speaking in complete and coherent sentences. Now, gradually, they were turning into "word salad," interesting tidbits of verbal creativity, but they were making less sense as the moments passed. At times, he acted happy and grandiose, at other times he sounded irritated and mad at his girlfriend. Throughout, Lance was pleading for me to help him understand what was going on. "I went to my squeeze's house last night and there," he paused a moment and continued, "Aren't they so, there, so beautiful, so . . . the clouds? It's really harmonious, Man, to feel it all crowding up so close. But why'd she kick me out, Man? Why, why wouldn't they think about it sometime even if there were a hurry which there shouldn't be. Should it be, Man? Should it BEEEE?"

In psychiatric terms, Lance was "decompensating" or else he was reacting to a drug that he had taken, possibly LSD. Disturbances in thought processes, especially from LSD, often come on gradually and get stronger with time. Like the police, I, too, might have missed his emerging condition if I had come earlier. Lance's uncle was growing visibly frightened. As I stood in the small front room, I glanced around again for weapons, any hard large objects. I was standing between Lance and the kitchen. Knives behind me, Lance in front of me. The front door, our exit, was behind Lance. His uncle had stopped talking and had retreated a few steps into the kitchen.

As confident as I was in my counseling abilities, this was beyond my sphere of expertise. Instead, it was time to play the role of cop, to protect the community, especially Lance's uncle and possibly myself. I knew that even on his good days, Lance argued often with his uncle, but I was afraid he might hear voices telling him to punish his uncle in some way. Or punish me. I could not leave Lance with his uncle and go for help so I began talking with Lancelot as warmly as I could, hoping to avoid anything that would provoke him. At the same time, I looked almost unconsciously around the room, checking again to be sure there was nothing my swashbuckling friend could grab. I told Lance that I thought we should take a ride in my car to visit his psychiatrist at the local mental health center. Maybe his psychiatrist, I suggested, formulating both my thoughts and my words in the same breath, could explain why his girlfriend rubbed him off. I began wondering, under my breath, about a contingency plan if he were not agreeable and refused to leave. Instead, he agreed, "Because it's such a beautiful day for a ride, Good Bud." Lance by now had conferred on me the honorary title "Good Bud," welcoming me to the brotherhood of his strange world. The sun was streaming brightly through the window, lighting gray and maroon threads on the worn carpet. "And besides, the fresh air could do one some good, you betcha."

It was undeniably a stroke of luck that Lance agreed so easily to go see his psychiatrist. He might have argued or created a standoff. I wondered whether he might get cold feet during the drive to the clinic. Would I have trouble with him while I was negotiating the car through traffic? My instincts told me that I could manage him. I'd never given Lance any reason to distrust me. I'd always been warm and consistent with him. He had begun to rely on me for emotional support. I took a gamble. I'd been his probation officer long enough by now that I felt confident that I could control his agitation and mood swings. I hoped no traffic snarls would delay us.

I knew that getting Lance to the mental health center was only the first battle; convincing someone at the mental health center to see him was not a foregone conclusion. While Lance continued talking, I telephoned the mental health center to see whether his psychiatrist was in. When the receptionist answered the telephone, I said we had an emergency with Lance. She said she remembered Lance. I explained that he needed to see the doctor right away. She said the psychiatrist was in but that she had no room for appointments today. "I'd be happy to let Lance see the doctor Friday." This was Tuesday. I hung up.

"The Doc's in, Lance and she'll see you, although we may have to wait a little bit. Is that okay?"

"Sure, my Good Bud. I don't mind. I like you. Let's take a ride in your car!"

"Then it's all set, Lance, let's go!"

Lance kept smiling his broad, friendly smile. His telling me over and over that he liked me seemed to reassure me that I was on the right track.

I drove Lancelot, Protector of the Kingdom, Far and Wide, to the mental health center. On the way, Lance started looking around and said he saw another knife. In my confusion, I momentarily worried that another probation officer or an arrested offender had left or concealed a knife in the backseat of the car I was driving, but I concluded that Lance was probably only hallucinating. Lance wasn't paranoid, I was. "Look at the beautiful rhodies, Lance," I said, hoping he would focus on flowers and become docile. Lance did in fact become increasingly docile and I felt myself relax. Before long, we reached the clinic. Together we walked into the office and up to the receptionist. Lance recognized the receptionist and she recognized him. He then asked in his typically loud voice, "Can you see the beautiful golden daggers? The golden ones, streaming, golden sunlight, piercing the green grass. Plunging into the ground. Deeply. Deeper." Lance was focusing on the beautiful green lawn beyond the reception office windows where bright sunlight now shimmered. She looked directly at me, avoiding further eye contact with Lance, and asked, "Are you here to schedule Friday's appointment?"

The receptionist had previously typed several psychiatric reports on Lance and knew about his crime and his fascination with knives. But she also knew that her duties included protecting her boss, the doctor, from disruptions. As Lance mumbled on more about the knives and swords, she began acting nervous and glanced around her work area. She discreetly removed a letter opener from the top of her desk to her desk drawer, locking it tightly with a small brass key. Then she explained that the doctor had no openings until Friday. "I'm sorry. It's impossible today."

While she spoke in her courteous but firm voice, Lance wandered behind the reception counter toward the windows, continuing to mumble incoherently about daggers and golden swords. My eyes darted from her to him. Then, while she waited for me to respond, she realized she was watching me watch Lance who was immediately behind her. He bumped into the receptionist who had risen from her swivel secretarial chair, startled. Her chair wheeled sideways, thumping into a file cabinet. Then Lance knocked a large vase of freshly cut tulips over. The vase broke and flooded her desk, water surging onto a pile of neatly stacked reports and files, quickly streaming toward her computer keyboard. Without explanation, the receptionist departed suddenly, leaving Lance and me standing alone. Almost immediately I heard the returning footsteps of two people. "Could be good, could be bad," I thought to myself. "Magic, or mayhem. It's either the doctor or the bouncer," and I mentally crossed my fingers.

Accompanying the sound of approaching footsteps, I heard the receptionist apologetically telling a woman in a smart gray suit that she was certain that it would save everyone a lot of time and trouble if she would see Lance right away. "Today it's magic," I concluded silently to myself. When I introduced myself to the psychiatrist and began to explain the situation, she invited me to wait in the reception area until she was done interviewing Lance, whereupon Lancelot declared in a loud voice: "I am Sir Lancelot, Protector of the Kingdom, Far and Wide. I can defend you. I can punish you. I will obey! I will come with my Ninjas, knives and all! The kniiives, they come, they coooome." Lance started elongating his syllables again, as he had earlier, as if imitating an amateur Shakespearean actor. This was no stage play, however. Lance was completely oblivious to the three of us as we stood there watching. He was

looking out the window behind the receptionist's desk. The sun
had broken completely through the clouds now, and the warm
day had turned bright and clear.

"On second thought," said the psychiatrist who was looking
directly at me, "please sit in with us. I may want to ask you
some questions too." By this time, I felt a growing need to see
a psychiatrist for my own peace of mind and we followed her
down the hallway to her office. Twenty minutes later, the psychiatrist agreed that Lance was "decompensating" and should
not go home to his uncle's. She asked whether I would be
willing to drive him to the state hospital, which I knew would
be a 2-hour drive, possibly more, depending on traffic. I tried
to picture myself driving through congested streets and free-
ways for hours, keeping one eye on traffic and the other eye on
Sir Lancelot, Protector of the Kingdom, Far and Wide.

Lance started talking about the knives and swords again.
Suddenly, the irony of Lance's name struck me. Lance. Knives.
Swords. Spears. Lances. A peculiar sensation came over me, as
if everything were standing still and I felt as if I were being
drawn hypnotically into Lance's trance. "How about taking him
to the city hospital?" I suggested. "And, how about authorizing
an involuntary commitment?"

Lance said the sun was beginning to shoot the knives toward
us now. "Look out!" he said, as he ducked involuntarily, avoiding the invisible knives and swords flying through his imaginary
battleground. The short drive to the local hospital sounded like
a cup of tea compared to the alternative, an automotive adven-
ture on the freeway. I knew that if the psychiatrist would certify
that Lance was "dangerous to himself and others," he could be
held at the hospital with a minimum of red tape. Without her
certifying he was "crackers," the hospital would probably not
admit him. She agreed.

We asked Lance about going to the hospital, and he con-
sented at once. It took no persuasion of any sort. He just said,
"Sure! I'll go voluntarily!" I felt surprised. Briefly. Then I
realized that the word "surprise" was no longer operative.

Anything could happen. Anything at all. So far, my luck had held out. "Just 10 more minutes," I silently said to myself, while planning our route to the hospital. As we walked out the door of the clinic to find the car, I glanced back and saw the psychiatrist heading back toward her office. For the time being, Lance's cooperation spared us all a great deal of extra work.

I drove Lance to the city hospital. The psychiatrist called ahead and Sir Lancelot went peacefully. He said he'd been there plenty of times before and he kept saying he was happy to ride shotgun with me "Because city traffic is really dangerous these days. You never can tell what will happen. That's why I never drive! But, I can protect us from anything. I am Sir Lancelot, Protector of the Kingdom, Far and Wide." He occasionally added, "Don't you worry about a thing. I like you. You're my bud. My goooood bud! I can protect you. I'll ride shotgun!" He seemed more fond of me than I liked and I wondered how he would feel about me later, after being committed. It was I, after all, who suggested to Lance that he take the drive to the hospital in the first place.

Lance was evaluated thoroughly at the hospital that afternoon. I had lunch in the hospital cafeteria and spent the afternoon answering questions, filling out forms, contacting Lance's uncle and brother, and untangling the confusion in the hospital staff's mind when they learned that he was a Criminal Insanity case, a "CI." They wanted to know why I couldn't arrest him and take him to the county jail or state mental hospital. As I explained to them, in this state, supervision of CIs is governed by an entirely different set of laws than those covering convicted criminals. For one, I had no powers of arrest in Lance's case under any circumstances. Eventually they understood he was their responsibility for the time being, and decided to hold him until a legal hearing in 72 hours to decide where he should go next. The good news was that I would not have to return later that week to testify, because Lance had voluntarily committed himself.

That Friday, Lance was transferred to the state hospital in a secure van. I later learned that doctors determined that he was not safe to be at large under any circumstances and they kept him for several months until they could stabilize him on medication and provide enough treatment so that he could be returned safely to the community. Regrettably, I never saw Lance again, but I miss him. I liked him. "But for the grace of God . . ." I often say to myself when I remember our few encounters.

I arrived back at the office at 10 minutes to 5:00 p.m. Closing time. I grabbed a handful of pink telephone message slips. "At least, my caseload is down one," I thought as I glanced at my in-box. Three new files sat in the in-box that I had left empty that morning. "Handle one, three spring up, like weeds in a garden," I thought. After all, it was Spring.

❖   ❖   ❖

The Corrections Agency

Most citizens have little idea what probation officers do in supervising criminal offenders. Most other parts of the criminal justice system (police, prosecuting attorneys, defense attorneys, judges, jails and prisons, etc.) have been given wide coverage in the news and entertainment media. Crime dramas abound on television and in motion picture theaters, as do documentaries on the successes and failures of police, the courts, and the prisons in the collective effort to catch, prosecute, and punish criminal offenders. Investigative journalism programs report on all aspects of crime. Even political elections for the nation's highest office have turned to publicity about the revolving door that shuttles offenders off the streets, into the jails, and back out to the streets again.

This media coverage, however, has done little to explain the significant role of probation officers. It is usually they who are most able to help you understand and deal with the convicted child molester. The purpose of this chapter is to explain more carefully the range of the demands on probation officers and what probation officers do when supervising child molesters and other sex offenders. Knowing this will give some perspective on the officer's responsibilities. It will also help you understand how to obtain information about the child molester and how to intervene if problems arise. Implicit in this discussion is the fact that workload demands in some instances can make it impossible to respond as quickly to the public's request for information as might be desired. Despite this fact, probation officers are the place to start when seeking this information. Chapter 8 outlined two aspects of the day-to-day responsibilities of the probation officer: the cop and the social worker. From a broader perspective, there are other issues that are vital to understanding the probation officer's job.

Complexity

One issue is the enormous complexity of correctional supervision and the probation officer's work. There is a wide variety of laws that the officer must understand, including not only the laws of the state where the officer is employed but sometimes the laws of other states as well. Lance's story illustrates one such complexity. Even the professional hospital staff responsible for mental illness did not realize the probation officer could not arrest Lance and take him to jail. In addition, the probation officer must have some basic understanding of human psychology to respond effectively to a vast number of situations that can jeopardize not only the safety of innocent citizens but at times the officer him- or herself. As Professor Thomas Ellsworth (1988) wrote recently, "We must understand the reality that in the 1980s probation staff members are forced to work with not only greater numbers of offenders but more dangerous ones as well" (p. 29).

Recently, the situation has only grown worse with the appearance of organized, armed gangs; more serious problems of drug abuse; and dwindling resources to help treat offenders. Furthermore, routine probation work requires a multitude of professional skills. The officer needs to understand and enforce court orders, and must

understand the basics of criminal investigation, surveillance techniques, and how to interview witnesses. The officer must be able to
determine when and how to search an offender's home, how to seize
evidence, and how to write complex reports that are used to prosecute violations of probation. Because probation officers often have
the authority to search an offender's home without a search warrant,
they not only have greater authority than police but, in some areas,
have commensurably more responsibility to act legally and professionally. The probation officer must be trained and prepared to arrest
offenders under supervision and to testify in court, to give public
presentations to schools and community groups, and know how to
interview victims sensitively. Finally, probation officers must be able
to work effectively with all of those citizens who are concerned about
specific offenders under their supervision. When you call the probation office, any one of these complex issues may arise. You must be
prepared for the fact that what you expected and what is obvious
and reasonable to you may be impossible under the officer's legal
constraints.

Workload

Another significant aspect of corrections is "workload." Unlike
some organizations, the corrections agency cannot refuse more
clients. It cannot develop a waiting list when too many offenders are
placed on probation. Jails can develop waiting lists telling inmates
when to report to jail and they can shorten offenders' sentences by
increasing the amount of "good time" allowable. Probation departments, however, are required to accept and supervise offenders as
soon as they walk out of the doors of the courthouse. As Joan
Petersilia (1987) of the RAND Corporation writes,

> Most probation systems across the country have experienced
> budget cuts because of fiscal limitations and the shift from
> rehabilitation to punishment. At the same time, however, the

public has demanded that criminals get harsher treatment, but also prison crowding has become so critical that the courts have increasingly used probation to catch the over-flow. . . . Between 1974 and 1983, the prison population increased by 48 percent, but the probation population jumped by 63 percent. . . . The Criminal Justice System is facing a severe dilemma. Probation caseloads are increasing at the same time that budgets are shrinking. (p. 56ff)

Unlike private industry, in corrections more employees are not hired because business is booming. Instead, the number of criminal offenders assigned to a probation officer simply increases and the caseload size, or workload, grows while agency administrators lobby elected officials for more staff. Because more staff means more taxes, lawmakers typically resist giving more money to corrections agencies until their problems become critical.

When new staff are hired and caseloads are reduced, the problem is not automatically solved. As the eminent sociologist and crimi-nologist, Daniel Glaser (1975) writes, as soon as caseload sizes are reduced, there is evidence that more paperwork and supervisory conferences are then demanded of probation officers, making the problem of workload a two-edged sword. Smaller caseload sizes may simply mean more red tape.

This dilemma is further complicated by the data that indicate more and more sex offenders are being sentenced to prison every year (Herrick, 1989). These offenders are in nearly every case released back into the community under correctional surveillance and supervision. As a result, the workload for probation officers grows.[1] Nevertheless, in our society the probation officer is often the public's most direct link between the offender and the court.

The remainder of this chapter will unravel the complexity of the corrections agency and the role of the probation officer. A list of essential questions to ask the probation officer about the agency will be provided (e.g., What can the probation officer do?), and it will provide a list of essential questions to ask about the offender (e.g.,

What did the sex offender do, in terms that I can understand?)
Knowing this will make your communication with the probation
officer much easier.

Legal Complexities

Changes in criminal statutes across the nation are making the laws
governing offenders more and more complex. The most significant
of these changes is the move away from open-ended, *indeterminate*
sentencing laws to more restrictive, *determinate* sentencing laws
(Smith, Rhine, & Jackson, 1990). (These terms will be discussed
more thoroughly below.) This shift means that formerly, probation
officers had significant authority to intervene, restrict, and control
the convicted sex offender, but under the new determinate laws, that
authority is sometimes seriously eroded. It cannot be safely assumed
that the probation officer can order a sex offender to do or not do
something, just because it makes good sense. In some instances, the
authority of the probation officer is so limited that it is essentially
nonexistent.

In one case, the author dealt with a repeat sex offender who was
released from prison with only one requirement, to pay court costs.
There were virtually no other conditions imposed on this offender.
The offender, who had very obvious mental problems, wanted
whatever counseling assistance that could be provided on a voluntary
basis. Although he continued to abuse drugs and alcohol and have
contact with minor children, there was legally nothing that could be
done to take him off the streets before he committed a new crime.

In other cases, usually under the indeterminate laws, the traditional authority of the probation officer remains fully intact. The
probation officer may exercise sufficient discretion and power over
the offender that nearly any reasonable condition can be imposed on
the offender under the probation officer's authority. In the state of
Washington, which appears to reflect the trend emerging nationally,
the laws have radically changed the authority of the probation officer
over some categories of sex offenders. In some circumstances, some

sex offenders are required to be in treatment programs while others are not and those sex offenders cannot be required to be in counseling even by the court in many cases. Sometimes, a neighbor can be notified that a sex offender is living next door, but at other times, the neighbor cannot be notified unless the offender gives his written legal consent. There are times when one sex offender is prohibited from having any contact with his victim or other children for 10 years, but another offender may have no restrictions against contact with children at all, including his victims.

Agency Complexities

Just as the laws are becoming more complex, the correctional agencies are also becoming more diverse, taking on a greater and greater variety of responsibilities and imposing more and more expectations on staff. Although the duties vary from state to state, most correctional agencies have duties requiring interviewing; surveillance and tracking offenders; monitoring reporting requirements; observing mental health status; overseeing payment of legal fees and monitoring specific requirements of court orders such as community service (court-ordered public work programs), jail sentences, curfew requirements, and registration with law enforcement agencies as criminal offenders; ensuring that sex offenders participating in a treatment program when ordered to do so and submit to testing for AIDS when required by court order; participating in urinalysis drug detection programs, attending Alcoholics Anonymous and Narcotics Anonymous meetings; ensuring that offenders remain within certain geographical localities and avoid others (schools and parks, for instance) and maintain work or educational programs as well as obey all laws; conducting searches of offenders' homes for suspected illegal activities; and arresting offenders who violate their court requirements. The 1990s have also seen the spread of computer technology in corrections, which requires probation officers not only to understand and use complex computer programs but also to provide many hours a week of data input into vast databases on thousands of offenders. This is only a partial list of some of the major duties taken on by the corrections agency.

In some areas, specialized units have been formed to attempt to deal with the growing number of new demands on corrections agencies. The oldest and most traditional specialization in supervising offenders is called *intensive supervision.* Usually, intensive supervision limits the number of offenders on a caseload and requires an increased number of contacts between the officer and the offender in the office and in the offender's home or workplace. Noted researcher Daniel Glaser's work suggests that smaller caseloads can result in more paper work and supervisory conferences and fewer contacts with offenders (National Institute of Law Enforcement and Criminal Justice, 1978). Nevertheless, smaller specialized caseloads and intensive supervision remain a primary focus of efforts to deal with the new public demand to hold offenders accountable (Burkhart, 1986; Byrne, 1986; Conrad, 1987).

As new laws are enacted, the agencies change their policies to reflect new attitudes and legal trends. At one point in time, an officer might have been authorized to talk routinely to neighbors about whether a sex offender was having any contact with children and to notify the neighbors that children might be in danger around the offender, but at another point in time, as a result of new legislation and agency policies, the probation officer might be completely prohibited from making such routine notifications to interested neighbors.

Added to these matters is the element of danger that is of increasing importance in the work of probation officers. Charles Lindner, JD, and Robert L Bonn, PhD, wrote about this succinctly in a 1996 issue of *Federal Probation,*

Field visits are often made to high crime areas where violence is commonplace. Many probationers reside in multi-dwelling buildings where the officer must climb several flights of stairs in dark or poorly lit hallways. Public housing projects are especially dangerous with elevators sometimes being stopped between floors, so that a mugger can enter through the emergency escape hatch in the ceiling. As a result, probation officers engaged in fieldwork are at some risk of being victimized not only by the offender, but also by persons frequenting the neighborhood. (p. 16)

Because of such complexities and the pace of change, the reader needs to find out directly from the probation officer exactly what he or she can and cannot do in working with the convicted child molester. Once that information is known, the person who does inquire will be far better situated to make a thoughtful and knowledgeable plan for dealing with the offender.

The Laws Under Which Sex Offenders Are Convicted

The laws governing sex offenders are complex, and they vary radically from one state to another. There is no common agreement among the states about what is and what is not child sexual abuse (Fraser, 1981). The difficulties about how to define child sexual abuse are discussed by many different authors (Kocen & Bulkley, 1983; Peters, Wyatt, & Finkelhor, 1988). Furthermore, offenders are not always convicted of a crime that they actually committed. For example, an offender may break into a home and molest a child but be convicted of burglary because the child was too young to be a credible witness. An offender may plead guilty to assault because his rape victim was too traumatized to testify or ran away from home and the offender was offered a plea bargain agreement to a reduced charge and shorter jail term. Or an offender may be charged with numerous counts of indecent liberties and plead guilty to only one or two on the prosecutor's offer to dismiss the others.

A *plea bargain* is an agreement between the defense and the prosecution about what the crime of conviction will be and what penalty will be recommended in exchange for the offender pleading guilty, rather than requiring the prosecution to conduct a full-scale trial. Plea bargain agreements constitute the vast majority of criminal convictions of child sexual abuse in the United States. As Dean Champion (1988) points out in his study of the sentencing practices of three states (Tennessee, Kentucky and Virginia), when 18,000 cases were reviewed, 94% of all child sex abusers pleaded guilty so that they could accept a plea bargain rather than face a court trial. It appears that this trend is being repeated throughout the nation.

The plea bargain serves purposes for the sex offender, the prosecuting attorney, and even the victim. By entering into a plea bargain, the child molester is able to escape a public trial and will usually get a shorter jail term. Also, the offender can often plead guilty to a less serious crime than the one he was originally charged with. The advantage to the prosecuting attorney is that plea bargain agreements save time, money, and reduce workload significantly although still maintaining some kind of control over the sex offender because the guilty plea usually results in some form of supervision and control by a probation officer, if only for a limited time. Plea bargain agreements also avoid risking further trauma to the child victim from testifying in criminal court. As a result, the crime a sex offender is convicted of on the record often does not tell what the offender actually did. *This means that someone working with a child molester needs to know not only the crime he was convicted of but also what the offender actually did.*

The Laws Under Which Offenders Are Sentenced

Once convicted, other laws determine what sentence the judge can impose on the offender. Sentencing laws differ from state to state and change considerably over time. In the 1990s, as the attention of communities and legislatures focuses more and more on child molesters, the pace of change is actually increasing. As a result of such changes, the correctional agency's role may change considerably as well. Most citizens usually assume that once the child molester is convicted, judges, prosecutors, and probation officers have nearly unlimited power over the sex offender. To an extent, this has generally been true in the past. Sometimes great power was wielded over the offender. In more recent times, however, the power is much more limited. Two terms, *determinate* and *indeterminate*, will clarify how laws differ in the treatment of offenders.

Indeterminate Sentencing Laws

Indeterminate sentencing laws, in use throughout most of this century, are those in which a maximum prison term is set by law, but the judge usually imposes a shorter sentence. So, how long an offender actually serves in jail or prison, or on probation or parole, is not automatically determined. Instead, the actual term an offender spends in jail or prison, or on probation or parole, depends on many different factors, such as how the judge assesses the seriousness of the crime and whether the offender complies with all conditions required of him or her. If the judge sentences the offender to prison, the actual prison term is usually determined by a parole board, not by the judge. The parole board considers such things as the seriousness of the crime, how the offender adjusts in prison, and whether he participates in rehabilitation programs during his prison sentence. After release, the length of parole is determined by how the offender adjusts during parole. Under an indeterminate system, a person who violates the requirements can be returned to jail or prison, often for a very long time. Generally, indeterminate laws are based on the concept of rehabilitation and require that the offender participate in a variety of programs to help lead a lawful, productive life.

Determinate Sentencing Laws

Determinate sentencing laws set an offender's jail or prison term based on a point system that takes into consideration how serious the crime is and the offender's prior convictions. State budget crises, unjust sentences for different racial groups, and prison overcrowding have been major reasons for the shift to determinate sentencing as well as the public's demand for "truth" in sentencing. The trend toward determinate sentencing has been the single most significant change in the criminal justice system during the past two decades

(Durham, 1991). Under most determinate sentencing laws, the judge's flexibility is reduced significantly. Also, the conditions that control an offender may be drastically reduced. The offender's punishment is determined by guidelines and not by the judge, a probation officer, or the parole board's knowledge of the offender and its opinions about the individual's case (for a discussion of these issues and current trends, see Durham, 1991). With only minor exceptions, the jail or prison term is set in advance based on the nature of the crime and the offender's past criminal convictions.

Determinate sentencing laws have made the criminal justice system very complex. Fortunately, it is not necessary to understand the complex laws. It is very important, however, that you find out what the probation officer can and cannot do with the child molester you are concerned about. To do this, you need to know what questions to ask. *Do not assume the probation officer has unlimited authority to control the offender. Ask what authority the probation officer actually has over the specific sex offender you are concerned about.*

Interstate Supervision of Offenders

Offenders do not always live within the county or the state where they were convicted. For example, an offender may be convicted of a sex offense in one state and move to another state. Usually he is supervised by a probation officer in the second state. In most instances, the sentencing laws of the second state do not govern this offender. Nevertheless, the rules of the corrections agency supervising him in the second state usually do apply based on an arrangement among all 50 states, called the Interstate Compact Agreement. If a sex offender's supervision is formally transferred to another state, he must almost always agree to comply with any and all requirements of the second state, regardless of what the original court required. Under these conditions, the second state will still have the basic documents about the offender, such as the presentence investigation report, the judgment and sentence, and the conditions of supervision imposed by the probation officer (as discussed below).

Basic Correctional Concepts

Despite the many variations that may occur among states and the differences in the laws for convicting and sentencing offenders, there are basic concepts that are fairly common throughout the United States. It should be noted that these are general definitions only and their specific use may vary from one locality to another. The following definitions apply primarily to felony offenders, although some important distinctions will be noted between felony and misdemeanor offenders.

The Corrections Agency

Corrections agencies provide surveillance and supervisory control of convicted offenders. These agencies are usually administered by state or county governments. In some areas, the state government administers the corrections agency for all felony offenders. In other areas, the counties administer the agencies. In still other areas, the state supervises some offenders, for example, felons released on parole from state prisons, and county governments supervise all felony offenders who received only county jail confinement and were released on probation.

Corrections agencies are known by many different names. The most common title is the Department of Corrections. Other titles are Probation and Parole Services, Department of Health and Social Services, Division of Corrections, Community Service Division, Adult and Juvenile Probation Services, Department of Offender Rehabilitation, Bureau of Correctional Services, or Division of Community Corrections. Sometimes, local county jails are also named the Department of Corrections but may have no authority over the offender after he leaves the jail.

To simplify this potential confusion, a convicted child molester is often given the business card of his probation officer or he has received correspondence from the agency. The reader can find out for sure who the offender's probation officer is by asking to see the business card or correspondence and by calling the probation officer identified if the offender doesn't seem to know.

The Probation Officer

The probation officer is that person who has responsibility to monitor the offender's compliance with the legal requirements of the sentence. The probation officer provides surveillance of and/or arrests the offender for violations, assists the offender in fulfilling his legal obligations, and reports violations to the court or parole board recommending what action should be taken for the violations. There are many different titles for the probation officer, including Probation Officer, Parole Officer, Probation and Parole Officer, Community Corrections Officer, Corrections Officer, Corrections Counselor, Corrections Agent, Parole Agent, and Caseworker. In this book the term *probation officer* is used for any person with responsibility for seeing that the offender complies with court or parole board orders while he is living in the community.

Probation

In most cases, probation is punishment imposed by a judge in which the offender must serve up to but no more than 1 year in a local county jail. Upon release from jail, the offender may be required to report to a corrections agency where he must follow rules imposed by the judge listed on the Judgment and Sentence (the court order) and follow the rules and regulations of the correctional agency as well. (More rarely, probation refers to a period of time after a prison sentence.)

Parole

Parole is a period of surveillance and control following a sentence of more than 1 year generally served at a state prison. Upon release, the offender reports to a corrections agency, and he must follow the requirements set down by a Parole Board and conform to the general rules of the corrections agency.

Judgment and Sentence

The Judgment and Sentence is the document that identifies the crime the offender is convicted of and the punishment imposed. It also specifies special requirements imposed by the judge and the date that the sentenced was imposed. This document can have several different names, such as the Order of Judgment, Order of Probation, and Conditions Upon Sentence. It can usually be easily identified because it is signed by a judge and is identified on the first page as the sentencing court order.

Order of Parole

The Order of Parole is the document that states the rules the parole board requires a person to follow after he is released from a state prison. Like the Judgment and Sentence, the Order of Parole can have a variety of names, nearly always including the word "parole."

Conditions of Probation/Parole

In addition to the rules in the Judgment and Sentence and the Order of Parole, offenders are usually required to follow the rules of the corrections agency. These rules can be found on a document usually titled something like the Conditions of Probation, the Standard Conditions of Parole, or the Standard Supervision Requirements. It is important that those working with the sex offender actually obtain and read a copy of this document because there are often conditions imposed by this document on the offender that do not appear on the Judgment and Sentence or on the Order of Parole.

Release of Confidential Information

Most information that the corrections agency has is protected by state and federal laws of confidentiality. However, a form called a Release of Confidential Information, which the sex offender can sign, gives the probation officer legal permission to share information about the offender with anyone chosen by the offender. Without such a signed release, the probation officer can usually only give out certain specified information, such as the name of the crime, the date of conviction, and when the offender entered and was released from custody. Only rarely will an offender refuse to sign a release when he understands that its purpose is to help him succeed under correctional supervision. *An offender who refuses to sign such a release should be considered dangerous, because he is usually trying to conceal important information.*

The Presentence Investigation Report

As described in Chapter 6, the Presentence Investigation Report is a written report, usually prepared by a probation officer, that is given to a judge detailing the offender's crime and personal history. The primary purpose of this document is to help the judge determine an appropriate sentence for the offender.

Felony

A felony is a criminal offense that is punishable by more than 1 year in jail. Usually, if more than 1 year is imposed the offender serves this time in a state facility commonly referred to as "prison," although some states have felons serving longer terms in county facilities.

Misdemeanor

A misdemeanor is a criminal offense that is punishable by a maximum term of less than 1 year in jail. When an offender is sentenced to a misdemeanor term, the confinement time is usually spent in a local jail, not in a state-run prison. However, the serious overcrowding in jails and prisons has begun to change where offenders serve their jail and prison terms.

What to Ask About the Convicted Child Molester

There are several key questions to ask when you want to find out more about a specific child molester. It is always preferable to request this information with the full knowledge and cooperation of the offender. Working on an open basis, with a clear idea of the information to be exchanged, is a significant step in combating secrecy that the offender relied on to commit his sexual crimes. A sex offender who is unwilling to sign a release of confidentiality is a poor risk to the safety of children and he may be a poor risk to the personal safety of adults as well. For example, he may be hiding other criminal activity or convictions, such as domestic violence or theft from friends. On the other hand, if the offender is willing to sign the release, an important step has been taken in ending the offender's reliance on secrecy and deception. The following are typical questions to ask the probation officer about the offender:

1. What crime was he convicted of?
2. What did he actually do?
3. When did he do it and over what period of time (i.e., how long did the molestation go on?)
4. What else is he known to have done that constituted a risk to the safety of children or others?
5. Were any charges plea bargained away? What did he allegedly do?
6. When was he sentenced?

7. What was his sentence?

8. How long does his sentence last?

9. How long will he be under the control of the corrections agency?

10. What are the court and agency conditions governing the offender's behavior?

11. Is the offender in compliance with those conditions?

12. Has he been charged with or convicted of any violations of the conditions of supervision? What, if any?

13. Has the offender been convicted of any other crimes?

14. What information does the probation officer want from you?

15. Will the probation officer notify you if there is any change in the offender's circumstances that would pose a risk to children?

16. Does the officer know about any other serious behavior or other serious criminal charges to be concerned about?

Summary

The laws under which sex offenders are tried and convicted vary from state to state. Plea bargaining may result in offenders pleading guilty to a crime that does not necessarily tell what the offender really did and, therefore, the crime of conviction may be an unreliable indicator of the offender's behavior and/or danger. Anyone who is asking about a convicted child molester should be sure to find out not only the crime he was convicted of but also what he actually did. At present, many states are revising their criminal codes and sentencing laws and those revisions will no doubt continue, especially owing to increasing concern over sex and drug offenders. The probation officer remains, despite these changes, the best person to communicate with regarding the convicted child molester, provided the offender is willing to sign a release. Communication of this sort is best when it is done openly so that all parties know they are talking to each other, including the offender himself. An offender who is not willing to sign a release for full disclosure of information is a poor risk.

Anyone wishing to understand the sex offender and his legal requirements should ask the probation officer supervising the offender what the powers and limitations of the agency are. Once this is understood, the wife of the offender (or a relative or an acquaintance) is in a much better position to communicate clearly and effectively with the offender and the probation officer. This communication will be less fraught with misunderstandings and time will not be wasted trying to persuade the probation officer to do something that is legally impossible. On the other hand, if someone has important information about an offender, such as a child molester drinking alcohol, she or he will know how to report the information. The earlier reports are made, the more quickly action can be taken to prevent problems from escalating.

Usually, a probation officer will consider sex offenses to be the most serious category of offenses. Workload pressures, as described at the beginning of this chapter, do sometimes prevent as quick a response as might seem warranted in some cases. For the most part, however, probation officers are interested in responding professionally and effectively. Their sympathies lie with victims and the law-abiding public. At the same time, probation officers are often the persons most capable of influencing the offender before problems get out of hand. Most probation officers accept both the role of the cop in enforcing compliance with rules and the role of the social worker in assisting the offender to be successful during his term of supervision.

Note

1. The requirements for correctional administrators are no less perplexing than those of the probation officer. For a discussion of the administrator's duties see Riveland (1991).

Community-Based
Treatment of Child Molesters

*This chapter describes the sex offender evaluation report,
basic concepts of treatment for child molesters, and the
importance of communication with the therapist who
is treating the child molester. Understanding each of
these topics is important in preventing the offender from
manipulating those around him, being sure that the
offender follows the rules and requirements of treatment,
and making decisions that increase the safety of children
and others who come in contact with the offender.*

◆   ◆   ◆

ALEX

Alex was 50, balding, wore thick glasses, and had gained
considerable weight over the years. Despite numerous failures
in marriage, he was quite successful in business. He ran his own
carpet-laying firm that usually netted a fair sum of money each

214

year, and he bragged to others by complaining about how much he had to pay in taxes. He liked having things his way, whether in business or in personal affairs, and he usually did. In business he made sure he got what he wanted by hustling jobs and making connections. During lean years, if he couldn't win his own contracts, he could always get well-paid work with major contracting firms in the area that knew of his work and reputation. He had become known over the years as "Mr. Consistency." He knew how a job needed to be done and made sure it was done right every time. Although he was on parole, there was never a day that he failed to work and earn good money.

Like many of his buddies, he drank alcohol, sometimes quite a bit in fact, although at other times he stayed completely sober. Alcohol never interfered with his work and no one ever complained to him about his drinking. Alex had developed strong, rough hands and thick wrists from years of carpet laying and, in the camaraderie of tavern life after a long day's work, he would challenge others to arm wrestling contests. Crowds would gather around, bystanders would make small wagers, and the fun would begin. He was a crowd-pleaser despite his boastful ways. He would make small wagers on these contests himself, but he would never wager a large sum, particularly if he knew the other competitor had a wife and children to support. "The money's just to make things interesting," he would say to his challenger. "I don't want to hurt your pocketbook. There'll be pain enough in your arm when we're done." He just wanted the challenge of good, wholesome competition, with a little bet on the side to go to whoever won. Usually, he won.

Few knew that Alex was on parole for rape. One of the requirements of his parole was that he complete counseling as directed by the parole officer. He was in a tough program for about a year, the kind of program that confronts sex offenders when they deny, minimize, or blame others for their sexually deviant acts. The pattern of his rapes was fairly clear, and Alex was as consistent in them as he was in his work. One victim described events vividly. She needed a ride home from a tavern and Alex offered her a ride. She accepted. He pretended to get lost and they ended up going down a lonely country road. From many years of working in the area, he knew all the main streets as a taxi driver would and he knew the back roads, too. The woman protested, but Alex continued to drive the truck, telling her there was a place to turn around just ahead. Alex then offered her some whiskey that he kept in a flask under the driver's seat. She refused, so Alex did not drink any either. But he ignored her demand to stop the truck, and she became more and more upset. She demanded to be let out or be taken back to town. Alex began to laugh, telling her that he couldn't leave her out here on a lonely road at night. Besides, he said, she owed him something for the long drive. He put his arm over her shoulder, attempting to entice her into sex which she steadfastly refused. By now she was afraid. The car was traveling too fast for her to jump out safely.

Suddenly, Alex pulled over to the side of the road and stopped the truck. He grabbed her by the wrist with his vice-like grip, a force unlike any she had known before, and he reached for a screwdriver on the cluttered dash board of the truck. He raped her at the side of the road while he held the screwdriver to her throat.

Despite the sheer terror she endured, not knowing whether she would live or die, she had made a point of memorizing everything she could about Alex, his physical appearance, his clothing, his voice, his age, his car, the route they took, and the interior of the car as well. She even observed, as Alex drove away, that his license plate was mud spattered, and only a few of the numbers could be read. But she remembered the scratches and dents in the dashboard of the vehicle, the cracked rearview mirror on the passenger's side, and the broken tail-light lens as she watched the truck pull away. She was determined to remember every detail and to see that her abductor got what he deserved. What Alex had in wrist strength, his victim had in spirit and determination.

As a result of her ability to remember so many specific details, Alex was soon apprehended, convicted, and sentenced to several years in the state prison. After his conviction, other women admitted to detectives that they too had been raped by Alex in a similar manner but, until now, they had been too traumatized to admit it. One felt guilty because she too had met Alex in a bar and had accepted several drinks from him before she was raped. She didn't feel she could make her charges stick. Another was worried about how her friends would react. His last victim, however, was determined and finally put an end to Alex's rapes. She was 15 years old.

After several years in prison, Alex was released on parole. His parole officer required that he enter one of the toughest sex offender treatment programs available. The therapist was a woman tougher than Alex in the game of wits that sex offenders play in therapy, and the group members were equally tough on each other. For about 6 months, Alex persisted in minimizing the seriousness of his crimes, saying, "I can't be held accountable for those others, after all, I wasn't convicted of them. I've been self-supporting all my life, never taken a dime of the state's money, and gone out of my way to be helpful and considerate to others." The group confronted Alex, telling him he wasn't looking at himself honestly. It was his last warning. Nobody believed his excuses and denials. They were especially angry about his blaming the victims, when it was apparent to all that he was a violent, predatory rapist and lucky that he wasn't still behind bars. The group told him so. When this pressure still failed to persuade him to admit to his problems and use group therapy appropriately, the members of the group and the therapist all agreed that he should be terminated from the program. The therapist promptly notified his parole officer by letter.

Around this time, Alex's parole officer transferred out of the area and supervision responsibilities went to a new officer who had essentially no training in dealing with sex offenders. By the time the new officer met with Alex to discuss being terminated from the treatment program, Alex said that he had already found another therapist who had agreed to take him into a new treatment program. The parole officer telephoned the new therapist to verify what Alex had said. The therapist reassured the officer that he was impressed with Alex's candor. However, the therapist failed to consult with Alex's previous therapist, feeling no need to do so, because Alex was now willing to work sincerely on his problems. The therapist indicated that seldom had he ever spoken with anyone who spoke so openly about his history of sexual offenses. Apparently the warning from the previous program had really done its job because, at last, the new therapist said to the new officer, Alex was really ready to work on his problems. The parole officer asked for a written report, which the therapist agreed to send.

When the two-page written report came in the mail some weeks later, the therapist described the openness shown by Alex, and he was especially impressed with Alex's religious conversion. The therapist indicated that he had met with Alex on several occasions and had talked with him about his history of rape. He had met with Alex's wife, too. Furthermore, the therapist indicated that he had worked successfully with criminal offenders before. He had been a pastoral counselor for years and he was persuaded that Alex, by virtue of his recent religious conversion, would be cured in 6 weeks. The prognosis was extremely good, the counselor wrote. He was absolutely confident that Alex had finally turned the corner on a life of crime.

Based on that report, the new parole officer went to another parole officer and reported that Alex's therapist said Alex would soon successfully complete treatment—without mentioning or realizing the importance of Alex's being terminated from the first program. The new officer explained that the therapist was quite pleased with Alex's openness and admissions of past misdeeds. Following a brief discussion, a report to the parole board was prepared indicating that Alex would be completing therapy successfully in about 6 weeks. Shortly afterwards, a discharge from active parole supervision was granted by the parole board. The officer's report requesting a discharge from parole read: "Alex has been on active parole supervision for two and a half years, participated in therapy most of that time, and the current therapist indicates that he is fully rehabilitated and is no longer in need of active parole supervision."

Six months later, Alex was arrested for attempted rape. He again attempted a rape, this time of a 13-year-old girl who needed a ride. He picked up the victim when she was standing at a bus stop in a snowstorm waiting for a delayed bus and the dropping temperature and increasing wind became hazardous. After picking her up, he again "got lost" driving her to her destination and ended up on a dark street. He offered the girl whiskey from a flask under his seat. When she refused, he threatened her, claiming she owed him something for the ride. In the darkness of the car, the girl had already placed her hand on the door handle and was planning her escape. When he asked her to have sex with him she remembered seeing the screwdriver on the dashboard. Without a moment's hesitation, she escaped out the door, before Alex had a chance to grab her, and ran to a nearby house. Despite her trauma, like the last victim she notified police, described the car (with the same mud-spattered license plates), and Alex was arrested again. Obviously, therapy had not affected Alex to any significant degree, despite what the counselor had claimed.

The story illustrates that sex offenders, whether child molesters or adult rapists, seldom adhere exclusively to one preferred sexual outlet. In this case, although Alex had mostly raped adult females, a child was clearly within his range of sexual assaults. This pattern has been well documented in careful scientific work conducted by Gene Abel and colleagues (Abel, Becker, Cunningham-Rathner, Mittleman, & Rouleau, 1988).

The psychological treatment of child molesters living in the community began growing significantly in the 1970s. A few institutional programs existed before that time, and a few trailblazers in the field did work and occasionally published articles and books on the subject. At the time, counseling child molesters in the community was still such a relatively new field that therapists were only beginning to ask some of the fundamental questions that needed to be addressed before any professional agreement, any scientific approach, could begin. Can a child molester be cured through psychological counseling? Can one who denies having such sexual problems be helped? How can child molesters be motivated to accept treatment if they initially are not interested? Can they benefit from therapy when it is ordered by the court? Is it better to allow them to participate on a strictly voluntary basis? Does treatment for child molesters require that the therapist discuss the offender's sexual behaviors and feelings directly, or can a therapist ignore sexual issues altogether and still successfully treat the offender by addressing problems such as low self-esteem?

In those early years, professional articles were relatively rare and real scientific study was even scarcer. Over the years, however, the professional literature has increased significantly. Although not all of the questions have been answered from a purely scientific standpoint, a broad consensus has emerged among professionals about some of the most important questions. This broad consensus does not mean that the answers have been scientifically proven but, rather, the experience of most professionals is in agreement in certain areas.

Important progress has been made concerning how to treat child molesters when one focuses on the primary issue of safety. One clear area of consensus is that specialized training and experience is required in the treatment of all sex offenders, whether child molesters or men who rape adult women. Fortunately, it is less common today for a therapist without training and expertise to undertake the treatment of a child molester, as happened in the case of Alex. Specialization has become expected in this field for a variety of reasons. In most cases, judges and prosecutors have become more sophisticated. They are simply less willing to approve a therapist who cannot demonstrate expertise in dealing with child molesters. Also, therapists now recognize that this area of treatment comprises a very specialized field, and they have become fully aware of the serious harm that can result from failing to evaluate and treat any sex offender carefully.

A second area of consensus is that controls over the offender's behavior are essential to community safety. The results of such controls in terms of safety to children and the community is evident to nearly every professional in the field. Judges and parole boards are more careful to specify rules and limits on the offender's behavior that must be adhered to if the offender wishes to remain free in the community. Therapists are more inclined to include extensive treatment rules in addition to those already ordered by the court. Probation officers are more active in contacting persons in the community to be sure that the rules are being followed. Both therapists and probation officers also recognize that if they fail to monitor sex offenders in a prudent manner, they may be held accountable for their failures in court.

Another area of agreement deals with sharing information. Therapists, prosecutors, probation officers, and others in the criminal justice field recognize the importance of effective planning and communication. Experience over the past 25 years has taught professionals that communication is beneficial not only in terms of the safety of children but also in terms of the offender's own well-being. Sharing information helps deter the offender's use of secrecy and manipulation. It appears to reduce his opportunity to groom and to set up a reoffense. As one noted therapist puts it, sharing information about the offender's history with those who know him is essential because doing so "destroys the secrecy necessary for commission of sexual aggression" (Pithers, Martin, & Cumming, 1989, p. 307). Communication is, therefore, seen as a cornerstone of responsible sex offender treatment.

Another area of emerging consensus is that effective communication needs to take place among those who know the offender on a personal basis. The impact of this communication on the safety of children should be clear by now. Many examples have illustrated how good communication has thwarted a child molester's attempts to break the rules and to reoffend. Also, therapists have a strong investment in seeing that the child molesters they treat actually benefit from therapy and do not reoffend against children. In most instances, the therapist knows that talking with the offender's wife, relatives, and employer can yield crucial information about how treatment is going. Those who know the offender on a personal basis can help the therapist by providing information about the offender.

There is also broad consensus that an offender in treatment must acknowledge his sexual misconduct. A survey spanning four states was recently reported in *Federal Probation;* it found, "With few exceptions, therapists interviewed at the sites stated that they would not accept into their programs offenders who absolutely denied sexual conduct with children. They firmly believed that individuals who deny abuse are not amenable to treatment" (research by Chapman & Smith, reported in Lurigio, Jones, & Smith, 1995, p. 74).

As awareness has grown that treating child molesters is a specialized field, therapists take increasing pride in applying what they know in a skillful and responsible manner. A considerable body of research, law, and clinical experience has been amassed in the past decade emphasizing good communication. This means that the therapist can provide important information to those who know the offender and who are working with him to make his treatment successful. What kinds of information can the therapist provide? Perhaps most important, the therapist can provide

1. The basic rules the offender is expected to follow
2. The offender's sexual history and pattern of sexual offenses
3. The situations that present the greatest danger for reoffense

To communicate effectively with the therapist, it will help the reader to have an understanding of the sex offender evaluation report, some idea of the methodologies and techniques that therapists use with child molesters, and an explanation of some of the basic terminology used. As in the previous chapter, suggestions will be given about how to tap into the therapist's information on the offender and how to assess whether adequate steps are being taken to ensure the safety of your own and others' children.

It is necessary to remind the reader that no individual book or article in the mental health or corrections field gives a complete definition or description of sex offender treatment, or conclusive answers about how child molesters should be treated. D. Richard Laws (1989) discussed this in his book on relapse prevention, which is only one kind of treatment aimed at child molesters:

> You must remember that relapse prevention (RP) as a treatment procedure is in its infancy and that RP as applied to sex offenders is approximately postnatal. . . . I would suggest that readers closely examine all assessment and treatment procedures . . . in order to decide which components will be best suited to your setting. Build your RP program around what will work best for you. . . . There is no definitive evidence, here or anywhere else, that RP or any other treatment is effective over the long haul with this difficult clientele. (p. viii)

Treatment of sex offenders not only is complex but also is changing dramatically. This is not to say that certain ideas or concepts are not widely accepted in the field. Be mindful, however, that individual therapists may have their own working definitions of concepts and treatment techniques that may differ from the discussion here. Even in the professional literature, major terms are defined in different ways. *What is most important is that the child molester not be allowed to obstruct good, clear communication between the therapist and others who know and work with the molester. If important questions arise about what is going on in therapy, ask the therapist directly for his or her explanation. Direct communication is always advisable and can increase the odds for successful treatment.*

The Sex Offender Evaluation Report

The sex offender evaluation report is valuable because it shows the wide variety of information available to the therapist. The sex offender evaluation report is unique in the mental health field. Only rarely are other kinds of mental health evaluations as thorough and exhaustive in their investigation of an individual's background. This is what makes the contents of the report so useful to you. The comprehensive sex offender evaluation report can help unlock the secrecy that has been perpetrated by the offender.

Briefly, the best sex offender evaluation report will contain the same personal history information that is found in the Presentence Investigation Report (PSI). The two reports are remarkably similar in many respects. However, there is usually additional information found in the sex offender evaluation report that is not found in the PSI. In most cases, the therapist is able to spend far more time in interviews with the offender and in gathering collateral reports, including psychological testing, than a probation officer could spend. Furthermore, the therapist is usually more clinically experienced and spends more time exploring the offender's sexual history. For these and other reasons, the sex offender evaluation report often contains a greater abundance of information that will be useful to others than the PSI.

What goes into the report? First, the report will usually contain detailed information regarding the sexual crime for which the offender was evaluated. Second, the report will include extensive information regarding all other forms of sexual activity the offender is known to have engaged in, including, possibly, crimes for which the offender has never been prosecuted. Often, an offender may have been involved in sexual crimes, for example, during childhood, but legal reasons and the lapse of time make it impractical to consider prosecution at the present time. Third, the report may include a detailed description of how the offender planned his sexual assault, how he groomed his victim and groomed others as well, how he set up and carried out the crime, and how he covered up his crime after it occurred. Finally, the report will often contain admissions and confessions by the offender to the therapist that the offender has never made known to anyone else.

It is not uncommon for the therapist to coax admissions and disclosures from the offender of which the wife, family members, even the offender's attorney, had no prior knowledge. For under-standable reasons, the offender may resist a completely honest disclosure to his wife but is willing to discuss his sexual history with his therapist. He is acutely embarrassed, ashamed, and fearful of being ostracized from the family forever if the wife and family members discover what he has been keeping secret all of his life. The skillful therapist recognizes this reluctance and has developed inter-viewing techniques to ease the offender into disclosing more and more about himself.

Therapists take many steps to verify the offender's truthfulness. These include giving psychological tests, reviewing police reports and criminal history records, conferring with probation officers, and consulting with those who know the offender on a personal basis. Furthermore, many therapists inform the offender that because a polygraph examination will be required, it is best that full disclosure be made during the evaluation process. The offender's belief in the polygraph examination can influence him to make far more admis-sions than he might otherwise be inclined to make. This is generally considered the greatest value of the polygraph examination, rather than whether it ever reveals the "absolute" truth. Research by Jan Hindman (*NDAA Bulletin,* 1988) confirms this point. She found that when not required to take a lie detector test, 67% of sex offenders claimed to have been abused as children. When they were told that they would have to take a lie detector test, only 29% of sex offenders claimed that they were abused as children (these results are described in the *National District Attorney's Association Bulletin,* 1988, pp. 1-3).

Gathering information from many sources is essential to a well-prepared sex offender evaluation report. Using many different sources helps persuade the offender to abandon the secrecy and dishonesty that would otherwise negate the positive effects of ther-apy. As with the PSI, weak evaluators rely only on what the offender tells the therapist. Such evaluations are of no value to anyone who truly wants to understand the offender. Previous chapters have described the offender's inclination to minimize, deceive, and, in short, to lie. When a report relies entirely on the offender's view of events (i.e., his self-report), the validity of the report is limited because of the good possibility that the offender is continuing to lie to the therapist. The importance of verifying the truthfulness of what an offender says cannot be overstated, whether in the evaluation process or during the course of treatment. Many noted experts share this view. Judith Herman (1990) writes, "when a treatment program minimizes the importance of the actual sexual behavior and does not provide any concrete method for monitoring it, failures are likely to go unrecognized, sometimes with disastrous consequences" (p. 184). Noted researchers and clinicians Gene Abel and colleagues (1978) share this view, stating,

> In recent years, however, it has become apparent that we must not only rely on this self-report, but also rely on concurring opinions. . . . Although some sexual aggressives accurately report their sexual behaviors and sexual arousal patterns, many either cannot or will not identify the extent of their sexual arousal or their need for control over their sexual behavior. Therapists thus relying exclusively on verbal reports in working with sexual aggressives are making decisions with limited or invalid information in many cases. (p. 318)

The recommendation not to rely exclusively upon what the offender tells the therapist is not to say that what the offender says about himself cannot be extremely useful. His own words help reveal the level of his denial or minimization. Also, some offenders are sometimes quite truthful in disclosing some of their personal and sexual history. They may reveal problems no one else would know about. From a practical standpoint, no evaluation or treatment can take place without the self-report.

A good sex offender evaluation report relies on police reports and victim statements, information from the wife and other family members, information from the corrections agency, a report from the victim's therapist if the victim is in therapy, information from the offender's employer, a polygraph examination, and plethysmograph information (an examination technique to be discussed below), and the results of psychological testing. Potential problems exist with any source of information. A psychological test may be invalid, a victim's statement may overstate or understate the nature of the abuse, an employer may overemphasize work-related problems or minimize problems that actually exist. Despite these potential problems, when many different sources are used, the offender is viewed from many perspectives. This approach increases the odds for a more accurate picture of the offender.

Thoroughness is an essential characteristic of a sex offender evaluation report. Thoroughness means that all important areas of the offender's life history have been evaluated and covered in the report wherever appropriate and that the report does not contain significant gaps in any areas. A report may properly dispense with a discussion of some areas, for example, military history or alcohol consumption, if those areas played no significant role in the offender's personal and sexual history. On the other hand, a report that failed to discuss those areas when they were a significant aspect of the offender's life would be seriously flawed. Because the safety and welfare of children may hang in the balance, such omissions should give rise to concern that the best job has not been done in evaluating the offender. It would be difficult to place as much trust in a therapist who demonstrated a failure to be thorough, because the therapist may also fail to impose adequate controls over the offender, which could potentially lead to reoffense.

Another essential component of a sex offender evaluation report is objectivity. Objectivity means that the report includes the verifiable facts or data upon which descriptions and conclusions about the offender are based. Data can include a wide variety of specific information, including the number of known victims, the nature of the sexual assaults, the known criminal convictions, the results of testing procedures, and specific important events in the offender's life. Without these specifics, there is no way to tell whether the therapist has exercised reasonable judgment. A therapist may feel, for example, that an offender with a history of 500 obscene phone calls, 500 incidents of indecent exposure, over 5 years of daily abuse of illegal drugs and alcohol, and a trail of a dozen victims is safe to be treated in the community. Readers, however, may not agree that such an offender can be treated safely in the community. A mother may not feel her children are safe around the offender under any circumstances. A judge might conclude that such an offender should be locked up. A probation officer might conclude that the offender should receive maximum attention from the moment he is assigned to the officer's caseload.

But if the therapist fails to provide the actual numbers of obscene phone calls, indecent exposures, the extent of drug abuse, and the number of victims, those relying on the report cannot make informed decisions for their own purposes. They are left making their decision based solely on the opinion of the therapist. What a therapist believes about a particular child molester may be at odds with what a prosecutor, a judge, or a mother of the victim(s) believes. All parties should be provided the data so that they can arrive at their own opinions. Working with child molesters, at a minimum, involves the combined knowledge, judgment, and expertise of as many persons as possible. Therefore, it is essential that the report include the actual numbers of known behaviors when they are available and not just opinions and conclusions of the evaluator. For a complete overview of the sex offender evaluation report and how to judge its contents, the reader is referred to O'Connell, Leberg, and Donaldson's (1990) *Working With Sex Offenders: Guidelines for Therapist Selection.*

Assessment and Treatment Tools

The specific techniques and strategies used by therapists to evaluate and treat offenders are currently evolving as therapists gain experience and research improves on the treatment of child molesters. Because of this, there is no definitive list or description of essential treatment methods. What is accepted for use by therapists today may be obsolete a few years from now. There is growing acceptance, however, of certain broad approaches to treatment. These approaches deserve discussion for three reasons. First, an offender can easily distort what these procedures are in a deliberate effort to confuse friends and acquaintances to gain their sympathy. In so doing, he can wrongly and dishonestly persuade others that he is justified in quitting a treatment program. Second, certain treatment techniques for child molesters have become widely accepted and are used almost universally (although they are identified by different names). Finally, knowing something about therapy in a general sense will help take the mystery out of sex offender treatment and enhance communication between the therapist and nonprofessionals.

The Plethysmograph Examination

Because the penile plethysmograph examination is one of those techniques that might be misunderstood or used by the offender to manipulate others, an overview may be helpful. Its use is of increasing importance, and noted expert H. E. Barbaree (1990) writes that the penile plethysmograph "has become an important part of a complete clinical assessment of sexual offenders" (p. 116). During the procedure, the offender is placed alone in a private room. The offender places a flexible band or "sleeve" around the shaft of his penis. The flexible band measures changes in the offender's penis. Some procedures measure the penis's diameter, others its volume. The sleeve is attached to an instrument that records the changes. If the penis becomes larger or erect, the recorded changes suggest that the offender is sexually aroused. As the penis becomes flaccid (and its size or volume is reduced), the results suggest that the offender is less sexually aroused (see Laws & Osborn, 1983, for a complete description of the penile plethysmograph laboratory).

While measurements are taken, the offender is shown a series of slides and/or listens to a series of audio tapes that describe a variety of potentially arousing situations. These may or may not be sexually arousing to the offender. Some slides typically involve children of different ages to measure the child molester's degree of sexual arousal to children. Other scenes involve adults, and some scenes depict violence to measure whether the offender is sexually aroused by acts of violence. The offender's responses to each scene is recorded and the examiner is able to measure and compare which situations are more and which situations are less sexually arousing to that particular offender.

Making accurate objective measurements of the child molester's sexual arousal patterns is essential for several reasons. First, the measurements provide a guide for the therapist, indicating which areas in the offender's sexual life need special attention. Second, the measurements can help suggest how strict the controls should be over the offender's life if he is allowed to remain in the community. Finally, with the therapist's guidance, the data from the plethysmograph examination can help others understand what precautions they may wish to take with the offender. If an offender, for example, has a very great arousal to very young children (toddlers), a mother may want to take exceptional measures to ensure that the offender is never around her own or others' young children unless the child molester is carefully supervised.

As with any treatment tool, there are limitations to the penile plethysmograph. Its use should not create a false sense of security if it is learned that an offender's arousal pattern to children is low. Nor should it be considered a panacea if the offender learns through therapy to reduce his arousal to children through behavioral treatment techniques. Such a reduction in arousal may last only as long as the offender continues to use techniques learned in his treatment program. If he does not continue to use the exercises learned, sexual arousal to children may return over time. Many questions about the treatment techniques to reduce deviant sexual arousal remain unanswered. Ultimately, when the penile plethysmograph is used the therapist should be consulted regarding what the results mean with respect to the individual offender and his family.

Ideally, the penile plethysmograph can help the therapist direct treatment in areas where the offender has highest deviant arousal. It can provide a more objective (measurable) means to assess whether the offender can learn to reduce his sexual attraction in those areas that are most problematic. In theory, if the offender can reduce his attraction to young children, for example, he will be less likely to molest them. As with any examination, it is not infallible. Researchers and clinicians alike note that offenders can deliberately reduce their measurable arousal to create the appearance that they are not aroused by children when in fact they really are. This is extremely important for clinicians to remember because the plethysmograph examination is dependent upon the full cooperation of the offender (Pithers & Laws, 1988).

If the offender describes the penile plethysmograph as a bizarre, painful, or reprehensible testing technique and offers it as a pretext for quitting treatment, one should consider seriously whether the offender is manipulating the listener, and the therapist should be consulted directly. Although it is an evaluation technique that the general public knows little about, the plethysmograph examination is one of the profession's most widely researched and thoroughly discussed treatment techniques. Generally speaking, those who use it strive to do so in a completely professional manner.

The Polygraph Examination

A second valuable tool used by an increasing number of therapists is the polygraph examination. When conducted by a trained and experienced examiner, this tool is quite valuable in assessing the offender's truthfulness in the evaluation process and his compliance with rules during the course of treatment. Nearly all therapists who use the polygraph examination are fully aware that polygraphs are not foolproof. They are only one more tool, but a significant tool, in unlocking secrecy and deception by child molesters.

The polygraph examination is not a "lie detector" in the strictest sense. Rather, the polygraph instrument records very small changes in a person's rate and depth of breathing, blood pressure, and perspiration. The examiner is trained to tell, based on those changes, whether the person is trying to deceive the examiner. The polygraph examination procedure with child molesters usually begins with a preexamination interview. During this interview, the legality of the polygraph is discussed and questions are raised about whether, for example, the person has medical problems that would influence the results. An atmosphere is established to persuade the person being tested that the examination is effective (Office of Technology Assessment, 1983). In the case of a child molester, the examiner may then review with the offender the information that the offender has previously provided to his therapist about his sexual history or his cooperation in therapy. The examiner records the answers carefully. Then, while the polygraph machine records the physiological changes in the offender's pulse, breathing, and perspiration, the examiner asks the offender certain specific questions derived from the preexamination interview. Finally, the examiner interprets the results to determine if the offender has tried to be deceptive.

Whether the results of polygraph examinations can be trusted is the focus of considerable debate, especially among convicted sex offenders who may have tried to persuade everybody they know that they are completely innocent. They may argue that polygraphs have wrongly shown innocent men to be guilty.

Although polygraphs are not universally accepted by the therapeutic community, the results of the U.S. Office of Technology Assessment (OTA) have lent considerable weight to their usefulness in criminal investigations. The OTA investigated research that had been conducted on the use of polygraph examinations in a variety of situations, both criminal and noncriminal. Although the OTA found that there is no scientific evidence supporting the validity (in the strict scientific sense of the word) of polygraph examinations in noncriminal preemployment interviews, they discussed the usefulness that polygraph examinations had in criminal investigations in their report. As other writers have noted,

> The use of the polygraph for the investigation of crimes is a well established practice. Known errors in field use are exceedingly rare. Where examinees are found to be deceptive during testing, the confession rate is consistently high. . . . Moreover, there is nothing about the polygraph technique that is likely to cause a false confession. (Ansley & Garwood, 1984, p. 3)

In most cases, if the offender is found to be attempting deception, the therapist discusses the results with the offender. Frequently, under carefully questioning by the therapist, the offender admits that he was attempting to conceal some additional aspect of his sexual history that he was afraid to admit. Or, he admits that he violated some rule that he hoped he could conceal from the therapist. In evaluating child molesters, the strength of the polygraph examination lies not in its proven scientific validity but in the offender's belief in its capacity to detect his deceptions. In other words, it causes many offenders to admit things that they would otherwise have tried to hide.

Controls

Controls are rules that the therapist makes to reduce the offender's opportunities to molest children. The therapist tries to identify those situations and behaviors that are considered risky for the offender and then establishes rules to reduce that risk. Depending on the circumstances of each case, the conditions may be quite numerous. Over 20 have been observed by this author being used in some programs. Below is a list of typical controls. It illustrates the variety of conditions and circumstances that therapists feel are important for controlling offenders (for a more exhaustive list, see O'Connell et al., 1990; Pithers et al., 1989). There is no standard list of controls for all child molesters because offenders differ greatly one from another. A high-risk situation for one may not be a high-risk situation for another. There are, however, many controls that are commonly applied to most offenders.

1. You shall have no contact with minor children without the therapist's written approval.
2. You shall not be employed in a position that places you in contact with or control over children.
3. You shall have no contact with any minors without the supervision of an adult chaperone who is fully informed of your offenses and the rules of your treatment program, and

who is approved in advance by your therapist and probation officer.

4. You shall not date, live with, or otherwise align yourself with any woman with minor children without the prior written approval of your therapist.

5. You shall not enter the family residence at any time without the prior written approval of your therapist and probation officer.

6. You shall not become involved as a supervisor, instructor, leader, or participant in any youth-oriented organizations.

7. You shall not use or possess alcohol.

8. You shall not use any illegal drugs.

9. You shall not participate in recreational activities involving children.

10. You shall not telephone or write to or contact in any other way your victim(s) or other children without the advance approval of your therapist.

Treatment

This section describes some methods of treating child molesters that are currently in use. The description certainly does not include all of the approaches that deserve attention. Information is presented here so that the reader will have at least a basic familiarity with some of those methods used and, therefore, not be totally in the dark when communicating with the offender, the therapist, or the probation officer. There is no substitute for asking the therapist to clarify any terminology that is not understood. It is also quite helpful to ask the therapist to explain what books and other material the offender is required to read, because reading such materials is a growing part of child molester treatment. Also, it might be helpful for you to ask the therapist for additional readings to help you to understand and work more effectively with the offender.

Behavioral Treatment

Behavioral treatment in its most basic form involves the systematic use of positive and negative reinforcers or consequences of some kind either to encourage or discourage certain behaviors, feelings, or sexual arousal patterns. Behavioral treatment includes a variety of techniques. One technique involves the offender imagining some deviant sexual act until he begins to feel sexually aroused, and then to imagine a powerful negative experience. This technique is sometimes called *covert sensitization.* Another technique involves the offender imagining, viewing slides, or listening to audio tapes of a high-risk sexual situation (such as playing with children in bathing suits at a beach) and then having the offender smell some foul odor, such as ammonia. This is called *olfactory conditioning. Masturbation satiation* requires the offender to masturbate to ejaculation while having an appropriate sexual fantasy, such as intercourse with an adult partner, after which the offender must continue masturbating to a deviant fantasy for as long as 2 hours. The purpose of this technique is to decrease the sexual attraction of the deviant stimuli (e.g., to children as sexual objects). These are only a few behavioral techniques that, on the surface, sound strange but are based on well-developed behavioral techniques for the treatment of child molesters.

An offender could easily distort or manipulate the lay person into believing the treatment program was unprofessional by describing treatment methods such as these, when in reality the treatment methods could reflect state-of-the-art, clinically sound, and fully professional treatment practices. Behavioral treatment methods such as these are being studied, reported, and discussed in professional journals. When used in conjunction with the penile plethysmograph, the therapist and the offender can more objectively measure whether the offender's sexual arousal to children is decreasing.

At present, there are no long-term studies demonstrating that behavioral treatment will be effective years after treatment has ended. However, if the offender is well motivated to continue using behavioral techniques after he completes therapy, it appears reasonable that he can effectively alter undesirable sexual arousal patterns in the long run. For a summary of many different behavioral treatment methods, see Schwartz (1988b).

Marital/Family Treatment

Another approach to treatment allows the offender's wife and sometimes even children to be involved. There is a strong movement among therapists to involve members of the family in the treatment process (McFarlane, 1983). This treatment strategy provides an excellent opportunity for the family members to learn what the offender's patterns are so that they can stop problems before they escalate (stopping such patterns will be discussed more thoroughly under Relapse Prevention later in this chapter). Family therapy can also help reduce secrecy, especially when children learn that it is both safe and important for them not to keep sexual abuse a secret. In family therapy, family members learn to communicate more effectively and to make better plans for the future. Marital counseling can help the husband and wife learn to talk openly about sexuality so that they can have more satisfying sex lives together. There are many other issues that can be discussed in marital therapy, including recognizing and stopping the use of anger and intimidation to control and coerce family members.

Group Treatment

In addition to individual treatment, therapists often work with child molesters in groups, which is one of the most common, if not the most important, kind of treatment for child molesters (McFarlane, 1983). In the group setting, child molesters discuss their sexual crimes and their interpersonal and sexual problems openly with one another. This approach can help reduce the child molester's defensiveness and denial of sexual problems. It can also help identify and correct the offender's multitude of erroneous beliefs about himself, about victims, and about other people. Erroneous beliefs are often referred to as *thinking errors* or *cognitive distortions*. For example, the child molester may claim and sincerely believe that the victim enjoyed being molested, that molesting the victim was the best way to educate her about sexual abuse, or that the family benefited overall from his sexual activities with the children. Although most people can see the obvious falsehood of such beliefs, many child molesters persist in believing such ideas to be true. Group treatment, including discussion and responses from other offenders, helps the child molester learn to recognize such faulty ideas and explore sexual abuse more rationally.

There are many different views on why group treatment is helpful with child molesters. Some practitioners believe that in the group setting there are other persons (i.e., other offenders) to scrutinize each offender's denial, minimization, lies, blaming, and manipulations. They can often point out such behaviors in ways that successfully encourage the offender to take a more honest look at himself. Also, the group setting helps child molesters recognize and confront the behaviors in others that they have had difficulty accepting in themselves. Thus, group treatment can lead to greater self-understanding. It is sometimes easier for the child molester to look honestly at his own sexual problems when he spends time with others who have already been through the painful process of admitting that they have a sexual problem. Finally, group treatment can also be a more efficient use of the therapist's time and help reduce the cost of treatment for the individual offender.

Relapse Prevention

Relapse prevention is a method of treatment that helps the child molester identify the patterns of events that he goes through leading up to an actual sexual assault. It then teaches him strategies that he can use to stop the pattern from continuing to the point of an assault. Those who know the offender can aid in this process by helping him recognize when he has entered such a reoffense pattern and support his efforts to break the pattern (Pithers, 1988). This "external supervisory dimension" of relapse prevention, according to William Pithers and colleagues,

entails the instruction of collateral contacts on the principles
of relapse prevention. All members of the collateral network
(e.g., spouse, employer, co-workers, friends) are informed
about apparently irrelevant decisions, high-risk situations,
lapses, the abstinence violation effect, and offense precursors. . . . Informing the offender's extended network about
his offense precursors destroys the secrecy necessary for
commission of sexual aggression. (Pithers et al., 1989, pp.
306-307)

For example, Alex, described at the beginning of this chapter,
had a distinct and elaborate relapse pattern that he repeated over
and over. The full details of Alex's pattern included leaving alcohol
in the truck; getting too busy with work to wash his truck; arguing
with his wife in the mornings about the lunches she fixed for him;
cluttering the cab of his truck with tools, including a screwdriver
placed handily on the dashboard; going to bars to meet women
rather than going home to face his wife after their morning argument; offering women, and sometimes young girls, rides; "getting
lost"; and forcibly raping the women.

The following is Jim's story, which illustrates many points where
the pattern can be broken. One of Jim's relapse patterns (offenders
can have more than one) included inviting his friends over for the
weekend without conferring with his wife, Mary, about having guests
and then demanding that Mary entertain the friends (whom she did
not particularly care for in the first place). He would insist that she
cook for them and baby-sit their children. Then Jim would stage a
loud argument with Mary in front of the guests, claiming she was a
poor hostess because there wasn't enough food for everyone. When
the guests left early, he would blame her for spoiling the weekend
and demand that she clean up the mess from the company entirely
alone while he drank beer and watched television. He would continue to argue with her until she developed a migraine headache and
went to bed. Then, Jim would send the children to bed, threatening
them if they made any noises, while he stayed up alone to drink
alcohol. Finally he would go into the eldest daughter's bedroom to

apologize for the scene he had made, he would cry, try to soothe her when she became upset, and ultimately molest the daughter, claiming she owed him something because no one else in the family treated him right.

Once Jim and his friends and family members recognize the offender's pattern, they can help stop or interrupt the pattern before it leads to molestation of the daughter. Inviting friends over on weekends would be the first sign for Jim and Mary, especially if Jim invites anyone without discussing it and making mutually agreeable plans with Mary. Drinking alcohol and loud arguments are similar warning signs. If they occur, Mary, by prior agreement, can ask Jim for a few moments alone to remind him that he is entering his relapse cycle. If the guests know about Jim's pattern of sexual molestation, they themselves can play an active role in interrupting Jim's cycle of relapsing by making sure that Mary has been consulted about the social occasion.

For some therapists, informing the wife, employer, relatives, and friends about the offender's pattern of offending is so important that the offender is *required* to sign confidentiality waivers so that these individuals can be informed, because informing those who know the offender can contribute so significantly to everyone's safety. It becomes doubly important when one considers the fact that child molesters are not generally reliable in reporting their own problems and behaviors to their therapists or the group. Being sure that members of the collateral network are fully knowledgeable about the offender is vital to the safety of potential victims (Pithers et al., 1989).

Relapse prevention alone will not solve all of the problems that may exist. For example, if Jim's wife is not given the counseling necessary to learn to be assertive with Jim, she may succumb to the same errors that were made in the past. Often, the wife and children will need a reliable support network that they can count on in times of crisis. Jim, too, may need someone he can call so that he can escape the dangerous situation he finds himself in. Jim's leaving the home and visiting such a knowledgeable friend is an *escape strategy*. Escape strategies are essential for relapse prevention to work. The reader can see that relapse prevention can be an effective intervention technique, but it requires the cooperation of everyone, including careful planning with a therapist.

Social Skills Training

Another significant trend in counseling for child molesters involves assessing how the offender has difficulty in getting along with adults. Some offenders have a difficult time making friends; others can make friends but have difficulty maintaining those relationships. Some offenders have difficulty talking openly about sex and some are too embarrassed to admit what they would like sexually, even when it is acceptable to themselves, their spouse, and their therapist. Some offenders have difficulty handling conflicts at work and others have difficulty talking to relatives without feeling frustrated and angry.

In social skills training, the therapist identifies those areas in which the offender may have trouble in social situations and teaches him how to handle those situations more successfully. This training is especially important when one considers the widely held belief that child molesters often gravitate toward children because they are unable to maintain successful and satisfying relationships with adults. If they are unable to feel good about being with adults, they are more likely to turn their attention to children, especially if they feel less threatened by interaction with children. Anna Salter (1988) writes,

> Given the social and sexual nature of human beings, an offender who is unable to meet his social and sexual needs with adults will almost invariably relapse to meeting those needs with children. The finest behavioral modification program to decrease deviant arousal will fail to prevent relapse unless the offender's ability to meet his needs in appropriate ways finds some success. Social and communication skills are key to the offender's ability to initiate and maintain adult relationships. (p. 122)

How to Gather Information
From the Therapist

If your husband, relative, or friend is involved in a specialized sexual deviance treatment program, there is a considerable amount of useful information that can be made available to you. With it, you can make decisions to better ensure the safety of yourself and your children. The information can also assist you in helping the offender stay out of trouble. The sex offender evaluation report, described above, has a great deal of such information. Gathering information does not stop, however, once the evaluation has been completed. Therapists continue to learn more and more about the offender over the course of treatment. Gradually, as more is learned, the therapist develops better ideas about the offender and how to deal with his problems. In most cases, the sexual deviance therapist is the best source for information about the child molester and the best person to suggest how others should deal with him generally and in specific high-risk situations.

As with requesting information from the corrections agency, the written permission of the offender is necessary before the therapist can release information about the offender. The therapist will have forms that the offender can sign authorizing the release of information to you. The therapist may already have required that the offender sign such a release. If not, asking the offender to sign such a release should be all that is required. As previously noted, if the offender is not willing to authorize the therapist to talk freely to you, extreme caution should be exercised in dealing with him.

Authorizing the release of information does not mean that the therapist is going to answer every question that you may have. The job of the therapist is, in part, to know what kinds of information are needed by different people in the offender's life. Therefore, the offender does not need to fear that all information will be released to anyone indiscriminately. Therapists are usually very careful in how they handle such sensitive information.

You do not need to know technical terms such as those in the psychological diagnoses of the offender. It is, of course, legitimate to ask the therapist for information that bears directly on your own and your children's safety. It is very rare for a therapist to refuse such a request if the offender has signed the appropriate release. However, the therapist should not be expected to answer every question. Therapists can only offer their best judgment, which is their best educated guess. Ultimately, protecting children from the offender rests on the shoulders of their caretakers, that is, their mother, grandparents, and other guardians.

Generally speaking, therapists welcome the opportunity to share information with others because doing so increases the chances for a safe and successful treatment. When more people know about the offender and know how to intervene if problems arise, the chances for reoffense and recidivism are reduced. In addition, talking with others, not only wives but employers, parents, friends, and ministers for example, provides the therapist with valuable information. This information can be vital to treating the offender safely.

It is customary for therapists to release their sex offender evaluation reports to other professional mental health counselors, such as victim therapists, because they know that those therapists will treat all written reports and other information in a professional manner. They can trust the other counselors to treat the information discreetly; to interpret data, diagnoses, and opinions correctly; and to work for the successful outcome of everyone involved. For that reason, the best way to gather information about the offender you know is through your own therapist if you are in treatment, unless the sex offender's therapist is willing to release a report directly to you. It is recommended that you gather any and all information that you can possibly obtain. Based on the experience of the author as a probation officer, it is more often the case that trouble develops from people not knowing enough, rather than knowing too much. Based on experience and trends in the treatment field as described earlier, it is much better to make the effort to find out everything possible so that you won't be left making decisions in the dark.

Some therapists are willing to meet individually with or invite spouses, chaperones, employers, ministers, and others to participate in counseling sessions with the offender. These meetings allow a freer exchange of information among all parties and help clear up misunderstandings. For the wife and other interested parties, meeting with the therapist and the offender together is perhaps the best way to learn about the offender and should be taken advantage of whenever the opportunity arises.

Some therapists also provide for the wives of offenders to participate in their own group meetings and treatment programs, during which they can learn about the multitude of problems related to sexual offenses and how they can plan for a successful family life, especially if the family decides to reunite. It may be initially painful to enter into a wives' group, but it provides the support of other people, usually wives and/or mothers of victims, who have already been through the experience and who can share useful ideas and important information.

When conferring with the therapist, one should at minimum attempt to learn (a) the basic criminal and sexual history known about the offender, (b) his pattern of sexual offending, and (c) the conditions and controls required by the therapist. The known criminal and sexual history (for crimes that have been both prosecuted and not) is important for a wife to determine the level of involvement she wants with the offender. A wife would be justifiably worried about staying with an offender if she learned that hers was the third marital relationship with the offender in which he sexually abused children. Similarly, a wife would want to know from the therapist if the offender had a history of domestic violence, even if he was never formally prosecuted or convicted.

Understanding the offender's pattern of sexual offense, especially the grooming process, is important because it can help the wife and others draw the line when the offender's behavior becomes questionable. For example, the therapist can help the wife see how the offender used anger or intimidation to manipulate her and can advise her about how to react if the offender makes similar attempts again.

Knowing the controls placed on the offender will help everyone understand what situations the therapist is most concerned about. The therapist may feel that use of alcohol or drugs is totally prohibited for the offender and any known violations of this stipulation should be reported immediately because drinking and using drugs are considered high-risk behaviors. Or, the therapist may feel that any contact, even, for example, talking with neighborhood children over the backyard fence, is a serious situation that should likewise be reported to the therapist. A therapist may have a policy that two unexcused absences from treatment are grounds for termination. In such situations, because a jail sentence may result, everyone should be concerned about the offender making up excuses to miss treatment appointments.

There are many other matters beyond those already mentioned that can be discussed with the therapist. These matters depend in large part on individual circumstances. One is what information the therapist would like to receive from you. Others are the anticipated length of treatment, what "homework" is assigned to the offender, and what suggested readings the therapist has for either the offender or other family members who are interested in learning more.

Usually, the therapist wants to know whether there are any major changes occurring in the circumstances of the family. If any children are returning to the family, for example, or perhaps returning from foster homes, or if nieces or nephews are staying with the family the therapist can make better treatment plans by taking these changes into account. Similarly, if the wife or children have been in a victims' treatment program and are now leaving treatment, knowing about it will help the therapist assess the offender's treatment needs and make future plans. If the wife decides to divorce the offender, knowing about this as soon as possible would assist in counseling the offender during the readjustment period.

It should be remembered, however, that the focus of treatment for the offender must always be the offender himself, except in those circumstances in which family members are directly involved in treatment. Gathering information from the therapist should not become a pretext for the wife or others to become involved therapeutically with the therapist, unless the therapist suggests it. In cases where the wife feels that her own needs are not being met or that her questions are not being answered to her satisfaction, she should find her own therapist, one who is knowledgeable and trained in the area of sexual abuse and who has the time to dedicate to her unique situation and needs. She should not try to get counseling for her own problems by asking repetitious or unending questions of the offender's therapist. Time is precious in treating offenders. Usually, the therapist has established fairly clear therapeutic goals. It is the therapist's job to set those goals and implement a treatment strategy to accomplish them. Doing this requires considerable professional judgment. Although the wife may feel that other matters are more pressing and more important, except in unusual circumstances the therapist must use the time and energy available to address the problems and treatment goals that have been established for the offender.

Despite the tremendous improvement in the rigor of sex offender evaluation and treatment over the past decade, there may still be questions regarding the adequacy and safety of a specific treatment program. In this author's experience, there are specific times when caution is called for. The first of these is any program's failure to complete a thorough and objective evaluation of the offender.[1] Here, there are many reasons for concern, the principal reason being that if a thorough and objective assessment has not been done, the program may lack sufficient information to set the necessary controls over the offender to protect potential victims. For example, the program may be treating the offender for one known incident of child molestation against a 7-year-old girl and appropriately advise you that he should not be around minor females. If a thorough evaluation was not completed, the therapist might remain unaware that the offender is also a risk to male children and has perhaps molested boys in the past. The story of Alex at the beginning of this chapter illustrates how such a situation can arise. In Alex's case, the combination of an untrained therapist and an inexperienced probation officer resulted in a situation that could have proven fatal for the next victim.

Caution is also advisable whenever treatment programs speak glowingly of their ability to successfully treat or cure offenders, especially in a short period of time. Generally speaking, successful treatment means that the offender has completed the various facets of the treatment program required by the therapist. This is different from saying the offender will not repeat his offense or that he is cured or is unlikely to molest children again. As researcher David Finkelhor (1986) writes,

> It cannot be said that [any researcher's] recidivism study provides strong evidence in favor of the positive effects of treatment. This, however, does not mean that treatment is ineffective. For one thing, there are many studies showing treatment "successes." . . . Unfortunately, the outcome measures in these treatment studies have been such things as attitude change, physiological arousal measures, and very short-term self-reports of offending behavior. The fact that these measures show improvement is encouraging, but not nearly as important as the question of whether or not they reoffend in the long run. . . . The fairest judgment at the present time is that good treatment programs for child molesters have not been evaluated yet in terms of their ability to reduce long-term recidivism. (p. 137)

Finkelhor's caution about sex offender treatment programs does not mean that treatment is not worthwhile. Practical experience suggests that treatment can provide significant benefits to the offender, the family, and the community. Certainly, the information learned about the offender from the evaluation process alone is a significant step forward for wives and others needing to make important decisions about their children's safety. Judith Herman (1990) compares treatment of sex offenders with treatment of alcoholics:

> [Alcohol] rehabilitation . . . has been shown to require at least 3 years of sustained abstinence. A similar time course should be anticipated for recovery even with cooperative, well-motivated sex offenders. Current claims of successful treatment outcome after 12 weeks . . . or 6 months . . . are unlikely to be borne out with careful follow-up. (p. 187)

Another reason to be cautious about a sex offender treatment program arises if the therapist makes specific predictions about any offender's risk not to reoffend. At present, there is no known way to assess reliably the risk that any individual child molester presents. For that matter, there is no accepted way of telling which criminals in general, whether they are child molesters or other violent offenders, are likely to repeat their violent acts. Making predictions of risk is a dilemma that continues to plague the entire criminal justice field.

> The difficulties [of mental health workers making predictions about offender dangerousness in criminal proceedings] could rather easily be resolved if some reliable instruments were readily available for the prediction of violent behaviors. Unfortunately, such instruments do not exist; and it is doubtful that they will ever attain the degree of reliability and accuracy that might be desired. (National Institute of Mental Health, 1981, p. iii; see also Prentky et al., 1989, for a discussion of an effort to understand the antecedents of sexual aggression)

Any therapist who refers to the child molester as being "no longer a risk to children" should, therefore, be viewed with suspicion. Currently, there are no significant professional books, journal articles, or published research reports that describe any child molester treatment methods that can entirely eliminate the risk presented by convicted child molesters. Even the radical medical procedure of castration is not a 100% effective cure (Starup, 1972). Instead, most knowledgeable professionals talk about offenders being similar to alcoholics in their recovery process. They are never cured but are rather in recovery for the rest of their lives.

Another reason to be cautious about a sex offender treatment program arises when the therapist fails to establish clear and carefully designed controls over the offender's behavior. Examples of such controls were given earlier. Failure to establish controls suggests that the therapist does not recognize the offender's lack of self-control and the important part that external controls play during treatment. By breaking society's rules against child sexual abuse, the offender has shown that he lacks the judgment and self-control to keep from harming children. An external control agent is necessary, and the therapist must play a significant part in establishing controls over the offender.

Similarly, caution is advisable whenever the therapist relies on nothing more than the controls imposed by the court. It is a mistake in general, and a critical error in terms of community safety, for a therapist to assume that a judge is able to decide what controls are necessary. Unfortunately, judges frequently lack sufficient information about the individual offender to determine all of the necessary rules that an offender should be required to follow. Specifying the exact conditions governing all of the offender's behavior is, practically speaking, beyond the abilities of the court (Goldfarb & Singer, 1973). Furthermore, circumstances change, and, for practical reasons, the offender cannot be brought back before the judge every time a situation arises requiring a new rule. Because of this, judges typically order the offender to participate in treatment with a therapist and to follow all rules required by the therapist.

Caution is also called for when a treatment program fails to address the offender's sexuality directly. Some experts write that offenders should not be readmitted into their families until their pattern of sexual arousal has been dealt with directly. "A common mistake is to focus the goals of the treatment plan on related problems rather than on the incest itself" (Spencer & Nicholson, 1988, p. 16). Programs that focus on the offender's social attitudes, relationships to others, his own victimization, stress management, and other issues of family therapy may make significant outward changes in the offender while internally he still finds himself sexually aroused by children. The program that fails to address the offender's sexuality directly, fails to recognize that, at best, sex offender treatment is entirely experimental. Such programs do not address the most direct cause of the offender's problem of offending because of the unwarranted belief that addressing those other areas will keep him from sexually offending in the future (Herman, 1990).

Caution is warranted whenever a therapist counsels the offender to ignore the requirements of official parties such as such as police, prosecutors, probation officers, or judges. A disagreement between the therapist and others can, in itself, be productive. When there is so much that is unknown about child molesters and their effective treatment, disagreements inevitably arise and listening to one another's opinions generally produces the wisest course of action. Even the best informed and well-meaning individuals sometimes disagree on specific issues. Nevertheless, suggesting that a child molester ignore a legal requirement encourages the very mental attitude that fostered his molestation in the first place: The offender ignored the laws and ethical values of society against molesting children.

Finally, caution should be exercised whenever a therapist fails to communicate with others in the community who have a legitimate interest in how the offender is doing. This means that therapists should be responsive to inquiries from probation officers, victim therapists, and others, including wives and family members. The importance of cooperation and teamwork in the treatment and supervision of child molesters is stressed by professionals in the field (Graves & Sgroi, 1982; O'Connell et al., 1990; Pithers in Marshall, Laws, & Barbaree, 1990).

Each of these cautions also suggests how to tell when the safest possible job is being done by the therapist. The therapist who bases the evaluation of the offender on a wide number of sources of data, and interviews persons other than the offender, probably has a better understanding of the offender's sexual deviance problem than the therapist who is not thorough and neglects to get information from many sources. The therapist who is careful to impose a number of controls on the offender's behavior recognizes the reality that the convicted child molester lacks the internal controls needed to avoid harming children. Imposing controls reflects concern for the offender by assisting him in a plan to reduce the chances that he will reoffend and be punished by more jail time, as well as concern for the safety of the community and its children.

Therapists who do not allow the offender to blame anyone but himself for his own behaviors are more likely to direct therapy in a way that teaches him that, ultimately, he is always responsible for his own behavior. There are no outs and no excuses. If he breaks any treatment rules or if he ever reoffends, the offender will be held accountable.

Therapists who meet with and/or confer with the wife, relatives, probation officers, victim therapists, friends, and acquaintances of the offender do not operate in isolation or in an information vacuum. They are more able to make adjustments in the treatment plan because they incorporate the observations of many people. They recognize that there is no panacea, no quick or easy cure for any child molester and, therefore, individualizing treatment is essential. Treatment is more likely to be successful when it takes into consideration all of the unique characteristics of the offender as well as the better known and understood patterns of sexual offending in general.

If any of the warning signs discussed in this chapter are present, or if questions or difficulties seem to exist, the following suggestions may be helpful. First, contact the therapist for an explanation about his or her approach to a particular offender. For example, if a therapist has not conducted a thorough evaluation of the offender, the therapist, if asked, might explain that no sexual deviance treatment is taking place at all. The offender has only requested vocational counseling. Perhaps the offender has been deceptive in suggesting that he was in treatment for his sexual deviance problems with the therapist. The therapist should have the opportunity to respond directly to concerns that might exist.

Second, one's own therapist should be consulted. For example, a sex offender therapist may indicate that the conditions and controls in the Judgment and Sentence are being required of the offender but that no further controls have been imposed by the therapist. The wife's therapist might obtain the Judgment and Sentence and the sex offender evaluation report and determine that, in this case, the Judgment and Sentence did list all of the conditions that were necessary. Consulting her own therapist, the wife might learn, for example, that the husband was being supervised by an elite team of probation officers who had extensive expertise and exercised the authority to impose adequate controls beyond any that the therapist might have wanted.

Consulting with others is always advisable. Talking to the probation officer, the caseworker, the prosecuting attorney,[2] and others can help resolve doubts or heighten concern where appropriate. One might learn from the prosecutor, for example, that a particular therapist had recently been formally disciplined (i.e., punished for unprofessional or unethical practice) by a state licensing authority and that the prosecutor has little confidence in the therapist's abilities. With such information, the wife could be justifiably concerned and cautious about relying too much on the recommendations of such a therapist. The key to preventing problems as well as solving problems and resolving doubts in working with the sex offender therapist is to increase communication as much as possible among all parties.

Notes

1. The importance of a thorough evaluation of convicted sex offenders has been recognized in law by the Washington State Legislature where most sex offenders cannot be treated in the community unless a complete and thorough evaluation has been completed.

2. More and more frequently, the offices of the prosecuting attorneys have special "Victim/Witness Programs" to help answer questions.

Epilogue

Eighteen months after checking Sir Lancelot into the mental ward at the local hospital, I was able to regain control over my caseload. Burt, the predatory molester whom I found on the street attempting to set up the paperboy was returned to prison and required to sit out the rest of his term without parole. He died of a heart attack before he was released. Dan, the school teacher, entered a treatment program for sex offenders and transferred out of my area. As in so many cases, I never heard from or about him again. Ben, the church youth counselor, committed suicide. Jerry, who used child care centers as his base for criminal activity, died in a shoot-out after a high speed chase in which he was attempting to escape from police. Rob, who begged me to arrest him, died of cancer precipitated by a life of alcohol and drug abuse. Gator also struck out. He was sentenced to life without parole after he got drunk and held up an espresso stand with a kitchen butter knife. He was so drunk he could barely walk and was arrested before he had traveled a block from the cart. The espresso saleslady had a cellular phone and police nabbed him within five minutes of the $20 robbery. His third assaultive conviction carried with it a price tag of over one million dollars under the state's new Three Strikes law mandating life in prison for serious violent repeat offenders. One million dollars is what it costs, conservatively, for one man to spend his life in prison without parole. I often wonder how much good we could do if we just kept him for half his life, let him out at age 60, and spent the $500,000 saved on treatment for victims of abuse. Billy, who allegedly attempted to entice the little boy into his car, had actually been at a 7:00 a.m. Alcoholics Anonymous meeting. Billy cleaned up his act, got sober, and is a counselor in a substance abuse treatment program today. My colleague's murder has never been solved.

I have never again faced the workload I had to endure for those 18 months during Sir Lancelot's time, although I occasionally hear about other probation officers going through similar difficulties and challenges. Perhaps an offender commits suicide and claims he did it because his probation officer demanded too much of him. Or an offender under supervision commits some heinous crime, a murder and bodily mutilation for instance, that was totally unforeseeable except through hindsight. These things are part of the profession and come with the territory. At times, it may be extremely difficult to have the best communication with a probation officer. Unlike most therapists, the corrections agency cannot reduce its workload by closing its doors to the never-ending onslaught of more offenders coming from court. Despite this fact, the probation officer and the sex offender therapist are your best bet for *taking charge* of the convicted child molester whether your goal is to protect yourself from ever being victimized again or to reunite your family in the safest way possible. Although circumstances are at times overwhelming for us all, we should never cease calling one another, asking for help. Calling one another, communicating, works. It doesn't work perfectly, but it's the best thing we have to overcome the cloak of secrecy, blaming, and manipulation in which child sexual abuse occurs.

References

Abel, G., Becker, J. V., Blanchard, E., & Djenderedjian, A. (1978, December). Differentiating sexual aggressives with penile measures. *Criminal Justice and Behavior, 5,* 315-327.

Abel, G., Becker, J. V., Cunningham-Rathner, J., Mittelman, M., & Rouleau, J. L. (1988). Multiple paraphilic diagnoses among sex offenders. *Bulletin of the American Academy of Psychiatry and the Law, 16*(2), 153-168.

Abel, G., Becker, J. V., Cunningham-Rathner, J., Rouleau, J. L., Kaplan, M., & Reich, J. (1986). *The treatment of child molesters* (Grant No. MH 36347-01 and 02). Washington, DC: National Institute of Mental Health.

Abel, G., & Rouleau, J. (1990). The nature and extent of sexual assault. In W. L. Marshall, D. R. Laws, & H. E. Barbaree (Eds.), *Handbook of sexual assault* (pp. 9-21). New York: Plenum.

Ansley, N., & Garwood, M. (1984). *The accuracy and utility of polygraph testing.* Washington, DC: Department of Defense.

Barbaree, H.E. (1990). Stimulus control of sexual arousal. In W. L. Marshall, D. R. Laws, & H. E. Barbaree (Eds.), *Handbook of sexual assault* (pp. 115-142). New York: Plenum.

Berliner, L., & Stevens, D. (1982). Clinical issues in child sexual abuse. In J. R. Conte & D. A. Shore (Eds.), *Social work and child sexual abuse* (pp. 93-109). New York: Haworth.

Brecher, E. (1978). *Treatment programs for sex offenders.* Washington, DC: National Institute of Law Enforcement and Criminal Justice.

Brodsky, S. L., & West, D. J. (1981). Life-skills treatment of sex offenders. *Law and Psychology Review, 6,* 97-167.

Browne, A., & Finkelhor, D. (1986). Impact of child sexual abuse: A review of the research. *Psychological Bulletin, 99,* 66-77.

Burkhart, W. R. (1986, June). Intensive probation supervision: An agenda for research and evaluation. *Federal Probation, L,* 75-77.

Burns, R. E. (1975). Why is the polygraph discriminated against by courts? In N. Ansley (Ed.), *Legal admissibility of the polygraph* (pp. 22-30). Springfield, IL: Charles C. Thomas.

Byrne, J. M. (1986, June). The control controversy: A preliminary examination of intensive probation supervision programs in the United States. *Federal Probation, L,* 4-16.

Champion, D. (1988, March). Child sexual abusers and sentencing severity. *Federal Probation, LII,* 53-57.

Chandler, H. P. (1987, June). Latter-day procedures in the sentencing and treatment of offenders in the federal courts. *Federal Probation, LI,* 14.

Conrad, J. P. (1987, June). The intensive revolution. *Federal Probation, LI,* 62-64.

Conte, J. R., & Berliner, L. (1981, December). Sexual abuse of children: Implications for practice. *Social Casework: The Journal of Contemporary Social Work,* pp. 601-606.

Crim, R. M. (1978). *Presentence report handbook.* Washington, DC: National Institute of Law Enforcement and Criminal Justice, LEAA.

Dougher, M. J. (1988). Clinical assessment of sex offenders. In B. Schwartz (Ed.), *A practitioner's guide to treating the incarcerated male sex offender* (pp. 77-84). Washington, DC: U.S. Department of Justice, National Institute of Corrections.

Durham, A. M. (1991, September). Then and now: The fruits of late 20th century penal reform. *Federal Probation, LV,* 28-36.

Ellsworth, T. (1988, December). Case supervision planning: The forgotten component of intensive probation supervision. *Federal Probation, LII,* 29.

English, K., Pullen, S., & Jones, L. (Eds.). (1996). *Managing adult sex offenders: A containment approach.* Lexington, KY: American Probation and Parole Association.

Finkelhor, D. (1979). What's wrong with sex between adults and children? (Ethics and the problem of sexual abuse). *Journal of the American Orthopsychiatric Association,* 692-697.

Finkelhor, D. (1986). *A sourcebook on child sexual abuse.* Beverly Hills, CA: Sage.

Fraser, B. (1981). Sexual child abuse: The legislation and the law in the United States. In P. Mrazek & C. Kempe (Eds.), *Sexually abused children and their families* (pp. 55-74). Elmsford, NY: Pergamon.

Freeman-Longo, R. E., & Wall, R. V. (1986, March). Changing a lifetime of sexual crime. *Psychology Today,* pp. 58-64.

Glaser, D. (1975, September). Achieving better questions: A half century's progress in correctional research. *Federal Probation, XXXIX,* 3-9.

Goldfarb, R. L., & Singer, L. R. (1973). *After conviction.* New York: Simon & Schuster.

Graves, P. A., & Sgroi, S. M. (1982). Law enforcement and child sexual abuse. In S. M. Sgroi (Ed.), *Handbook of clinical intervention in child sexual abuse* (pp. 309-333). Lexington, MA: Lexington Books.

Green, R. (1988). Comprehensive treatment planning for sex offenders. In B. Schwartz (Ed.), *A practitioner's guide to treating the incarcerated male sex offender* (pp.

71-74). Washington, DC: U.S. Department of Justice, National Institute of Corrections.

Groth, A. N., Hobson, W. F., & Gary, T. S. (1982). The child molester: Clinical observations. In J. R. Conte & D. A. Shore (Eds.), *Social work and child sexual abuse* (pp. 129-144). New York: Haworth.

Herman, J. (1981). *Father-daughter incest.* Cambridge, MA: Harvard University Press.

Herman, J. (1990). Sex offenders: A feminist perspective. In W. L. Marshall, D. R. Laws, & H. E. Barbaree (Eds.), *Handbook of sexual assault* (pp. 177-193). New York: Plenum.

Herrick, E. (1989, January-February). Survey: More sex offenders in prison, but trend slows. *Corrections Compendium, 14,* 1.

Howells, K. (1981). Adult sexual interest in children: Considerations relevant to theories of etiology. In M. Cook & K. Howells (Eds.), *Adult sexual interest in children* (pp. 55-94). London: Academic Press.

Jamieson, K., & Flanagan, T. (Eds.). (1989). *Sourcebook of criminal justice statistics* (pp. 481-489). Washington, DC: Bureau of Justice Statistics.

Journal of the American Medical Association. Council on Scientific Affairs. (1986, September 5). 256(9), 1172-1175.

Knefelkamp, D. E. (1988, June). *Investigative strategies and the use of polygraph in child abuse investigations.* Paper presented at the Northwest Polygraph Association's Seminar.

Kocen, L., & Bulkley, J. (1983). Analysis of criminal child sex offense statutes. In J. Bulkley (Ed.), *Child sexual abuse and the law.* Washington, DC: American Bar Association.

Lanning, K. (1986). *Child molesters: A behavioral analysis for law enforcement officers investigating cases of child sexual exploitation.* Quantico, VA: Behavioral Science Unit, Federal Bureau of Investigation.

Laws, D., & Osborn, C. (1983). How to build and operate a behavioral laboratory to evaluate and treat sexual deviance. In J. Greer & I. Stuart (Eds.), *The sexual aggressor, current perspectives on treatment* (pp. 293-335). New York: Van Nostrand Reinhold.

Laws, D. R. (1989). *Relapse prevention with sex offenders.* New York: Guilford.

Lilies, R. E., & Childs, D. (1986, Fall). Similarities in family dynamics of incest and alcohol abuse: Issues for clinicians. *Alcohol Health and Research World, 4,* 66-69.

Lindner, C., & Bonn, R. L. (June, 1996). Probation Officer Victimization and Fieldwork Practices: Results of a National Study. *Federal Probation, L,* 16-23.

Lurigio, A. J., Jones, M., & Smith, B. E. (1995, September). Child sexual abuse: Its causes, consequences, and implications for probation practice. *Federal Probation, LIX,* 69-76.

McDonald, H. C. (1982). *Survival.* New York: Ballantine.

McFarlane, K. (1983). Program considerations in the treatment of incest offenders. In J. Greer & I. Stuart (Eds.), *The sexual aggressor* (pp. 62-79). New York: Van Nostrand Reinhold.

Marshall, W., & Barbaree, H. (1990). Outcome of comprehensive cognitive-behavioral treatment programs. In W. L. Marshall, D. Laws, & H. E. Barbaree (Eds.), *Handbook of sexual assault* (pp. 363-385). New York: Plenum.

Marshall, W. L., Laws, D., & Barbaree, H. E. (Eds.). (1990). *Handbook of sexual assault.* New York: Plenum.

Meiselman, K. (1979). *Incest: A psychological study of causes and effects with treatment recommendations.* San Francisco: Jossey-Bass.

National District Attorney's Association Bulletin (1988). Vol. 7, No. 4, 1-3.

National Institute of Law Enforcement and Criminal Justice. (1978, June). *Exemplary project validation report: Intensive service project, Philadelphia County, Pennsylvania.* Cambridge, MA: Abt.

National Institute of Mental Health. (1981). *The clinical prediction of violent behavior.* Washington, DC: U. S. Department of Health and Human Services, Public Health Services, Alcohol, Drug Abuse, and Mental Health Administration.

O'Connell, M., Leberg, E., & Donaldson, C. (1990). *Working with sex offenders: Guidelines for therapist selection.* Newbury Park, CA: Sage.

Office of Technology Assessment. (1983). *Scientific validity of polygraph testing: A research review and evaluation. A technical memorandum* (OTA-TM-H-15). Washington, DC: Author.

Parsons, J. B. (1964, March). The presentence investigation report must be preserved as a confidential document. *Federal Probation, XXVIII.*

Peters, S., Wyatt, G., & Finkelhor, D. (1986). Prevalence. In D. Finkelhor (Ed.), *A sourcebook on child sexual abuse* (pp. 15-59). Newbury Park, CA: Sage.

Petersilia, J. (1987, June). Probation and felony offenders. *Federal Probation, LI* 56.

Pithers, W. (1988). Relapse prevention. In B. Schwartz (Ed.), *A practitioner's guide to treating the incarcerated male sex offender* (pp. 123-140). Washington, DC: National Institute of Corrections.

Pithers, W., & Laws, D. R. (1988). The penile plethysmograph. In Schwartz, B. (Ed.), *A practitioner's guide to treating the incarcerated male sex offender* (pp. 85-94). Washington, DC: U.S. Department of Justice, National Institute of Corrections.

Pithers, W., Martin, G., & Cumming, G. (1989). Vermont Treatment Program for Sexual Aggressors. In D. R. Laws (Ed.), *Relapse prevention with sex offenders* (pp. 293-310). New York: Guilford.

Prentky, R. A., Knight, R. A., Sims-Knight, J. E., Straus, H., Rokous, F., & Cerce, D. (1989). Developmental antecedents of sexual aggression. *Development and Psychology, 1*, 153-169.

Riveland, C. (1991, June). Being a director of corrections in the 1990s. *Federal Probation, LV,* 10-11.

Salter, A. (1988). *Treating child sex offenders and victims: A practical guide.* Newbury Park, CA: Sage.

Schwartz, B. (1988a). Characteristics and typologies of sex offenders. In B. Schwartz (Ed.), *A practitioners guide to treating the incarcerated male sex offender* (pp. 15-28). Washington, DC: U.S. Department of Justice, National Institute of Corrections.

Schwartz, B. (Ed.) (1988b). *A practitioner's guide to treating the incarcerated male sex offender.* Washington, DC: U.S. Department of Justice, National Institute of Corrections.

Sgroi, S. M. (1982). Family treatment of child sexual abuse. In J. R. Conte & D. A. Shore (Eds.), *Social work and child sexual abuse* (pp. 109-128). New York: Haworth.

Smith, W. R., Rhine, E. E., & Jackson, R. W. (1990, October). Parole practices in the United States. *Corrections Today, 51* 22-28.

Spencer, C. C., & Nicholson, M. A. (1988). Incest investigation and treatment planning by child protective services. In L. Walker (Ed.), *Handbook on sexual abuse of children* (pp. 152-174). New York: Springer.

Starup, G. (1972). Castration: The total treatment. In H. Resnik & M. Wolfgang (Eds.), *Sexual behaviors: Social, clinical, and legal aspects* (pp. 361-382). Boston: Little, Brown.

Steele, N. (1988). Aftercare treatment programs. In B. Schwartz (Ed.), *A practitioner's guide to treating the incarcerated male sex offender* (pp. 117-122). Washington, DC: National Institute of Corrections.

Thornburgh, D. (1991, June). *National Institute of Justice reports.* Washington, DC: U.S. Department of Justice.

U.S. Advisory Board on Child Abuse and Neglect. (1990). *Child abuse and neglect: Critical first steps in response to a national emergency* (Stock Number 017-093-00204-5). Washington, DC: Government Printing Office.

U.S. Department of Justice. (1989). *Compendium of state privacy and security, 1989 overview. Privacy and security of criminal history information.* Washington DC: Bureau of Justice Statistics, Office of Justice Programs.

Zastrow, W. G. (1971, December). Disclosure of the presentence investigation report. *Federal Probation, XXXV,* 22.

Index

About the Author

ERIC LEBERG, a Probation and Parole Officer for the Washington State Department of Corrections since 1975, has investigated and supervised hundreds of sex offenders in virtually every category of offender from fetishists and exhibitionists to child murderers. With Michael O'Connell and Craig Donaldson, he coauthored *Working With Sex Offenders: Guidelines for Therapist Selection* (Sage, 1991), which received universal praise from reviewers and readers alike. He teaches classes on sex offenders and professional issues at Western University's Human Services Program. He served as Chair of the Washington State Department of Health Advisory Committee on the Certification of Sex Offender Therapists. This was the nation's first certification requirement for those who treat sex offenders. He is a member of the American Professional Society on the Abuse of Children and has received its Honor Roll recognition, in part for the development of an annotated and indexed bibliography of more than 600 professional articles on adult sex offenders. He received his master's degree in social work from the University of Denver in 1973. He received a bachelor of arts degree in Spanish literature from

Pomona College in 1968. It was his ability to speak Spanish that first brought him to the field of social work when he was employed as a caseworker with migrant farm workers in Yakima County, Washington. He has also worked in Children's Protective Services and has conducted child custody evaluations for Snohomish County Superior Court. He has been married for 25 years to his wife Carolyn, plays jazz flute and guitar, and is an avid basketball player and bird watcher.